The MVS JCL Primer

The MVS JCL Primer

Saba Zamir

Chander Ranade

McGraw-Hill, Inc.

New York   San Francisco   Washington, D.C.   Auckland   Bogotá
Caracas   Lisbon   London   Madrid   Mexico City   Milan
Montreal   New Delhi   San Juan   Singapore
Sydney   Tokyo   Toronto

Library of Congress Cataloging-in-Publication Data

Zamir, Saba.
    The MVS JCL primer / Saba Zamir & Chander Ranade.
        p.   cm.
    Includes index
    ISBN 0-07-072702-3
    1. IBM MVS. 2. Job Control Language (Computer program language)
    I. Ranade, Chander. II. Title.
    QA76.6.Z35   1994
    005.4'3—dc20   94-25954
                                                  CIP

     6 7 8 9 0 DOC/DOC 9 0 9

ISBN 0-07-072702-3

The sponsoring editor for this book was Jerry Papke, the editing supervisor was Jim Halston, and the production supervisor was Suzanne W. Babeuf.

Printed and bound by R. R. Donnelley & Sons Company.

*This book is dedicated to the memory of
Uncle Shabbir,
for his wisdom, grace,
and love for life and people,
and for enriching my life in my younger days.
I am indebted.*

Saba Zamir

*To my husband, Jeewan
and my children, Ram and Sunita.*

Chander Ranade

Contents

Part 2   Utilities

Preface

Job Control Language, or JCL for short, is a powerful, flexible, and unique language that runs in an IBM mainframe environment. In addition to the qualities that we have just listed, might we add that at first glance, it appears to be quite incomprehensible and most user-unfriendly!

A JCL job is a collection of statements that specify the resources required to run the job to the operating system. Unless you know JCL, you can not execute your programs on the IBM mainframe, since it is IBM's means of communication between programs written in a computer language, such as COBOL, and the MVS operating system.

Given that JCL is an inescapable fact of life for those of you who work in this environment, and that it is not one of the most enjoyable or easy languages to work with, the question arises, what can be done to make your task of mastering this language as easy, quick, and painless as possible?

The authors have written this book with the above premise in mind. This book is designed to teach JCL to you as quickly and effortlessly as possible.

Who This Book Is For

This book is for anyone who needs to learn JCL, and knows nothing whatsoever about the language. The book can also be used by those who are already familiar with the language, but wish to gain a better understanding of some of its parameters and concepts. There are no prerequisites for this book, although it is assumed that you have a general understanding of computers, and that you know some basic COBOL. Even if you don't know COBOL, you may use this book, since complete explanations of COBOL programs are provided whenever they are referenced.

A Word on the Style

This book has been written in such a way that each chapter is self-contained and self-explanatory. What this means is that you don't need to read the prior chapter in order to gain an understanding of a subsequent one. Numerous examples are used. Generally speaking, each example is designed to explain one parameter of the language only, so that you gain a complete and thorough understanding of each parameter described (without confusing it with the functionality of another), before reading about the next.

Also, since our lives become more busy and hectic each day, we have endeavored to write this book so that you can practically breeze through it, and yet understand what you are reading.

Believe it or not, you will find learning JCL to be a pleasant and painless undertaking!

What Is Included

Part 1 discusses the basics by describing some of the most heavily used parameters in JCL.

Part 2 contains descriptions of some of the more commonly used IBM-supplied utility programs, and explanations of the JCL required to execute them.

Part 3 is devoted to a discussion of Virtual Storage Access Methods (VSAM) and Access Method Services (AMS). It also contains a discussion on JES2 and JES3 subsystems, and some of the most commonly used parameters in these environments.

After reading this book, you will not only understand JCL, but will also have an understanding of VSAM, AMS, and JES2 and JES3.

Final Word

After reading this book, you will find that the difficulty and mystery associated with JCL will be a thing of the past. You will be able to run JCL jobs and debug any errors that may be encountered in the process with a high degree of confidence.

Acknowledgments

The authors wish to thank several people that have made this book possible.

First of all, we must thank Carol Lehn for her thorough, expert review of this book. Her suggestions and comments increased the quality and usefulness of this book, and we are indebted to her for her input. The authors would also like to thank Jan and Hirday Ranade, for taking the time to review the book, and offer useful suggestions.

Mr. Gerald Papke, our very understanding (and sympathetic) senior editor at McGraw-Hill, provided us with encouragement throughout this project. Thanks are also owed to Jay Ranade, series editor, for his contribution in this project.

Chander Ranade would like to thank her son, Ram, for the multiple trips that he made on her behalf, which helped ease her life tremendously. Chander would also like to thank her husband, Jeewan, for being so understanding during the countless weekends that were spent writing this book.

Saba Zamir would like to thank her parents, Ammi and Abjani, and her aunt, Khala Jaan, for always being there for her. Saba would also like to thank her husband, David, for his quiet, thoughtful support, and her son, Richad, for being so wonderful, and teaching her the fine art of typing with her left hand, while balancing him with her right one! Finally, Saba would like to thank her cousin, Nadeem Nasir, for the support that he gave in his own unique way at a time that she needed it most. She is indebted to him.

Saba Zamir
Chander Ranade

Part

1

MVS JCL

1

Basic Concepts
Of JCL

1.1 INTRODUCTION TO JCL

A mainframe has to be one of the most awe-inspiring creations of mankind. If you are moving from a PC-based environment to that of a mainframe, then it is likely that you have heard comments such as "Now you can get to work with a REAL computer!" from colleagues. If you are right out of college, then you may not even be aware of what a mainframe is, except in the context of having to *dial in* to something that performed your tasks for you. We cannot help but agree with the reputation that has been built around a mainframe; it is one of the most complex creations of mankind that has graced the face of this earth! And IBM mainframes are no exception to the rule. They have existed, in all of their complexity, for more than a quarter of a century, with minimal changes in their basic hardware architecture, their operating system (which is MVS), and mode of user access to it.

So what does all of this have to do with JCL? JCL is not a procedural language, like COBOL, Assembler, or C. It is not an object oriented language, like C++ or SmallTalk. Instead, it has a uniquely identifying character of its own, it is a *Job Control Language*. It is a means of communication between a program that can be written in COBOL, Assembler or PL/1, and the MVS operating system. If you have ever written a program (and it is unlikely that you haven't), which accesses files or writes output, then it will be the JCL that will identify to the operating system the resources that your program expects to use. It is the interface between the requirements or instructions in your program, and the MVS operating system that your program will run in. Without JCL, your programs will not run on an IBM mainframe.

1.2 WHY JCL?

Those of you who have some experience programming in other languages may be taken aback when you are introduced to JCL. For example, if you wrote a C program in a UNIX environment, all you had to do was compile it, and the executable was ready to be run simply by typing "a.out" at the system prompt. If you wrote a program in a PC or MS/DOS environment, most probably your interface with the operating system was menu driven, and all you had to do to run a program was click on the "Compile" button, and then the "Run" button, (or type equivalent commands at the system prompt), and that was that! But if a program has to be run in an IBM mainframe environment, first you have to learn JCL, then you have to write the program, then write the correct interface for it, and then you have to run it. (Incidentally, you also have to learn how to access the ISPF Menu, more on this later.) Why does life have to be so difficult in the mainframe environment? Let's take a little time to understand why this is so.

JCL was created at a time when "user-friendly" environments were not an issue, instead, power and flexibility were. At first sight, JCL may seem arcane, incomprehensible, almost a little bit like Greek! However, at the same time, JCL is also a very powerful and flexible language that helps customize the use of local and remote resources available to one or more computers. Regardless, it was and is a fact of life, and there is no escaping it.

Since its inception, billions of dollars have been invested in the creation of applications and utilities that will run in this architecture. In addtion to the benefits it provides, JCL continues to be a driving force in the mainframe arena, since it is not financially feasible for many companies to switch to different environments, particularly if their existing applications would become incompatible in them. A re-write of existing applications for different environments would be an expensive, time-consuming, and formidable undertaking!

We now devote the remainder of this book to an explanation of the parameters and syntax of JCL. Note: the apparent difficulty of this language will be made easier before you conclude this chapter!

1.3 RELATIONSHIP BETWEEN COBOL PROGRAMS AND JCL

As stated earlier, JCL is a means of communication between a program written in COBOL, Assembler or PL/1, and the MVS operating system. All sample programs in this book will be written in COBOL. We now present a very simple COBOL program that writes the statement "THIS STATEMENT WILL BE WRITTEN TO PRINTER" to a printer. Here's the program:

```
IDENTIFICATION DIVISION.
PROGRAM-ID.    PROGRAM1.
DATE-WRITTEN.  OCT 1, 1992.
DATE-COMPILED.
AUTHOR.   CHANDER RANADE.
**
ENVIRONMENT DIVISION.
CONFIGURATION SECTION.
SOURCE-COMPUTER.
  IBM-370.
INPUT-OUTPUT SECTION.
FILE-CONTROL.
  SELECT IN-FILE     ASSIGN TO INPUT1.
  SELECT PRINT-FILE  ASSIGN TO REPORT1.
**
DATA DIVISION.
FILE SECTION.
FD  IN-FILE
    LABEL RECORDS ARE STANDARD.
01  IN-REC          PIC X(40).
FD  PRINT-FILE
    LABEL RECORDS ARE STANDARD.
01  PRINT-REC       PIC X(133).
*
WORKING-STORAGE SECTION.
01  NO-DATA-FLAG    PIC X(3)  VALUE SPACES.
    88   NO-MORE-DATA       VALUE 'YES'.
**
PROCEDURE DIVISION.
A000-MAIN.
    PERFORM A000-OPEN-FILES.
    PERFORM B000-PROCESSING THRU B000-EXIT
       UNTIL NO-MORE-DATA.
    PERFORM C000-CLOSE-FILES THRU C000-EXIT.
    STOP RUN.
*
A000-OPEN-FILES.
    OPEN INPUT IN-FILE.
    OPEN OUTPUT PRINT-FILE.
*
B000-PROCESSING.
    READ IN-FILE
      AT END
    MOVE 'YES' TO NO-DATA-FLAG
      GO TO B000-EXIT.
    MOVE IN-REC TO PRINT-REC.
      WRITE PRINT-REC.
*
B000-EXIT.
      EXIT.
*
C000-CLOSE-FILES.
    CLOSE IN-FILE PRINT-FILE.
```

```
C000-EXIT.
    EXIT.
```

Before proceeding further, we will describe the main components of the COBOL program just presented. We will go into considerable detail in the description of this simple program, and we ask that the COBOL experts among you bear with this explanation. It is necessary for us to take this approach now, in order to show you exactly how the JCL statements correspond to the contents of this program.

As you are undoubtedly aware, all COBOL programs are divided into four main parts. The first is called the IDENTIFICATION DIVISION, this identifies the name of the program, the date the program was written, and so forth:

```
IDENTIFICATION DIVISION.
PROGRAM-ID.   PROGRAM1.
DATE-WRITTEN.   OCT 1, 1992.
DATE-COMPILED.
AUTHOR.  CHANDER RANADE.
```

The second part of a COBOL program is called the ENVIRONMENT DIVISION. It identifies the environment in which the program will be run. This is the division that is directly related to the JCL statements that will introduce the program to the operating system. We ask that you pay special attention to this section of the code:

```
ENVIRONMENT DIVISION.
CONFIGURATION SECTION.
SOURCE-COMPUTER.
  IBM-370.
INPUT-OUTPUT SECTION.
FILE-CONTROL.
  SELECT IN-FILE   ASSIGN TO INPUT1.
  SELECT PRINT-FILE    ASSIGN TO REPORT1.
```

Notice that the source computer is identified as the IBM-370. The FILE-CONTROL section identifies the input and output files that will be used by the program. In our program, "IN-FILE" is assigned to "INPUT1", and "PRINT-FILE" is assigned to "REPORT1". "IN-FILE" and "PRINT-FILE" are user-defined names in the COBOL program. "INPUT1" and "REPORT1" will be referenced in the JCL segment that relates to this program. The exact correspondence between the COBOL program and the JCL statements will become clear at the conclusion of this section, when we will present the JCL statements required to run this program. The third part of the COBOL program is called the DATA DIVISION. This section of the program describes the structure of the files that will be utilized by the program:

```
DATA DIVISION.
FILE SECTION.
FD  IN-FILE
    LABEL RECORDS ARE STANDARD.
01  IN-REC    PIC X(40).
FD  PRINT-FILE
    LABEL RECORDS ARE STANDARD.
01  PRINT-REC   PIC X(133).
```

As you can see, the symbol FD (File Description) is followed by the names of the input and output files (IN-FILE and PRINT-FILE) referenced earlier on by the program, and their structure.   IN-FILE references the input file and PRINT FILE references the file to which the output will be written. Each record in IN-FILE is forty characters long. Each record in PRINT-FILE is 133 characters, which is the standard number of columns across wide printer paper.

The WORKING-STORAGE SECTION   is a sub-set of the DATA DIVISION. It identifies variables utilized by the program:

```
WORKING-STORAGE SECTION.
01  NO-DATA-FLAG  PIC X(3)  VALUE SPACES.
    88   NO-MORE-DATA     VALUE 'YES'.
```

Our program defines two flags: NO-DATA-FLAG and NO-MORE-DATA.   NO-DATA-FLAG is 3 characters long and is initialized to spaces. NO-MORE-DATA is an 88 level condition-name entry.

The last part of a COBOL program consists of the PROCEDURE DIVISION. As the name implies, this contains the main logic of the program. Our PROCEDURE DIVISION can be logically divided into three sections. The first section is called A000-MAIN. This section contains the main processing logic of the program:

```
A000-MAIN.
    PERFORM A000-OPEN-FILES.
    PERFORM B000-PROCESSING THRU B000-EXIT
       UNTIL NO-MORE-DATA.
    PERFORM C000-CLOSE-FILES THRU C000-EXIT.
    STOP RUN.
```

As you can see, this section instructs the execution of procedures A000-OPEN-FILES,   B000-PROCESSING, and C000-CLOSE-FILES. These procedures are defined immediately after:

```
A000-OPEN-FILES.
    OPEN INPUT IN-FILE.
    OPEN OUTPUT PRINT-FILE.
```

This procedure opens the files that will be utilized by the program.

IN-FILE is designated as the file from which input will be obtained. PRINT-FILE is designated as the file to which the output of the program will be written. Notice that reference is made to IN-FILE and PRINT-FILE, the same names that are described in the FD section of the program. Keep in mind that the JCL references the symbolic names that follow the "ASSIGN TO" statements in the FILE-CONTROL section.

The procedure B000-PROCESSING is the main processing loop in the program:

```
B000-PROCESSING.
    READ IN-FILE
      AT END
    MOVE 'YES' TO NO-DATA-FLAG
      GO TO B000-EXIT.
    MOVE IN-REC TO PRINT-REC.
      WRITE PRINT-REC.
```

In this procedure, IN-FILE is read. Then, the contents of IN-REC are moved to PRINT-REC, and PRINT-REC is written to the printer. When the end-of-file is reached, 'YES' is moved to NO-DATA-FLAG, and then B000-EXIT is executed. The following procedure performs a simple exit:

```
B000-EXIT.
    EXIT.
```

C000-CLOSE-FILES closes all files accessed by the program:

```
C000-CLOSE-FILES.
    CLOSE IN-FILE PRINT-FILE.
```

Once again, notice that IN-FILE and PRINT-FILE, the names described in the FILE SECTION of the program, are referenced.

1.4 CORRESPONDING JCL

OK. Now let's understand the JCL statements that will execute that COBOL program. As you read through the remainder of this chapter, keep in mind that for now we will be explaining the main components of the JCL statements only briefly. More detailed explanations will follow in subsequent chapters. Here's the JCL:

```
//JOB1      JOB    (A189),'C RANADE',CLASS=A,PRTY=6
//STEP001   EXEC   PGM=PROGRAM1
//INPUT1    DD     DSN=INFILE,DISP=SHR
```

```
//REPORT1   DD      SYSOUT=A
//
```

As you preview the segment, notice:

- Each line begins with the symbols //

- The last line is // by itself. This is called the null statement, as it indicates the end of the current job.

- Each statement consists of *fields*. Consider a field to be a group of characters that convey certain information about the job to the operating system. In the following JCL statement:

```
//JOB1    JOB   (A189),'C RANADE',CLASS=A,PRTY=6
```

JOB1 is a field, JOB is a field, (A189) is a field, and so on. All JCL statements can be categorized as consisting of five types of fields.

1.5 COMPONENTS OF JCL STATEMENTS

As we just stated, all JCL statements can consist of up to five types of fields:

- //. The two forward slashes are required at the beginning of each JCL statement in Columns 1 and 2.

- The *name* field. This is an optional field and, if coded, must immediately follow the //, starting in Column 3.

- The *operation* field, which indicates the operation that is to be performed.

- The *operand*. This field must appear one or more spaces after the operation. Multiple operands in one statement are separated from each other via commas. This must start in Column 16.

- *Comments*. Comments begin one space after the last operand. Our simple example has no comments.

The statements in our sample JCL can be categorized into the five different fields types as follows:

//	Name	Operation	Operand	Comments
//	JOB1	JOB	(N189), 'C RANADE', CLASS=A, PRTY=6	
//	STEP001	EXEC	PGM=PROGRAM1	
//	INPUT1	DD	DSN=INFILE, DISP=SHR	
//	REPORT1	DD	SYSOUT=A	
//				

Now take another look at the Operand field. You will notice that some operands are enclosed in parenthesis (A189), others in quotes ('C RANADE'), while others have an equal sign between them (CLASS=A, PRTY=6). In JCL, you can have two types of parameters: *positional* and *keyword*. These parameters will be explained in detail in the next chapter. For now, it is enough for you to understand that positional parameters are called as such because of the position in which they appear in the operand field; they must be displayed in a certain order. Also, they must always precede keyword parameters. Keyword parameters, on the other hand, can appear in any order. They contain a keyword followed by an equal sign, followed by variable information.

1.6 GENERALIZED GROUPING OF JCL STATEMENTS

Before we explain each individual statement, let us take another brief detour and explain how all JCL segments can be more or less divided into three logical groupings.

The first group identifies the job being submitted to the operating system. The following is a statement that does this:

```
//JOB1 JOB    (A189),'C RANADE',CLASS=A,PRTY=6
```

The next group identifies the name of the program that is to be executed. Here's the statement that does this:

```
//STEP001    EXEC  PGM=PROGRAM1
```

The final group defines the data sets or input and output files being utilized by the COBOL program. Here's the JCL statements in our example that do so:

```
//INPUT1    DD    DSN=INFILE,DISP=SHR
//REPORT1   DD    SYSOUT=A
```

Now, keep in mind that all JCL segments are more or less always divided in terms of functionality into these three generalized groups.

We now describe the parameters in each statement, based on the logical groupings just described.

1.7 JOB IDENTIFICATION

Let's take another look at the first statement:

```
//JOB1    JOB (A189),'C RANADE',CLASS=A,PRTY=6
```

As indicated previously, all JCL statements must be preceded by the //. These symbols must appear in Columns 1 and 2 of each line. The next field

```
..JOB1...
```

identifies the name of the job to the operating system. Our job will now be recognized by the operating system as JOB1.

The next field

```
...JOB...
```

is called the JOB statement. All statements that follow this will now relate to this job, until another null or JOB statement is encountered. In our example, no job other than JOB1 is specified. The next field

```
...  (A189),...
```

is an optional positional parameter. We include this parameter in our simple example since it is almost always included in all JCL segments. This field identifies the user. It conveys accounting information that is used for billing computer time to the user.

The next field

```
...'C RANADE',...
```

specifies the name of the programmer or some other identifying characteristic. Although this parameter is also optional, we include it in our example because it is good practice to always indicate who wrote the JCL segment.

The next two fields are keyword parameters, and relate to each other:

```
...CLASS=A,PRTY=6
```

A *class* is a designation that is assigned to a group of users. Class designations vary with different installations, so check with your systems programmer for the CLASS that you have been assigned to. Then, each job which is run within a class is assigned a priority number (PRTY). The higher the number, the higher the priority of the job. For example, a job with priority number 1 will run after a job with priority number 6. In our example, JOB1 is assigned to the CLASS called A, and given a priority of 6.

1.8 PROGRAM IDENTIFICATION

The second statement in our example identifies the name of the program that is to be executed:

```
//STEP001    EXEC   PGM=PROGRAM1
```

STEP001 is the name of the job step. It is an optional parameter. However, if multiple jobs are being executed at the same time, the job step name becomes important in tracing the job with an error condition. This parameter will be explained in greater detail later on in the book. We include it in our example because we want you to get into the habit of including a job step name each time you write any JCL.

The next field

```
...EXEC...
```

specifies the beginning of the job step. All statements that follow this statement now belong to this step, until a null or another EXEC statement is encountered.

The next field

```
...PGM=PROGRAM1...
```

is a keyword parameter that identifies the name of the program that is to be executed.

1.9 INPUT/OUTPUT FILE IDENTIFICATION

The final grouping of a JCL segment identifies the input and output files utilized by the program. The statements that do so in our example are:

```
//INPUT1    DD   DSN=INFILE,DISP=SHR
//REPORT1   DD   SYSOUT=A
```

The fields `INPUT1` and `REPORT1` must correspond to the name specified in ASSIGN To part of the FILE-CONTROL section of the COBOL program:

```
FILE-CONTROL.
   SELECT IN-FILE        ASSIGN TO INPUT1.
   SELECT PRINT-FILE     ASSIGN TO REPORT1.
```

The next field

```
...DD...
```

is called the *Data Definition* field. Its main function is to describe the data set (or file) that the program will read from, or write to. It is a required field.
   The next field

```
...DSN=INFILE...
```

identifies the name of the file that input will be read from as `INFILE`.

The final field

```
...DISP=SHR
```

indicates that multiple users can access the file INFILE at the same time. `DISP` stands for `DISPOSITION`, and `SHR` stands for `SHAREABLE`.
   The next statement identifies the location to which output will be written. The field:

```
...SYSOUT=A
```

is the `SYSOUT` parameter, which routes output to the printer. The "A" after the equal sign is traditionally the class assigned to the printer.

1.10 PROGRAM EXECUTION AND OUTPUT

When the job is submitted, the COBOL program executes, and the following output is produced at the printer:

THIS STATEMENT WILL BE WRITTEN TO PRINTER

The above statement is in the input file, which is specified as INFILE. The next chapter will describe what happens when errors are encountered.

1.11 REVIEW

This chapter introduced you to the basics of JCL. To review briefly, each job submitted must have a JOB statement (identifies the job being submitted to the operating system), an EXEC statement (identifies the program to be executed), and DD statements (identify the input and output files utilized by the program). JCL is a collection of statements that specify details about the job to be run by the operating system. Each statement is a collection of name fields, operations, operands (positional and keyword parameters) and possible comments. We briefly described a few of these parameters in order to give you a feel for the language. However, you now know enough to write a complete JCL segment that will execute a program of your choice. The next chapter will describe how to input information using the ISPF editor, how to submit the job, and will also describe other JCL parameters in greater detail.

2

Basic Concepts, Continued

2.1 INTRODUCTION

In the previous chapter we described how a COBOL program writes output to the printer, and the JCL statements that run it. In this chapter we will modify the COBOL program to write output to disk and tape, and explain the corresponding JCL statements.

2.2 COBOL REVISITED

The following is the COBOL program that will write output to tape and disk:

```
IDENTIFICATION DIVISION.
PROGRAM-ID.  PROGRAM1.
DATE-WRITTEN.  OCT 1, 1992.
DATE-COMPILED.
AUTHOR. CHANDER RANADE.
**
ENVIRONMENT DIVISION.
CONFIGURATION SECTION.
SOURCE-COMPUTER.
  IBM-370.
INPUT-OUTPUT SECTION.
FILE-CONTROL.
  SELECT IN-FILE ASSIGN TO INPUT1.
   SELECT DISK-FILE ASSIGN TO DISK1.
   SELECT TAPE-FILE ASSIGN TO TAPE1.
```

```
**
DATA DIVISION.
FILE SECTION.
FD  IN-FILE
    BLOCK CONTAINS 0 RECORDS
    LABEL RECORDS ARE STANDARD.
01  IN-REC   PIC X(40).
FD  DISK-FILE
    BLOCK CONTAINS 0 RECORDS
    LABEL RECORDS ARE STANDARD.
01  DISK-REC PIC X(40).
FD  TAPE-FILE
    BLOCK CONTAINS 0 RECORDS
    LABEL RECORDS ARE STANDARD.
01  TAPE-REC PIC X(40).
*
WORKING-STORAGE SECTION.
01  NO-DATA-FLAG  PIC X(3) VALUE SPACES.
    88  NO-MORE-DATA     VALUE 'YES'.
**
PROCEDURE DIVISION.
A000-MAIN.
    PERFORM A000-OPEN-FILES.
    PERFORM B000-PROCESSING THRU B000-EXIT
       UNTIL NO-MORE-DATA.
    PERFORM C000-CLOSE-FILES.
    STOP RUN.
*
A000-OPEN-FILES.
    OPEN INPUT IN-FILE.
    OPEN OUTPUT DISK-FILE TAPE-FILE.
*
B000-PROCESSING.
    READ IN-FILE
       AT END
    MOVE 'YES' TO NO-DATA-FLAG
       GO TO B000-EXIT.
    MOVE IN-REC TO DISK-REC.
       WRITE DISK-REC.
    MOVE IN-REC TO TAPE-REC.
       WRITE TAPE-REC.
    GO TO B000-PROCESSING.
*
B000-EXIT.
    EXIT.
*
C000-CLOSE-FILES.
    CLOSE IN-FILE DISK-FILE TAPE-FILE.
```

The following statements in the INPUT-OUTPUT SECTION identify the two new output files that will be created by the program:

```
SELECT DISK-FILE ASSIGN TO DISK1.
SELECT TAPE-FILE ASSIGN TO TAPE1.
```

DISK-FILE and TAPE-FILE are user defined names which will be referenced in the corresponding JCL segment that will execute this program.

The structure of these files is defined in the DATA DIVISION:

```
FD    DISK-FILE
      BLOCK CONTAINS 0 RECORDS
      LABEL RECORDS ARE STANDARD.
01    DISK-REC PIC X(40).
FD    TAPE-FILE
      BLOCK CONTAINS 0 RECORDS
      LABEL RECORDS ARE STANDARD.
01    TAPE-REC PIC X(40).
```

The statement

```
BLOCK CONTAINS 0 RECORDS
```

is used to specify that the actual size of the block of the referenced file will be specified in the corresponding JCL. A block is a specific number of storage bytes on a direct access storage device.

The statement

```
LABEL RECORDS ARE STANDARD
```

is used to specify that the label for the file being processed will conform to standard system specifications. Labels are a method of identification for files created on a tape or a disk, and are processed by special routines in the operating system. Generally speaking, installations adopt a standard format for its label records. We will now describe the concept of labels.

A tape or disk unit is often referred to as a *volume*. A volume may have one or more complete or partial files stored on it. Thus, in order to access a specific file on a volume, the volume must be identified, and the start and end of files that are stored on that volume must also be identified.

In an MVS operating system, a *volume label record*, which is at the beginning of each volume, identifies characteristics for that volume. For each data file stored on that volume, there exists a *header label* record, and a *trailer label* record. The header label record identifies the start of a file, and other characteristics for it. A trailer label record marks the end of the file. Data records for the file exist between the header and trailer labels.

The following statements in the PROCEDURE DIVISION open the input and output files:

```
OPEN INPUT IN-FILE.
OPEN OUTPUT DISK-FILE TAPE-FILE.
```

The following statements write to these files:

```
MOVE IN-REC TO DISK-REC.
    WRITE DISK-REC.
MOVE IN-REC TO TAPE-REC.
    WRITE TAPE-REC.
```

and all files are closed in the procedure C000-CLOSE-FILES:

```
C000-CLOSE-FILES.
    CLOSE IN-FILE DISK-FILE TAPE-FILE.
```

The next section describes the JCL that will run this program:

2.3 CORRESPONDING JCL

Here's the JCL that will execute this program:

```
//JOB1     JOB  (A189),'F CLAPTON',CLASS=A,PRTY=6
//STEP001 EXEC PGM=PROGRAM1
//INPUT1   DD   DSN=INFILE,DISP=SHR
//DISK1    DD   DSN=DISK.OUTPUT,
//              DISP=(NEW,CATLG,DELETE),
//              UNIT=DISK,
//              SPACE=(TRK,(1,1),RLSE),
//              DCB=(RECFM=FB,LRECL=40,BLKSIZE=400)
//TAPE1    DD   DSN=TAPE.OUTPUT,
//              DISP=(NEW,CATLG,DELETE),
//              UNIT=TAPE,
//              DCB=(RECFM=FB,LRECL=40,BLKSIZE=400)
//
```

As you review this JCL, keep in mind how the statements can be functionally divided into three generalized groupings. The first group identifies the job being submitted to the operating system. This is the first statement:

```
//JOB1        JOB  (A189),'C RANADE',CLASS=A,PRTY=6
```

The next group identifies the name of the program that is to be executed. This is the second statement:

```
//STEP001    EXEC  PGM=PROGRAM1
```

These statements are exactly the same as the segment that we used in Chapter 1 to output to the printer. Please refer to it if you need to refresh your memory.

The third group defines the data sets or input and output files that will be utilized by the COBOL program that is to be executed. This is the group of statements that we will now explain in detail.

2.4 WRITING TO DISK

Here's the JCL that writes to disk:

```
//DISK1   DD      DSN=DISK.OUTPUT,
//                DISP=(NEW,CATLG,DELETE),
//                UNIT=DISK,
//                SPACE=(TRK,(1,1),RLSE),
//                DCB=(RECFM=FB,LRECL=40,BLKSIZE=400)
```

The above group of statements can be divided into five types of fields, which are the //, the *Name, Operation, Operand* and *Comments* fields. We display these subdivisions in table format in Figure 2.1. The Comments grouping has been omitted.

Now let's understand these statements. The first two characters are the //. As always, all JCL statements must be preceded by the //. Next is the *Name* field, identified as DISK1. DISK1 corresponds to the name of the file specified in the FILE-CONTROL section of the COBOL program. Next comes the *Data Definition* field, identified as DD. The parameters that follow this field describe the data set that the program will write to. These parameters are found in the *Operand* field.

Recall from Chapter 1 that the operand field contains both *positional* and *keyword* parameters. Positional parameters are so called because of the position in which they appear, and must precede keyword parameters. Keyword parameters can appear in any order, and they consist of a keyword followed by an equal sign and variable information. We now describe each of these parameters.

//	Name	Oper.	Operand
//	DISK1	DD	DSN=DISK.OUTPUT, DISP=(NEW,CATLG,DELETE), UNIT=DISK, SPACE=(TRK,(1,1),RLSE), DCB=(RECFM=FB,LRECL=40,BLKSIZE=400)

Fig 2.1 JCL Divided Into Fields

2.4.1 THE DSN PARAMETER

This is a keyword parameter. It identifies the *Data Set Name* of the file that output will be written to. In our example, output will be written to a file called DISK.OUTPUT.

2.4.2 THE DISP PARAMETER

DISP is also a keyword parameter. It specifies the current *DISP*osition of the dataset. Up to three positional subparameters can be coded on the DISP parameter, and they are used to specify three things:

■ The current status of the data set. The current status specifies whether the data set pre-exists, or if it has to be created. If the data set already exists, the current status is used to specify whether the current job has exclusive access to it, or whether other jobs are allowed to share access to it.

■ The status of the data set upon normal execution of a job, i.e. the job executes without errors. Upon normal execution of a job, a data set can be saved or cataloged.

■ The status of the data set upon abnormal execution of the job, i.e. the job terminates abnormally. Upon abnormal execution of a job, the data set can be saved or deleted.

Now, let's take another look at the DISP statement as it appears in our sample JCL:

```
...DISP=(NEW,CATLG,DELETE)
```

NEW, CATLG, and DELETE are the positional subparameters. Since they are positional, they must appear in the order specified.

The first positional subparameter is NEW. The presence of this subparameter indicates the status of the dataset at the start of the job; it's a new dataset.

The next subparameter is CATLG, and is used to specify the disposition of the dataset if the job executes successfully. The CATLG subparameter, in conjunction with the NEW subparamter, indicates that an entry for this dataset will be placed in the system catalogs.

The last subparameter is DELETE, and is used to indicate the disposition of the dataset, if the job terminates abnormally. DELETE indicates that the dataset should be deleted.

The DISP statement can have other subparameters besides the ones just described. These will be explained in subsequent chapters.

Summarizing, we are specifying the name of the dataset to be written to as DISK.OUTPUT. It is a new dataset. If the job executes successfully, then we would like it to be cataloged in the system catalogs. In case of error, we would like the dataset to be purged or deleted, so that space is not wasted.

2.4.3 THE UNIT PARAMETER

This is a keyword parameter that specifies the physical device on which a data set is to be placed. The statement:

```
...UNIT=DISK
```

requests that the unit assigned the name DISK be used to create the dataset. DISK is an arbitrary name which is assigned by the installation to various units of devices. If there is more than one device which has been assigned the name DISK, then the first available one will be used.

2.4.4 THE SPACE PARAMETER

SPACE is a keyword parameter. It requests space for the dataset, and specifies alternatives, in case sufficient space is not allocated initially. Here's the corresponding JCL statement:

```
//              SPACE=(TRK,(1,1),RLSE),
```

TRK indicates that space is being requested in tracks. Space can also be requested in cylinders or blocks. A request in terms of cylinders would look like this:

```
//              SPACE=(CYL,(1,1),RLSE)
```

The request for different types of space is dependent on the individual needs of the program, or the physical limitations that may exist at your installation. All of this will be explained in detail later on in the book.

Let's continue. The keyword TRK is followed by numbers that are enclosed in parentheses:

```
//              SPACE=(TRK,(1,1),RLSE),
```

The first number references the unit of primary space requested. The second number indicates the unit of secondary space. Consider primary space to be the request for space that we expect to require; think of it as an "educated guess." Secondary space is a request for subsequent space, just in case the amount specified in the primary space is not enough! If enough space is still not allocated, then an error condition will occur. Error conditions will be described in subsequent chapters.

In our example, we request one track of primary space. We expect one track to be sufficient for storing the output file that will be created by the COBOL program that will be executed. However, as a safety precaution, we also request secondary space, just in case one track is not enough. For now, consider primary space to be the initial allocation, and secondary space the subsequent allocation, if the amount of primary allocation is deficient. (1,1) is the specification of the request in physical units.

Let's continue with the statement. Following the track specification we see the keyword RLSE. This is an optional subparameter. It is used to specify that any space not utilized by the job should be released for other job requests after successful completion. It is good practice to use this option.

2.4.5 The DCB Parameter

Continuing with the JCL, the DCB parameter is encountered next:

```
//         DCB=(RECFM=FB,LRECL=40,BLKSIZE=400)
```

This is the Data Control Block parameter. In an MVS operating system, data contained within data sets can be identified in various ways. For example, data records can be of fixed or variable length, and of different sizes. The Data Control Block parameter is used to supply information to the executing program about the physical characteristics of the data in a data set. These physical characteristics must correspond with those specified in the DATA DIVISION of the COBOL program.

Here's the COBOL segment that corresponds to this statement:

```
FD   DISK-FILE
     BLOCK CONTAINS 0 RECORDS
     LABEL RECORDS ARE STANDARD.
01   DISK-REC PIC X(40).
```

Now take a look at the JCL. The first subparameter is RECFM. This specifies the record format as FB, or *Fixed Block*. A fixed block record can be of the specified length only. You can also have *Variable Block* records. These would have been specified like this:

```
//          DCB=(RECFM=VB)
```

A variable block can be of any length.

The next subparameter is LRECL. This specifies the logical record length of the dataset. We are specifying the logical record length to be 40 bytes, and this corresponds to the specification in the COBOL program:

```
01     DISK-REC PIC X(40).
```

If there is no correspondence between the JCL specification and the COBOL program, an error will occur.

BLKSIZE specifies the size of one block. A block is a specific number of bytes of storage on a direct access storage device. It can contain one or more records of a file. In our example, we specify block size as 400 bytes. Thus, at 40 bytes per record, ten records can be stored in one block.

2.5 WRITING TO TAPE

Here's the JCL that writes to tape:

```
//TAPE1 DD DSN=TAPE.OUTPUT,
//          DISP=(NEW,CATLG,DELETE),
//          UNIT=TAPE,
//          DCB=(RECFM=FB,LRECL=40,BLKSIZE=400)
//
```

There are three differences in this group of statements and the one that we used to write to disk. The first one is the difference in the name field. In this group, it is TAPE1, in the prior group it was DISK1. Second, the dataset name is TAPE.OUTPUT, instead of DISK.OUTPUT. Third, the UNIT parameter is TAPE, instead of DISK. Aside from these differences, all other parameters are the same. Take a few moments now to mentally review the meaning of the subparameters. If you are unsure of anything, reread this chapter before continuing.

2.6 PROGRAM OUTPUT

Upon submitting the JCL to execute the COBOL program, the contents of `IN-FILE` will be written to a file on a disk called `DISK.OUTPUT`, and then will be written to a file on a tape called `TAPE.OUTPUT`. As the program executes, multiple messages are generated from the device designated in the job as the output device. These messages will be explained throughout the book. For now, it is important that you understand only one thing. If your program executes without any errors, then a condition code of 0 will be generated. A condition code is a number which is returned by the system after the execution of your job. Different numbers imply different meanings. A condition code of 0 implies a successful execution. Any numbers returned (other than zero) must be looked up in the appropriate system manuals to determine their meaning.

2.7 AN INTRODUCTION TO ISPF

As indicated previously, the only way to execute a COBOL program is via JCL. However, before a group of JCL can be submitted to the operating system, it has to be typed to a file and stored on a disk. In other words, you need to create and edit a file with the appropriate JCL. In the IBM mainframe environment, you create and edit files through what is called the *ISPF/PDF Primary Option Menu*. We now describe briefly how you can access this menu, and also a few options that are available in this menu. Since this is only an introduction, we refer you to the ISPF manual for further reference.

2.8 ACCESSING ISPF

As you log in to the system, you may or may not be placed directly into the ISPF main menu. If you are not, all you have to do is type `ISPF` at the command line and the menu displayed in Figure 2.2 (or something very close to it) will appear on the screen.

```
----------- ISPF/PDF PRIMARY OPTION MENU ---------
OPTION ===>

 0 ISPF PARMS   - SPECIFY TERMINAL AND USER PARAMETERS
 1 BROWSE       - DISPLAY SOURCE DATA OR OUTPUT LISTINGS
 2 EDIT         - CREATE OR CHANGE SOURCE DATA
 3 UTILITIES    - PERFORM UTILITY FUNCTIONS
 4 FOREGROUND   - INVOKE LANGUAGE PROCESSORS IN FOREGROUND
 5 BATCH        - SUBMIT JOB FOR LANGUAGE PROCESSING
 6 COMMAND      - ENTER TSO COMMAND, CLIST, OR REXX EXEC
 7 DIALOG TEST  - PERFORM DIALOG TESTING
 8 LM UTILITIES- PERFORM LIBRARY ADMINISTRATOR UTILITY FUNCTION
 9 IBM PRODUCTS- ADDITIONAL IBM PROGRAM DEVELOPMENT PRODUCTS
10 SCLM         - SOFTWARE CONFIGURATION AND LIBRARY MANAGER
 C CHANGES      - DISPLAY SUMMARY OF CHANGES FOR THIS RELEASE
 I IOF          - INTERACTIVE OUTPUT FACILITY
 O OTHER PROD.  - ADDITIONAL NON IBM PROGRAM PRODUCTS
 T TUTORIAL     - DISPLAY INFORMATION ABOUT ISPF/PDF
 X EXIT         - TERMINATE ISPF USING LOG AND LIST DEFAULTS

ENTER END COMMAND TO TERMINATE ISPF.
```

Figure 2.2 The ISPF/PDF Primary Option Menu

In the upper right hand corner of the screen will appear information which relates to yourself, the current system time, and so on. Here's what appeared on our screen:

```
USERID   - MA08
TIME     - 16:55
TERMINAL - 3278
PF KEYS  - 24
DATE     - 92.260
```

The display indicates that our terminal type is a 3278, and tells us that we have access to 24 function keys, and displays the date in julian format (day number 260, 1992). The cursor will position itself next to the OPTION ===> field.

As you take another look at the menu, notice that ISPF allows the user to interact with the operating system in a variety of ways: as a user, a programmer, a system administrator, and so on. In this chapter we will describe the screens that display on choosing option 0 (ISPF PARMS) and option 2 (EDIT). Please refer to the ISPF manual if you require further details.

2.8.1 ISPF PARMS Option

Enter 0 on the command line next to the OPTION prompt. Doing so will result in a display of the following screen:

```
-----------  ISPF PARAMETER OPTIONS  ---------
OPTION  ===>

1 TERMINAL   - SPECIFY TERMINAL CHARACTERISTICS
2 LOG/LIST   - SPECIFY ISPF LOG AND LIST DEFAULTS
3 PF KEYS    - SPECIFY PF KEYS FOR 3278 TERMINAL WITH 24 PF KEYS
4 DISPLAY    - SPECIFY SCREEN DISPLAY CHARACTERISTICS
5 LIST       - SPECIFY LIST DATA SET CHARACTERISTICS
6 GRAPHIC    - SPECIFY GDDM GRAPHIC PRINT PARAMETERS
7 ENVIRON    - SPECIFY ENVIRON COMMAND SETTINGS
8 KEYLIST    - MODIFY KEYLIST(S)
9 DIALOG TEST - SPECIFY DIALOG TEST OPTION
```

Figure 2.3 ISPF Parameter Options

The options available in this menu are used to customize the terminal and user environment. We now type 3 next to OPTION. Doing so will result in a listing of the mapping of available function keys. The screen displayed in Figure 2.4 appears. Please note that the mapping for function keys at your site can be different from the one displayed at our installation.

```
-----------  PF KEY DEFINITIONS AND LABELS - PRIMARY KEYS-----
OPTION  ===>

PF13 ===> HELP
PF14 ===> SPLIT
PF15 ===> END
PF16 ===> RETURN
PF17 ===> RFIND
PF18 ===> RCHANGE
PF19 ===> UP
PF20 ===> DOWN
PF21 ===> SWAP
PF22 ===> LEFT
PF23 ===> RIGHT
PF24 ===> CURSOR

PRESS ENTER KEY TO DISPLAY ALTERNATE KEYS, ENTER END COMMAND TO
EXIT
```

Figure 2.4 Primary PF Key Mapping

We press the ENTER key to display the alternate mapping.   The screen in Figure 2.5 displays:

```
-----------  PF KEY DEFINITIONS AND LABELS - ALTERNATE KEYS --
OPTION   ===>

PF1   ===> HELP
PF2   ===> SPLIT
PF3   ===> END
PF4   ===> RETURN
PF5   ===> RFIND
PF6   ===> RCHANGE
PF7   ===> UP
PF8   ===> DOWN
PF9   ===> SWAP
PF10  ===> LEFT
PF11  ===> RIGHT
PF12  ===> CURSOR

PRESS ENTER KEY TO DISPLAY ALTERNATE KEYS, ENTER END COMMAND TO
EXIT
```

Figure 2.5 Alternate PF Key Mapping

2.8.2 The Edit Screens

The screen displayed in Figure 2.6 displays on choosing option number 2 from the main ISPF screen.

```
-----------------  EDIT - ENTRY PANEL --------------------
COMMAND ===>

ISPF LIBRARY:
   PROJECT ===> MA08
   GROUP   ===> TEST    ===>         ===>         ===>
   TYPE    ===> JCLLIB
   MEMBER  ===> TESTJCL (BLANK OR PATTERN FOR MEMBER SEL. LIST)

OTHER PARTITIONED OR SEQUENTIAL DATA SET:
   DATA SET NAME   ===>
   MEMBER          ===>   (IF NOT CATAL GEO)

DATA SET PASSWORD ===>   (IF PASSWORD PROTECTED)

PROFILE NAME      ===>   (BLANK DEFAULTS TO DATA SET TYPE)

INITIAL MACRO     ===>   LMF LOCK  ===> YES (YES, NO OR NEVER)

FORMAT NAME       ===>   MIXED MODE ===> NO   (YES OR NO)
```

Figure 2.6 The EDIT Screen

Entry is required for the following prompts. We display these prompts along with the appropriate response:

```
ISPF LIBRARY:
   PROJECT ===> MA08
   GROUP   ===> TEST    ===>          ===>          ===>
   TYPE    ===> JCLLIB
   MEMBER  ===> TESTJCL (BLANK OR PATTERN FOR MEMBER SEL. LIST)
```

You need to check with your installation for the required entry in these fields. Please note that you need to press the Tab key to go from one field to the next. If you press the Enter key, the system will assume that you are ready to exit from this screen and proceed to the next one.

Entry is optional for the following prompts:

```
OTHER PARTITIONED OR SEQUENTIAL DATA SET:
   DATA SET NAME   ===>
   MEMBER          ===>    (IF NOT CATAL GEO)

DATA SET PASSWORD ===>    (IF PASSWORD PROTECTED)

PROFILE NAME      ===>    (BLANK DEFAULTS TO DATA SET TYPE)

INITIAL MACRO     ===>   LMF LOCK   ===> YES (YES, NO OR NEVER)

FORMAT NAME       ===>   MIXED MODE ===> NO  (YES OR NO)
```

We enter information only in the required fields for now. Recall that while input for the required fields varies for different installations, it is usually designated by the system administrator.

Before proceeding to the next screen, let's take a moment to understand the input. And even before we do that, let us add a small disclaimer. For now, it is not important that you understand the meaning of each field in the ISPF screens. It would be best if you ask the designated personnel at your installation what to enter. As you continue to read this chapter, the screens will start to make much more sense.

Let us now continue. For this example, MA08 is entered in response to the PROJECT prompt. This is our user ID, and corresponds to the user ID that appears on the right hand of the screen on entry to the ISPF menu. TEST is entered as response to GROUP. TESTJCL is entered as response to MEMBER. This is the name of the file that we wish to create and edit.

After entering this information, the *ENTER* key is pressed, and the edit screen is displayed. We describe this screen next.

2.9 INPUTTING INFORMATION

Figure 2.7 illustrates how the edit screen looks. The first line displays information about the file being edited. The top and bottom of the screen display TOP OF DATA and BOTTOM OF DATA, respectively.

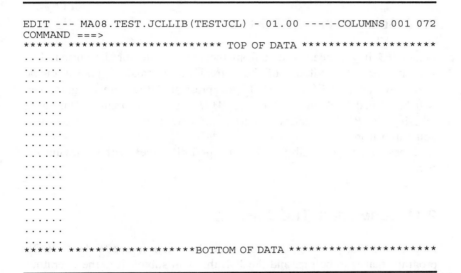

```
EDIT --- MA08.TEST.JCLLIB(TESTJCL) - 01.00 -----COLUMNS 001 072
COMMAND ===>
****** ********************** TOP OF DATA ********************
 . . . . . .
 . . . . . .
 . . . . . .
 . . . . . .
 . . . . . .
 . . . . . .
 . . . . . .
 . . . . . .
 . . . . . .
 . . . . . .
 . . . . . .
 . . . . . .
 . . . . . .
 . . . . . .
 . . . . . .
 . . . . . .
 . . . . . .
****** *******************BOTTOM OF DATA *********************
```

Figure 2.7 Entry into Edit Screen

Now you are ready for input. As we proceed through this tutorial, we will be accessing specific function keys to do the job. Please note that these function keys may be defined differently at your site; check with your system administrator for further details.

Enter I to enter information in the file, and press the *ENTER* key. On doing so, the dots will disappear, and line numbers will appear instead. The cursor will be positioned on the first line. You are now ready to input information.

Hit *ENTER* at the end of each line. If you hit *ENTER* at the end of the first line, then all of the blank lines on your screen will be lost.

If you make a mistake while typing, and you have not hit *ENTER* yet, simply hit the *BACKSPACE* key until the cursor is positioned where you want it to be. Correct the mistake by typing over it, and press the ENTER key when you are done.

Once you have typed the JCL, (or whatever you may be editing at the time), hit *PF12 (Programmeable Function Key number 12)*, and this will place you at the command line. Type SAVE to save the file, and hit *ENTER*. The name of the file will be displayed in the top left-hand corner, and the message MEMBER HAS BEEN SAVED will be displayed in the upper right-hand corner.

If you don't want to save the file, hit *PF12* to get to the *COMMAND* line. Then type CANCEL on the command line and hit ENTER. The file will not be saved.

2.10 SOME USEFUL PF KEYS

Press *PF3* if you need to exit from the input mode for the current file, save its contents, exit out of the current screen, and be placed in the *EDIT-ENTRY PANEL* screen. If you press the *PF3* screen again, you will be placed back in the *ISPF PRIMARY OPTION* menu. Basically, pressing the *PF3* key takes you from the current screen to the one that you came from.

Press *PF4* if you wish to exit from the Edit screen without saving the file.

2.11 SUBMITTING THE JOB

Please note that you would need to use the editor to create the COBOL program that is to be run, and the JCL that will submit it to the operating system. Once this is done, the COBOL program is compiled and link-edited (these terms will be explained later on in the book), and then submitted to the operating system for execution. We now explain how a program is executed from the ISPF editor screen.

Bring up the file that contains the JCL used to execute the COBOL program (this file was presented in Section 2.3) on your screen while in Edit mode and type SUB or SUBMIT on the command line. Then hit the *ENTER* key. Your job will be submitted.

2.12 REVIEW

You now know how to create and edit files, and submit jobs to the operating system. You also know a few preliminaries about ISPF, and the function of a few useful function keys. In a nutshell, you really know the basics required to run a program in the IBM mainframe environment! The remainder of the book will go into more detailed descriptions of JCL statements. But most of what follows will build on the fundamentals described in Chapters 1 and 2. You should feel confident about what you have learned so far, before proceeding to the next chapter.

The JOB Statement

3.1 INTRODUCTION

The first two chapters exposed you to some fundamental aspects of JCL. The statements that you encountered there will now be discussed in much greater detail. This chapter is devoted to explaining the JOB statement.

3.2 AN OVERVIEW

In JCL, a job can be considered as a unit of work that has to be executed. It contains several JCL statements that instruct the operating system on what to do.

As you should be aware by now, in an IBM mainframe environment, all resources required by a program have to be specified. In a job statement, the following issues become significant:

- The start of a new job must be specified.

- A name should be provided for a job, so that it can be differentiated from other jobs. Without a name, no job can be executed.

- A job is billed for its usage of CPU time, resources, and so on. In order to bill it, an account number has to be provided.

- The name of the programmer of the job can be specified.

- Jobs can be differentiated in many ways. For instance, there can be jobs that utilize a lot of CPU time, those in which usage of CPU time is not that significant, jobs that would take a very long time to execute, those that require a relatively short amount of time, those that have a higher priority than others, and so on. Thus, the job has to be categorized.

- As a job executes, many kinds of messages are output. Some of these messages are generated by the program that is being executed. The device to which these messages will be written must be specified.

- Messages are generated by the job step itself, indicating the status of the job, errors, status of data, and so on. If these messages are to be listed, then the device to which these messages will be written to must also be specified.

- A job can be explicitly assigned a priority.

- A job can be held for later execution.

- Comments can and should be added, indicating the nature of the job being executed, and so on.

3.3 CORRESPONDING JCL

Table 3.1 indicates the JCL parameter that is used to convey the information listed in Section 3.2, if one is available. If there is no specific JCL parameter, then the text indicates how the information can be coded. All JCL parameters are capitalized.

3.4 THE JOB STATEMENT

This is the very first statement in any JCL segment. It identifies the beginning of a job to the operating system. Hence, if this statement is missing, the operating system will be unable to execute the job. Like all JCL statements, it can be divided into four fields.

Positional and/or keyword parameters are coded in the operands field. Positional parameters must precede the keyword parameters, if both exist.

The format of this statement looks like this:

//	Name	Operation	Operands	Comments
//	jobname	JOB	operands <positional/ keyword parameters >	comments

Table 3.1 JCL Parameters on the JOB Statement

Function	Corresponding JCL Parameter
Specification of the start of a job	JOB
Specification of job name	jobname
Specification of accounting information	(accounting information)
Specification of programmer name	,name
Categorization of job	CLASS
Specification of output class to job log	MSGCLASS
Specification of printing the system messages	MSGLEVEL
Assignment of priority to a job	PRTY
Holding a job for later execution	TYPRUN

3.5 RULES FOR CODING JOB STATEMENT

The following rules must be adhered to when coding this statement:

- A valid name must be assigned to the job that is being submitted. This is called *jobname*, and it must follow the initial two slashes that precede all JCL statements.

- The word JOB must be coded in the operation field.

- Positional parameters can be coded in the operands field.

- Keyword parameters can also be coded in the operands field. Keyword parameters cannot precede positional parameters.

- Comments can be coded, as in any JCL statement. Comments are recognized as such by coding as follows:

```
//*comment
```

Comments can be specified on the same line as the JCL statement by placing at least one space between the end of the JCL parameters and the beginning of the comment.

We will now discuss each parameter in greater detail.

3.6 JOBNAME

The *jobname* must start in Column 3, immediately following the double slashes. It must be followed by at least one space. As stated previously, it must be the first statement for the particular job being submitted at the time.

3.6.1 Rules for Coding

Valid names can be 1 to 8 alphanumeric characters in length. The #, @ and $ symbols (also called national symbols) can also be included in the name. The first character of the name must be alphabetic or national; it cannot be numeric.

3.6.2 Some Examples

Here are a few examples of valid jobnames:

```
//QYGBCXXX
//C31249
//R45MR@67
//@12345
//W7
```

The following are examples of a few jobnames that are not valid:

```
//123JRC
```

The above example is invalid because a number is coded as the first character.

```
// ABC
```

The above example is invalid because there is a space between the // and the start of the job name.

```
//ABCDEFGHI
```

The above example is invalid because the jobname is longer than 8 characters.

Your installation may assign jobnames for your jobs.

As you are aware, more than one job can be submitted in succession within the same JCl. If more than one job is submitted, then each job should be given a unique name. If two jobs are submitted with the same name, then the second job will execute after the first has terminated. If errors are generated for either one of the jobs, then they will be identified by the jobname, and confusion can result as to which job actually generated the error. Hence, the recommendation by the authors is to identify each job with a unique name.

3.7 Positional Parameters

Positional parameters must precede keyword parameters. The following two positional parameters will be described:

- Job Accounting Information parameter

- Programmer name parameter

Since these are positional parameters, they must be coded in the order just presented. A discussion follows of each.

3.8 Job Accounting Information Parameter

Accounting information in an IBM mainframe environment is used to bill or charge back any job that is run on the mainframe. The accounting information parameter identifies the account number which will be billed for the CPU time utilized on the mainframe.

3.8.1 Syntax

Here's the syntax of this parameter:

(account-number,additional-accounting-information)
or
'account-number,additional-accounting-information'
or
account-number
or
,additional-accounting-information

3.8.2 Rules for Coding

The following rules must be adhered to, when coding this parameter:

- Parentheses or apostrophes must be used if additional accounting information is coded.

- Parentheses or apostrophes may be omitted if only the account number is coded.

- If both parameters are coded, then they must be separated from each other by a comma.

- If only additional accounting information is coded, then the absence of the account number must be indicated via a comma. This is because these are positional parameters; if one is omitted, then its absence must be indicated in this way.

- If the accounting information parameters contain any special characters, the parameter should be enclosed within single quotes. If the special character itself is a single quote, then another single quote should precede it.

Although these parameters are optional as far as JCL is concerned, they are probably required by your installation.

As far as the contents of these parameters are concerned, you don't have to do much thinking here, because your installation will give you exact instructions on how to code this. The basic rule that you must adhere to is to insert a comma between each parameter, and enclose them within parentheses or apostrophes. Note: both of these cases are acceptable.

3.8.3 Some Examples

Examples are presented illustrating the rules just stated.

Example 1

```
//JOB1 JOB (A123,DEPT1)
```

Each parameter of this statement is discussed.

JOB1 is the name of the job. It immediately follows the initial two slashes that precede every JCL statement. JOB is the operation. A123 is the account number. DEPT1 is additional accounting information. Since both parameters are coded, they are enclosed within parentheses.

Example 2

```
//JOB1 JOB 'A123,DEPT1'
```

In this example, apostrophes are used to enclose the accounting information parameters, instead of brackets.

Example 3

```
//JOB1 JOB (A123,'DEPT/MIS',124)
```

In this example, the special character (/) is included in the additional information parameter. For this reason, that particular parameter is enclosd in single quotes.

Example 4

```
//JOB1 JOB (A123,'DEPT''S MGR',124)
```

In this example the DEPT'S MGR is coded as 'DEPT''S MGR'. The apostrophe before the apostrophe is required, if an apostrophe is contained within the sub-parameter.

Example 5

```
//JOB1 JOB A123
```

In this example, only the account number is coded, and additional information is skipped.

Example 6

```
//JOB1 (,DEPT1)
```

In this example, the account number is skipped. The comma is required because these are positional parameters. If a parameter that would appear in Position 1 is skipped, its absence must be indicated via a comma.

3.9 PROGRAMMER-NAME PARAMETER

The *Programmer-Name* parameter follows the *Job-Accounting Information* parameter. It can specify two things:

- Your name

- Information related to the job being submitted

3.9.1 Syntax

There are no special syntax requirements for this parameter, except that it should be coded immediately after the accounting information parameter.

3.9.2 Rules for Coding

The following rules must be adhered to while coding this parameter:

- It can be from 1 to 20 characters long.

- If the name contains any special characters, such as a blank, comma, hyphen (/), single quote, asterisk, dollar sign, plus, minus, or equal sign (=), or brackets, then it must be enclosed within apostrophes.

- If the name contains a single quote, than two single quotes must be used.

- A hyphen (-) is a special character that cannot be embedded within the programmer-name parameter.

It is possible that this parameter may be mandatory at your installation. Check with your systems programmer for further information.

3.9.3 Some Examples

Examples follow.

Example 1

```
//JOB1 JOB (A123),SABA
```

The parameters in this statement are:

The double (//) slashes are required at the start of each JCL statement, in Columns 1 and 2. JOB1 is the job name and immediately follows the double slashes. JOB is the operation.

(A123) is the account number. SABA is the programmer name parameter.

Example 2

```
//JOB1 JOB (A123),'O''SULLIVAN'
```

In this example, the name O'Sullivan is coded as 'O''SULLIVAN'. The apostrophe before the apostrophe is required.

Example 3

```
//JOB1 JOB (A123),'CHANDER K. RANADE'
```

In this example, spaces and a period are included in the name. These are special characters. Therefore, the entire name is once again enclosed within apostrophes.

Example 4

```
//JOB1 JOB ,ZAMIR
```

In this example, the accounting information parameter is skipped, while the programmer name parameter is coded. Since these are positional parameters, the absence of the accounting parameter is indicated via a comma.

3.10 Keyword Parameters

Keyword parameters must follow positional parameters. However, unlike positional parameters, they can be coded in any order. The following keyword parameters will be described in this chapter:

- CLASS

- PRTY

- MSGCLASS

- MSGLEVEL

- TYPRUN

3.11 THE CLASS PARAMETER.

The CLASS parameter assigns what is called a *jobclass* to a job. A *jobclass* identifies the nature of the job that is to be submitted. Some jobs can be short-running, others can take a long time, still others may utilize heavy resources, require one or more tapes, and so on. The jobclass is used to identify these characteristics to the operating system, thereby categorizing the job being submitted.

3.11.1 Syntax

Here's the syntax:

    CLASS=jobclass

where jobclass is any character between A-Z or number between 0-9.

3.11.2 Rules for Coding

- This parameter must follow positional parameters on the job statement.

The JOBCLASS parameter is usually assigned by your installation. Sometimes a default value is assigned to this parameter. If this is the case, then you do not need to code it in your JCL. Check with your installation as to whether your job has been assigned a default class.

3.11.3 Some Examples

To follow are some examples that illustrate the use of this parameter.

Example 1

```
//JOB1 JOB (A123),RANADE,CLASS=K
```

An explanation of each parameter follows.

First, there are the double slashes that precede each JCL statement. JOB1 is the job name.   JOB is the keyword identifying the JOB statement.

(A123) is the account number.   RANADE is the programmer name parameter.   CLASS=K is assigned to the CLASS parameter.

At the time that an MVS system is generated (this is called a *SYSGEN*; it is synonymous with loading a new operating system on a computer), various defaults are established.   At this time, different letters and numbers are designated as classes to help categorize the nature of the jobs that will be submitted once the system is up.   Hence, the letter *K* is installation defined.   It can mean anything.   For example, it could be used to indicate a job that uses a lot of CPU time, or one that is a low priority.

Example 2

```
//JOB2 JOB (A123),RANADE,CLASS=8
```

In this example, class is assigned the number 8.   Hence, job JOB2 will contain the characteristics assigned to class 8.

3.12 PRTY PARAMETER

The PRTY parameter is related to the CLASS parameter.   It assigns priority to jobs which belong to the same class.

3.12.1 Syntax

Here's the syntax:

```
PRTY=priority
```

where priority is a number between 0 to 14, or 0 to 15, depending on what job entry subsystem is being run at the time.   In an IBM mainframe environment, *JES2* or *JES3* are the names assigned to different types of subsystems within the operating system. These subsystems will be described in detail later on in the book. Don't be too concerned about this for now. Sub-systems are transparent to the users.

3.12.2 Rules for Coding

- The PRTY parameter must follow positional parameters on the JOB statement.

A job with a higher number takes precedence over a job with a lower number. A job with priority 10 will run before a job with priority 3. If two jobs have the same jobclass and same priority, then they will be executed in the order in which they are submitted. Please note that priority is assigned to jobs within the same classes.

3.12.3 Some Examples

Here are a few examples that illustrate what has just been said:

Example 1

```
//JOB1 JOB (A123),ZAMIR,CLASS=8,PRTY=6
//JOB2 JOB (B123),ZAMIR,CLASS=8,PRTY=9
```

An explanation of each parameter follows:
JOB1 and JOB2 are the job names of two jobs. JOB is the keyword identifying the JOB statement. A123 and B123 are the account numbers. ZAMIR is the programmer name parameter. CLASS=8 is the CLASS parameter. PRTY=6 and PRTY=9 are the assignments to the priority parameter.
JOB2 will execute before JOB1, because it has a higher priority number (9) than JOB1 (6).

Example 2

```
//JOB3 JOB (A123),RANADE,CLASS=K,PRTY=6
//JOB4 JOB (B123),RANADE,CLASS=9,PRTY=9
```

In this example, JOB4 will execute before JOB3, since it has a higher priority number than JOB3. Notice that the CLASS assignments are not the same.

3.13 MSGCLASS PARAMETER

Messages can be categorized into two types. First, there are those that relate to the system and the JCL. Second, there are those that are output by the program or procedure being executed. Let us explain this in greater detail.

As a job executes, the operating system outputs messages that specify the events that take place each step along the way. This includes messages related to the system, and those that have to do with the JCL that is being executed. In addition to this, the job that you submit may be executing a program or procedure that writes the output to the printer, a tape or a disk. The MSGCLASS parameter determines the output device to which system messages and JCL messages are written.

3.13.1 Syntax

The syntax of the MSGCLASS parameter looks like this:

    MSGCLASS=output-class-name

where *output-class-name* can be any alphabetic (A-Z) or numeric (0-9) character. The *output-class-name* is related to a specific output device to which messages are routed.

3.13.2 Rules for Coding

- The MSGCLASS parameter must follow positional parameters on the JOB statement.

3.13.3 Some Examples

Examples follow.

Example 1

```
//JOB1 JOB  (A123),RANADE,CLASS=K,
//          PRTY=6,MSGCLASS=A
```

In this example, JOB1 is the jobname, JOB is the keyword identifying the JOB statement, (A123) is the account number, RANADE is the programmer name, CLASS is set to K, priority is set to 6, and MSGCLASS is set to A. Usually, MSGCLASS=A designates the printer.

Example 2

```
//JOB1 JOB (A123),RANADE,CLASS=K,
//          PRTY=6,MSGCLASS=1
```

In this example, MSGCLASS is set to 1. The number 1 could specify a printer, or any other output device.

3.14 MSGLEVEL PARAMETER

The MSGLEVEL parameter is used to specify the JCL and allocation messages which will be recorded on the output device specified in MSGCLASS.

As a JCL job is submitted, all kinds of messages are generated by the system. These messages can be roughly categorized as follows:

- First, log messages indicating job name, user name, etc. are routed to the output device.

- Next, JCL statements comprising that job are output.

- Next, messages related to the execution of the job will be output.

- Finally, the output of the program being executed is output.

In addition to this, allocation messages are also printed. These messages print at the beginning of a job step, indicating the allocation of data sets to devices. They also print at the end of the job step, indicating the dispositions of data sets used by the job.

3.14.1 Syntax

The syntax of the MSGLEVEL parameter is as follows:

    MSGLEVEL=(statements,messages)

or

    MSGLEVEL=statements

or

    MSGLEVEL=(,messages)

where *statements* may be the number 0, 1, or 2, and *messages* is a value which can be 0 or 1.

Coding a 0 in *statements* will result in messages related to the JOB statement only being output.

Coding a 1 will result in all JCL in the job being submitted being output. In addition to this, if any cataloged procedures are invoked, then their JCL will also be output. If symbolic parameters are used, then they will also be output, but only after they have been substituted. (Cataloged procedures and symbolic parameters will be described later on in the book.)

Coding a 2 will result in only the input JCL statements being printed.

In the messages field, you can code a 0 or a 1.

Coding a 0 will result in only allocation/termination messages being output if the job terminates abnormally.

Coding a 1 will result in all allocation/termination messages being output, regardless of whether the job terminates normally or abnormally.

3.14.2 Rules for Coding

■ The MSGLEVEL parameter must be coded after positional parameters on the JOB statement.

If this parameter is not coded, then all messages will be output.
If it is coded, then specific output can be requested.

3.14.3 Some Examples

Example 1

```
//JOB1   JOB   (A123),'RANADE',MSGLEVEL=(1,1)
```

In this example, JOB1 is the jobname, JOB is the keyword identifying the JOB statement, (A123) is the accounting number, RANADE is the programmer name, and MSGLEVEL is set to (1,1). All JCL will be printed, including allocation messages.

Example 2

```
//JOB1   JOB   (A123),'RANADE',MSGLEVEL=0
```

In this example, only the JOB statement will be printed.

Example 3

```
//JOB1   JOB   (A123),'RANADE',MSGLEVEL=(,1)
```

In this example, only allocation messages will be output.

3.15 TYPRUN PARAMETER

The TYPRUN parameter is used to specify a special type of job processing, such as whether a job is to be held until it is released, and whether its execution is to be suppressed altogether.

3.15.1 Syntax

The syntax of this parameter follows:

TYPRUN=HOLD

or

TYPRUN=SCAN

Specification of the HOLD parameter results in the job being held until further notice. This parameter is useful when jobs which utilize a lot of resources are required to be held until a time when the system is relatively unused.

Specification of the SCAN parameter results in the JCL being scanned for syntax errors and reports them to the requested output media. Syntactical errors are comprised of invalid keywords, illegal characters and incorrect use of parentheses. The job will not be executed when this parameter is used, even if there are no errors. Use of the SCAN parameter is a good practice.

3.15.2 Rules for Coding

■ The TYPRUN parameter should be coded after the positional parameters.

■ Make sure that a job which is being held is ultimately released by the operator, or it will remain in the input queue for a duration of time that is fixed by the installation.

3.15.3 Some Examples

Example 1

```
//JOB1  JOB  (A123),'RANADE',TYPRUN=HOLD
```

In this example, JOB1 will be held until it is released by the operator.

Example 2

```
//JOB1   JOB   (A123),'RANADE',TYPRUN=SCAN
```

In this example, the JCL will be checked for syntax errors.

3.16 THINGS THAT CAN GO WRONG

In an IBM mainframe environment, error messages are generated to the output device if your job does not execute properly. All error messages have a code associated with them. A description of these error codes can be found in the appropriate manual, where they are listed in alphabetical order.

Often, it is difficult to trace exactly which JCL statement resulted in which error. In Table 3.2, we provide a generalized correspondence between some common errors, and the error code and message that is generated from it. You may use this information in two ways: either match up the error code generated in your code with what is listed; or, if you have trouble tracing the exact statement generating the error, scan through the section titled *Probable Cause of Error* and try to match it up with your JCL.

3.17 REVIEW

In this chapter we discussed the JOB statement and described its parameters in detail

Table 3.3 indicates the basic syntax of each parameter or related information.

Table 3.2 Some Common Errors

JCL Error Code	Description	Probable Cause of Error
IEF642I	Excessive parameter length on the JOB statement	Invalid name assigned to JOB statement
IEF196I	Unknown job code	Coding key word in NAME field
IEF632I	Format error in the CLASS field	Coding CLASS parameter before positional parameters Similar messages will be generated on coding keyword parameters before positional parameters
IEF639I	Invalid class designation in the CLASS field	Assigning an invalid jobclass to CLASS
IEF644I	Invalid numeric in the PRTY field	Assigning a non-numeric character to PRTY
IEF643I	Unidentified positional parameter in the TYPRUN field	Misspelling the assignment to TYPRUN Similar messages will be generated on misspelling other designations to parameters
	Enter JOBNAME character(s)	Forgetting to code JOB name parameter

Table 3.3 Parameters on the JOB Statement

JCL Parameter	Syntax
JOB	JOB
jobname	jobname where jobname is 1 to 8 alphanumeric characters and/or national symbols. The first character cannot be numeric. jobname must start in Column 3, immediately following the double slashes.
accounting information	account number (account number, additional information) where account number is a number assigned by your installation, and additional information is anything else required to be coded by your installation. Parentheses are not required if additional information is not coded. They are required if it is coded.
programmer name	programmer-name 'programmer name' where programmer-name is a 1 to 20 alphanumeric characters identifying name. It is enclosed in apostrophes if it contains any special characters.
CLASS	CLASS=class where class is any alphabetic or numeric character symbolizing the category in which that job is being placed.

MSGCLASS	MSGCLASS=class where class is any alphabetic or numeric character symbolizing the output device.
MSGLEVEL	MSGLEVEL=(n1, n2) where n1 is a number between 0 and 2, indicating the JCL messages to be output. n2 is either 0 or 1, indicating whether or not the message is to be printed.
PRTY	PRTY=priority where priority is a number between 0 to 14, or 0 to 15, depending on job entry subsystem
TYPRUN	TYPRUN=function where function can be HOLD or SCAN

The EXEC Statement

4.1 INTRODUCTION

In Chapter 3 you became familiar with the JOB statement. A job may consist of one or more job steps. A job step is a unit of work that is submitted to the operating system in the form of a collection of JCL statements. The EXEC statement is the first statement of each job step.

This leads us to the question: what is a unit of work? A unit of work can be the execution of a program. Or, it can be the execution of a procedure that is pre-written and available for general use by users of the system. Procedures such as these are called cataloged procedures; their name and location are recorded or cataloged by the system. This chapter will describe, in detail, the EXEC statement used to execute a program. We will describe the EXEC statement coded for cataloged procedures later on in the book.

4.2 AN OVERVIEW

As always, any kind of resources that will be required for the proper execution of the job and the program must be specified to the operating system. The following issues become significant:

- The system must be told the location of the program that is to be executed.

■ The location specified may be universal for all job steps within that job, or specific to a particular job step within that job.

■ The program to be executed must be identified, and its name must be specified.

■ Since a job can consist of multiple job steps, each job step must be identified, and have a name.

■ It is possible that each job step is to be billed to a different account. Hence, an account number can be specified for specific job steps.

■ The program that is being executed may require values to be passed to it, when it is run. There has to be some way to input values to the program.

■ A job step may have specific storage requirements. These must be specified.

■ A job step may have a greater or higher priority than other steps within that job and its priority must be specified to the system.

■ Certain job steps can be more important than others, and thus should be allowed free access to system resources. Conversely, other job steps may not be that important, and can be restricted in their use of system resources. If this is so, then the job step should be categorized appropriately.

■ A program may terminate abnormally within a job. If a job consists of several job steps, it may not be necessary to rerun each job step prior to the one that terminated with an error. Thus, the job should have the capability of being restarted at any point.

4.3 CORRESPONDING JCL

Table 4.1 presents the JCL parameters used to specify the information just listed. The remainder of this chapter will explain each parameter in detail.

Table 4.1 JCL Parameters on the EXEC Statement

Function	JCL Parameter
Specification of location of program to be executed, location being universal for all job steps within a job	JOBLIB
Specification of location of program to be executed, location being specific to a job step	STEPLIB
Specification of program name	PGM
Specification of job step name	stepname
Specification of account number for particular job step	ACCT
Sending values to a program when it is executed	PARM
Specification of storage requirements for a job step	ADDRSPC
Assignment of priority to a job step	DPRTY=(value1,value2)
Specification of rate of access to system resources	PERFORM
Specification of restart at a job step in case of abnormal termination	RD

4.4 SYNTAX

The syntax of the EXEC statement looks like this:

//stepname EXEC PGM=program-name, keyword parameters

where stepname is the name assigned to the job step, EXEC is the EXEC statement, program-name is the name of the program, (this is a positional parameter) and keyword parameters follow the positional parameters.

The syntax that you see here executes a program. The syntax for executing cataloged procedures will be explained later in the book.

4.5 RULES FOR CODING

The following rules apply to coding the EXEC statement.

- The EXEC statement must exist for each job step. A maximum of 255 EXEC statements can be specified within a single job.

- *stepname* is optional. However, a valid and unique stepname must be coded for each job step if certain tasks are to be implemented. More on this in the next section.

- Positional parameters can be coded in the operands field. The PGM parameter will be described later on in this chapter.

- Keyword parameters can also be coded in the *OPERAND* field. As usual, keyword parameters must follow positional parameters.

4.6 STEPNAME

The *stepname* is an optional field. However, since system messages reference stepnames, it is strongly recommended that you give unique and meaningful names to each step. Under certain conditions, its presence is essential. We will describe these conditions later on in this section. For now, we describe the syntax and rules for coding.

4.6.1 Syntax

There are no special syntax requirements for this parameter.

4.6.2 Rules for Coding

The following rules must be adhered to when coding a stepname:

- The stepname must consist of 1 through 8 alphanumeric (A-Z,0-9) and national characters (#, @, $). The first character must be alphabetic or national.

- It must be coded in Column 3, immediately after // in Columns 1 and 2.

- The stepname must be followed by at least one blank.

4.6.3 Some Examples

Example 1

```
//STEP01 EXEC PGM=PROGRAM1
```

STEP01 is the name of the step. EXEC is coded in the operation field. PGM is the positional parameter. PROGRAM1 is being executed.

Example 2

```
//#1     EXEC PGM=PROGRAM1
```

In this example, the stepname is #1. A national character is valid as the first character in a stepname.

4.6.4 Conditions in which STEPNAME is Mandatory

There are certain conditions under which coding the stepname is mandatory. This is when reference is made to a step that has been previously executed. Three different scenarios will be presented that will help you understand when stepnames are mandatory.

First, within a job, you may have reason to reference a previously executed job step. For example, assume that one job step produces a temporary dataset that is to be used as input by the second job step. In this case, the prior job step must be referenced. This is called a refer-back statement and a stepname is mandatory.

Stepnames are mandatory when an overriding parameter is used. Overriding parameters are explained in Chapter 10.

Finally, one job may consist of several job steps. If one step fails, and the others are successful, there may be no need to restart the entire job; you may only need to restart from the step that failed. This is done via the restart parameter. Stepname is mandatory when the restart parameter is used.

All three parameters will be described in detail later on in the book. For the time being, it is only necessary to understand the conditions in which stepname is mandatory.

4.7 POSITIONAL PARAMETERS OF THE EXEC STATEMENT

As you are aware, positional parameters are characterized by the order in which they appear, and they must precede keyword parameters. Let's look at the PGM parameter.

4.8 THE PGM PARAMETER

The PGM parameter identifies the name of the program that is to be executed.

4.8.1 Syntax

Here's the syntax:

//stepname EXEC PGM=program-name

This chapter will describe the PGM parameter only.

4.8.2 Rules for Coding

- The program name specified in the PGM parameter must exist either in the system libraries, in temporary libraries, or in private libraries.

    The system libraries contain all of the IBM-supplied programs, such as compilers, editors, utility programs, etc. Temporary libraries and private libraries are user-defined.

- The program must be a member of a partitioned data set.

    Partitioned data sets are placed on direct access volumes. A partitioned data set is analogous to multiple stacks of objects placed together. In order to access an object, you have to pick the appropriate stack, and then go through it sequentially.

4.9 KEYWORD PARAMETERS OF THE EXEC STATEMENT

Keyword parameters must follow positional parameters. Unlike positional parameters, they can be coded in any sequence.

A job can have many EXEC steps. The keyword parameter coded for a job step will apply only to that step. The following keyword parameters will be explained in this chapter:

- ACCT

- PARM

- ADDRSPC

- DPRTY

- PERFORM

- RD

The following parameters will be explained in Chapter 5:

- COND

- REGION

- TIME

4.10 THE ACCT PARAMETER

The ACCT parameter is used to supply accounting information for the job step that it is used in. This parameter is rarely used in the EXEC statement. However, if it is, then the information to be coded is usually supplied by your installation.

4.10.1 Syntax

Here's the syntax:

    ACCT=(account-information,account-information...)
or
    ACCT=account-information

where *account-information* consists of one or more subparameters defined by your installation.

4.10.2 Rules for Coding

- If the account information consists of more than one subparameter, then each must be separated from the next via a comma.

- If a subparameter consists of any special characters (besides a hyphen), then the special characters must be enclosed in apostrophes.

- The maximum number of characters that you can include in accounting information, including the commas, is 142.

4.10.3 Some Examples

Example 1

```
//STEP1 EXEC   PGM=PROGRAM1,ACCT=(A123,RR)
```

STEP1 is the stepname. EXEC is the operation. PROGRAM1 is being executed. The accounting information that follows the ACCT parameter is specific to this job step only.

Example 2

```
//STEP2   EXEC   PGM=PROGRAM1,ACCT=1234
```

The parentheses are omitted, since there is only one subparameter for ACCT.

Example 3

```
//STEP3   EXEC   PGM=PROGRAM1,
//               ACCT=(RR,47,'B=3456')
```

Three subparameters are included for ACCT. Since the last subparameter includes a special character (=), it is enclosed in apostrophes.

4.11 THE PARM PARAMETER

The PARM parameter is used to supply information to a program as it executes. It is a very useful parameter.

4.11.1 Syntax

Here's the syntax:

PARM=value

where *value* is a string from 1 to 100 characters long.

4.11.2 Rules for Coding

- If the string contains special characters, then it must be enclosed within apostrophes.

- If the string is composed of several sub-strings, then each sub-string must be separated from the next by a comma, and the entire string must be enclosed within parentheses or apostrophes.

4.11.3 Some Examples

Example 1

```
//STEP1   EXEC   PGM=PROGRAM1,PARM=PRINT
```

STEP1 is the stepname. EXEC is the operation. PROGRAM1 is being executed, and the string "PRINT" is supplied to it during execution.

Example 2

```
//STEP2   EXEC   PGM=PROGRAM2,PARM='13+10'
```

In this example, a special character (+) is included in the string, and therefore the string is enclosed in apostrophes. The apostrophes are not passed to the program as part of the string.

Example 3

```
//STEP3   EXEC   PGM=PROGRAM3,PARM=(SALLY,MARY,ANDY)
```

In this example, the string is enclosed within parentheses. The parentheses are not passed to the program as part of the string.

4.12 Relationship of PARM to COBOL Program

We will now explain how the PARM parameter defined in JCL is linked to a COBOL program. Here's the JCL:

```
//JOB1       JOB   (A123),'C RANADE',
//                 CLASS=O,
//                 MSGCLASS=A
//JOBLIB     DD    DSN=NI.X100.LOADLIB,
//                 DISP=SHR
//STEP1      EXEC  PGM=PROGRAM1,
//                 PARM=PRINT
//INPUT1     DD    DSN=MA08.T.INFILE,
//                 DISP=SHR
//REPORT1    DD    SYSOUT=T
//
```

JOB1 is the jobname. (A123) is the accounting information for this job. 'C RANADE' is the programmer name. The program is assigned to CLASS O and MSGCLASS is set to A.

This example includes the JOBLIB statement, which indicates the location of the program that is being executed by the EXEC satement. The JOBLIB statement (and STEPLIB, which is related) will be explained towards the end of the chapter. For now, it is enough that you understand that the program (PROGRAM1) is a member of the partitioned data set NI.X100.LOADLIB.

STEP1 is the name of the jobstep. The program (PROGRAM1) is executed, and the string PRINT is passed to this program at the time that it is executed.

INPUT1 and REPORT1 are names assigned to *Data Definition* (DD) statements. The DD statement will be described in detail in later chapters. For now, it is enough for you to understand that input to the program is provided from the partitioned data set file called MA08.T.INFILE. The SYSOUT parameter, which specifies the devices to which the output will be routed, is set to T. *T* is installation defined. Disposition for both data sets is SHR, i.e. shared, implying that multiple users may access these data sets at the same time.

Now take a look at the COBOL program. Make special note of the LINKAGE SECTION. This is where the JCL PARM parameter links to the program.

```
        IDENTIFICATION DIVISION.
        PROGRAM-ID.    PROGRAM1.
      *
        ENVIRONMENT DIVISION.
```

```
    CONFIGURATION SECTION.
    SOURCE-COMPUTER.
      IBM-370.
    OBJECT-COMPUTER.
      IBM-370.
    INPUT-OUTPUT SECTION.
    FILE-CONTROL.
     SELECT IN-FILE    ASSIGN TO INPUT1.
     SELECT PRINT-FILE  ASSIGN TO REPORT1.
*
    DATA DIVISION.
    FILE SECTION.
    FD   IN-FILE
        LABEL RECORDS ARE STANDARD.
    01 IN-REC              PIC X(40).
    FD   PRINT-FILE
        BLOCK CONTAINS 0 RECORDS
        LABEL RECORDS ARE STANDARD.
    01   PRINT-REC         PIC X(133).
    WORKING-STORAGE SECTION.
    01   NO-DATA-FLAG      PIC X(3)   VALUE SPACES.
        88   NO-MORE-DATA              VALUE 'YES'.
*
    LINKAGE SECTION.
    01 PARM-FIELD.
        05   PARM-LENGTH              PIC S9(04) COMP.
        05   PARM-INDICATOR           PIC X(05).
*
    PROCEDURE DIVISION USING PARM-FIELD.
*
    A000-MAIN.
        PERFORM A000-OPEN-FILES.
        PERFORM A000-CHECK-PARM THRU A000-PARM-EXIT.
        PERFORM B000-PROCESSING THRU B000-EXIT UNTIL
           NO-MORE-DATA.
        PERFORM C000-CLOSE-FILES.
        STOP RUN.
*
    A000-OPEN-FILES.
        OPEN INPUT IN-FILE.
        OPEN OUTPUT PRINT-FILE.
*
    A000-CHECK-PARM.
        IF PARM-INDICATOR = 'PRINT'
           NEXT SENTENCE
        ELSE
           PERFORM C000-CLOSE-FILES.
*
    A000-PARM-EXIT.
        EXIT.
*
    B000-PROCESSING.
        READ IN-FILE
          AT END
```

```
               MOVE 'YES' TO NO-DATA-FLAG
               GO TO B000-EXIT.
          MOVE IN-REC TO PRINT-REC
          WRITE PRINT-REC.
          GO TO B000-PROCESSING.
  *
    B000-EXIT.
       EXIT.
  *
    C000-CLOSE-FILES.
       CLOSE IN-FILE PRINT-FILE.
```

Take another look at the LINKAGE SECTION:

```
LINKAGE SECTION.
01 PARM-FIELD.
      05   PARM-LENGTH              PIC S9(04) COMP.
      05   PARM-INDICATOR           PIC X(05).
```

PARM-LENGTH is the length of the PARM field. PARM-INDICATOR specifies the number of characters that will be passed to the program. Five characters will be supplied to the program. PARM-LENGTH and PARM-INDICATOR are user-defined fields, based on the string that is passed to the program.

If there is a LINKAGE SECTION in the program, PROCEDURE DIVISION must be coded as follows:

```
PROCEDURE DIVISION USING PARM-FIELD
```

Now take another look at the following statements in the procedure division:

```
A000-CHECK-PARM.
   IF PARM-INDICATOR = 'PRINT'
      NEXT SENTENCE
   ELSE
      PERFORM C000-CLOSE-FILES.
```

If PARM-INDICATOR is equal to the string PRINT, the next statement is executed. If it isn't, the procedure C000-CLOSE-FILES is executed, which closes the input and output files and exits the program.

4.13 THE JOBLIB AND STEPLIB STATEMENTS

Before continuing with the seldom-used keyword parameters, we will describe the JOBLIB and STEPLIB statements. It is not enough to know the name of the program that is to be executed. The system needs to know where that program resides. The EXEC statement identifies the member name only. Its location in the system has to be specified by the JOBLIB or STEPLIB statements. We will now briefly describe these statements.

4.14 THE JOBLIB STATEMENT

Recall that the first statement in any job is the JOB statement. The JOBLIB statement immediately follows this; it is a DD (Data Definition) statement, and it specifies where the program that is specified by the EXEC statement resides.

The EXEC statements for one or more jobsteps that comprise that job follow the JOBLIB statement. The same JOBLIB statement can apply to all subsequent EXEC statements.

4.14.1 Rules for Coding

- The JOBLIB statement must immediately follow the JOB statement.

- It must precede the EXEC statement.

- It cannot be used in a cataloged procedure.

- If its location is uncataloged, that is, name and location are not recorded by the system, it must specify the unit and volume serial number of the device containing the program to be executed.

4.14.2 Some Examples

Example 1

```
//JOB1    JOB   (A123),RANADE
//JOBLIB  DD    DSN=MI.TEST.LOADLIB,DISP=SHR
//STEP1   EXEC  PGM=PROGRAM1
```

In this example, JOB1 is the name of the job being submitted. (A123) is the accounting information parameter, RANADE is the programmer name.

Immediately following the JOB statement is the JOBLIB DD statement. This is used to specify the location of the program that is to be executed. In this example, PROGRAM1 is being executed, and it is a member of the partitioned data set MI.TEST.LOADLIB.

Example 2

```
//JOB1    JOB   (A123),RANADE
//JOBLIB  DD    DSN=MI.TEST.LOADLIB,
//              DISP=SHR
//STEP1   EXEC  PGM=PROGRAM1
//STEP2   EXEC  PGM=PROGRAM2
//
```

In this example, both PROGRAM1 and PROGRAM2 exist in the library called MI.TEST.LOADLIB.

Example 3

```
//JOB2    JOB   (A123),RANADE
//JOBLIB  DD    DSN=PROGRAM2,
//              DISP=SHR,
//              UNIT=3331,
//              VOL=SER=PACK1
```

In this example, the UNIT and VOL parameters are used with the JOBLIB statement. This is because PROGRAM2 is uncataloged. The UNIT and VOL parameters will be described later on in the book. For now, you should simply understand that you must use these parameters if the library that the program resides in is uncataloged.

4.15 THE STEPLIB STATEMENT

The function of the STEPLIB statement is the same as the JOBLIB statement. However, this statement is coded after the EXEC statement, instead of before it, and is effective only for that job step, instead of the entire job.

4.15.1 Rules for Coding

- The STEPLIB statement can be placed anywhere in the job step, it does not have to immediately follow the EXEC statement.

- The STEPLIB statement can be coded in cataloged procedures.

- Unit and volume parameters must be specified for data sets that are uncataloged.

4.15.2 An Example

Example 1

```
//JOB1     JOB   (1234),ZAMIR
//STEP1    EXEC  PGM=PROGRAM1
//STEPLIB  DD    DSN=PROD.LOADLIB1,DISP=SHR
//STEP2    EXEC  PGM=PROGRAM2
//STEPLIB  DD    DSN=PROD.LOADLIB2,DISP=SHR
```

JOB1 is the name of the job being submitted.   (1234) is the accounting parameter for this job. ZAMIR is the programmer name. STEP1 is executing PROGRAM1.   This program resides in PROD.LOADLIB1. STEP2 is executing PROGRAM2, which is a member residing at PROD.LOADLIB2.   Remember, the DD statements are applicable only for the job step in which they appear, not the entire job.

4.16 CODING BOTH JOBLIB AND STEPLIB STATEMENTS

If both the JOBLIB and STEPLIB statements are coded, then the STEPLIB specification will override that of the JOBLIB for that jobstep. The specification of the JOBLIB will continue for any jobstep that does not have a corresponding STEPLIB statement.

If the same library is used for all jobsteps, then it is good practice to code the JOBLIB statement.

4.16.1 An Example

Here's an example that illustrates the use of both statements:

```
//JOB1     JOB   (A123),'C RANADE',
//               CLASS=O,
//               MSGCLASS=T
//JOBLIB   DD    DSN=A100.TEST.LOADLIB,
//               DISP=SHR
//STEP1    EXEC  PGM=PROGRAM1
//STEPLIB  DD    DSN=B100.TEST.LOADLIB,
//               DISP=SHR
//STEP2    EXEC  PGM=PROGRAM2
//STEP3    EXEC  PGM=PROGRAM3
//STEPLIB  DD    DSN=C100.TEST.LOADLIB,
//               DISP=SHR
//
```

JOB1 is the name of the job being submitted. This job consists of 3 steps: STEP1, STEP2, and STEP3, each of which execute PROGRAM1, PROGRAM2, and PROGRAM3 respectively. STEP1 specifies that PROGRAM1 resides in B100.TEST.LOADLIB. STEP3 specifies that PROGRAM3 resides in C100.TEST.LOADLIB. In STEP2, there is no STEPLIB statement. Therefore, A100.TEST.LOADLIB, which is the specification in the JOBLIB statement, will be searched for PROGRAM2.

4.17 LESS FREQUENTLY USED PARAMETERS

We now continue with the keyword parameters that can be coded on the EXEC statement. These parameters are rarely used. However, we describe them for the sake of completeness. The following parameters will be described:

- ADDRSPC

- DPRTY

- PERFORM

- RD

4.18 THE ADDRSPC PARAMETER

The purpose of this parameter is to indicate to the system that the job step is to use either virtual or real storage. Virtual storage results in program addresses being independent of the addresses that actually exist in a computer. (An address is a location in memory where data is stored.) The technical term for this feature is "paging." Setting ADDRSPC to VIRT results in that job step being paged. If ADDRSPC is set to REAL, then the job step is locked into real storage only.

4.18.1 Syntax

The syntax of this parameter is like this:

    ADDRSPC=VIRT
or
    ADDRSPC=REAL

where *VIRT* indicates virtual storage, and *REAL* indicates real storage. If *ADDRSPC* is omitted, virtual is the default.

4.18.2 Some Examples

Example 1

```
//JOB1   EXEC PGM=PROGRAM1,
//             ADDRSPC=VIRT
```

In this example, PROGRAM1 will be paged.

Example 2

```
//JOB2   EXEC PGM=PROGRAM2,
//             ADDRSPC=REAL
```

In this example, PROGRAM2 will utilize real storage only, and will not be paged.

4.19 THE DPRTY PARAMETER

This parameter is used to assign a dispatching priority to the job step. Dispatching priority is used by the system to determine the order in which tasks are to be executed. Dispatching priority is different from CLASS priority, in that CLASS assigns a priority to the job, and DPRTY assigns a priority to the job step.

4.19.1 Syntax

Following is the syntax:

DPRTY=(value1,value2)

where *value1* is a number from 0 to 15 that specifies the priority of the job step. The higher the number, the higher the priority. *value2* is also a number between 0 and 15. *DPRTY* is computed as follows:

DPRTY=(value1)*(16) + value2

4.19.2 Some Examples

Example 1

```
//JOB1    JOB    (A123),'RANADE'
//STEP1   EXEC   PGM=PROGRAM1,
//               DPRTY=(12,9)
```

The priority in STEP1 is determined like this:

$$(12*16) + 9 = 192 + 9 = 201$$

If the DPRTY parameter is not coded, then the system assigns the APG <Automatic Priority Group> priority to the job step. This priority is installation defined. Please talk to your system administrator for further details.

4.20 THE PERFORM PARAMETER

The PERFORM parameter is used to specify the performance group for the job step. A performance group determines the rate at which the job steps in a program have access to system resources, and is helpful in optimizing system performance.

4.20.1 Syntax

The syntax of the PERFORM parameter looks like this:

```
PERFORM=n
```

where n is a number from 1 to 999. This number must define a performance group that has been defined by your installation.

4.20.2 An Example

Here's an example:

```
//JOB1    JOB    (A123),'LEVITZ'
//STEP1   EXEC   PGM=PROGRAM1,
//               PERFORM=10
```

In this example, JOB1 is the name of the job, JOB is the operation, (A123) is the accounting information, and LEVITZ is the programmer name. In STEP1, PROGRAM1 is executed, and the PERFORM parameter is set to 10. Thus, STEP1 is assigned the performance group 10. The number 10 will be installation defined, and will specify a rate at which the program being executed will be able to access storage processors.

If this parameter is omitted, the system uses a built-in default.

4.21 THE RD PARAMETER

The RD parameter (*Restart Definition*) is used to specify automatic restart of a job if it abends. It also fully or partially suppresses the *CHKPT* (checkpoint) macro instruction, so that no checkpoints are taken as a program executes. A *checkpoint* is taken by the system to record the status of a program as it executes. The advantage of checkpoints is that if a job abends, it can be restarted from the last successful checkpoint, rather than from the beginning of the run. Please note that the proper placement of checkpoints requires careful planning.

4.21.1 Syntax

The syntax for this parameter looks like this:

    RD=R
or
    RD=RNC
or
    RD=NR
or
    RD=NC

where *R* is for *R*estart, *RNC* is for *R*estart with *N*o *C*heckpoint, *NR* stands for *N*o *A*utomatic *R*estart, and *NC* stands for *N*o *C*heckpoint.
When *R* is used, automatic restart is indicated and the CHKPT macro is not suppressed. When *RNC* is used, automatic restart is indicated, but the CHKPT macro is suppressed. When *NR* is used, automatic restart is suppressed but the CHKPT macro is not. When *NC* is used, automatic restart is suppressed and so is the CHKPT macro.

4.21.2 Some Examples

Example 1

```
//JOB1     JOB  (A123),'BECKER'
//STEP1    EXEC PGM=PROGRAM1,
//              RD=R
```

In this example, the operator can perform automatic step restart if the job abends. The CHKPT macro is not suppressed.

Example 2

```
//JOB2     JOB  (B123),'CAMASTRA'
//STEP2    EXEC PGM=PROGRAM2,
//              RD=RNC
```

In this example, the operator can perform automatic step restart if the job step fails. Checkpoints are suppressed.

Example 3

```
//JOB3     JOB  (C123),'LORENZO'
//STEP3    EXEC PGM=PROGRAM3,
//              RD=NR
```

In this example automatic restart is not permitted. The CHKPT macro is not suppressed.

4.22 THINGS THAT CAN GO WRONG

Once again, we present a generalized correspondence between the error messages that are generated if a job does not execute properly, their description, and their probable cause. You may use the information presented in Table 4.2 in two ways: to find a correspondence between the error codes listed and those that are generated by your listing, or, if you do not know exactly which JCL statement could be generating the error, scan through the column titled Probable Cause of Error, and try to trace it this way.

Table 4.2 Error Codes on the EXEC Statement

Error Code	Description	Probable Cause of Error
IEF605I IEF607I	Unidentified operation field JOB has no steps	Forgetting to code the EXEC statement
IEF647I	First character of name not alphabetic or not national on the EXEC statement	Coding an invalid stepname.
CSV003I	Requested module xxxxx not found where xxxxx is module name	Executing a non-existing program
IEF636I	Misplaced JOBLIB statement	Coding JOBLIB after STEPNAME
IEF606I	Misplaced DD statement	Coding STEPLIB before EXEC
IEF626I	Incorrect use of PLUS in the PARM field	Coding the special character (+) in the PARM field, without enclosing in apostrophes Similar messages will be generated on incorrect assignments
IEF605I	Unidentified operation field	Continuing a JCL statement on the next line, without coding a comma as the last character on the prior line
IEF621I	Expected continuation not received	Continuing a JCL statement on the next line, without coding a // on this line

IKFI77I	User error found. Debug output follows... <Debug output>	Specifying incorrect information in COBOL program to the JCL that executes it

4.23 REVIEW

In this chapter we discussed the EXEC statement and described some of its parameters in detail.

Table 4.3 indicates the basic syntax of each parameter and related information.

Table 4.3 Additional Parameters on the EXEC Statement

JCL Parameter	Syntax
JOBLIB	JOBLIB where JOBLIB is coded immediately after the // in columns 1 and 2 and it immediately follows the JOB statement
STEPLIB	STEPLIB where STEPLIB is coded immediately after the // in columns 1 and 2 and it follows the EXEC statement
EXEC	EXEC an EXEC must exist for each job step

stepname	stepname
	where stepname is 1 to 8 alphanumeric characters and/or national symbols. The first character cannot be numeric.
	stepname must start in Column 3, immediately following the double slashes.
ACCT	ACCT=(account-information)
	where account-information consists of one or more subparameters defined by your installation
	Parentheses are not required if only one subparameter is coded.
	Enclosing apostrophes are required if any special characters are included
PARM	PARM=value
	where value is a string from 1 to 100 characters
	Parentheses are required if string consists of multiple sub-strings
	Enclosing apostrophes are required if any special characters are included
ADDRSPC	ADDRSPC=VIRT ADDRSPC=REAL
	where VIRT indicates virtual storage and REAL indicates REAL storage

DPRTY	DPRTY=value1,value2
	where value1 and value2 are numbers from 0 to 15
	The higher the number, the higher the priority
PERFORM	PERFORM=n
	where n is a number from 1 to 999
RD	RD=R RD=RNC RD=NR RD=NC
	where R, RNC, NR and NC indicate various combinations that do or do not allow automatic restart of a step, if it abends.

JOB and EXEC Statements Additional Parameters

5.1 Introduction

In this chapter we will describe certain parameters that can be coded both in the JOB and EXEC statements. But first, an overview of some additional features that can be specified to the operating system, by coding them on the JOB and EXEC statements.

5.2 An Overview

Recall that a JOB statement is used to specify information related to the job that is being submitted, while an EXEC statement is used to specify information related to the program or procedure that is being executed. The following issues become significant:

- If storage is limited, then the operating system can be instructed to assign only a specific amount of storage for a job or a job step.

- In Chapter 2 we described condition codes. These are generated at the end of each job, and indicate the status of the job. A job often consists of several job steps, and sometimes the input of one job step is the output of a prior one. But what would happen if this step did not execute as expected? The operating system can be instructed on what to do, based on the condition codes generated at the end of a job or each step, thereby controlling the execution of subsequent jobs or job steps.

■ Sometimes, time is at a premium, and it may be necessary to limit the amount of time that a job or job step is allowed to utilize. The operating system can be instructed as to how much time it should allow a job or job step to execute, before it is terminated.

5.3 CORRESPONDING JCL

Table 5.1 indicates the JCL parameters that are used to convey the information listed in Section 5.2.

Table 5.1 JCL Parameters on the JOB and EXEC Statements

Function	Corresponding JCL Parameter
Specification of storage space for all job steps	REGION coded on the JOB statement
Specification of storage space for a specific job step	REGION coded on the EXEC statement
Checking condition codes of all job steps	COND coded on the JOB statement
Checking condition code of a specific job step	COND coded on the EXEC statement
Specification of amount of time that a job can utilize	TIME coded on the JOB statement
Specification of amount of time that a step can utilize	TIME coded on the EXEC statement

5.4 THE REGION PARAMETER

At the time that a job is run, a default amount of work space is automatically assigned to it. This default can be overridden via the REGION parameter.

5.4.1 Syntax

Here's the syntax:

    REGION=value1K
or
    REGION=value2M

where *value1* is the storage in multiples of 1024 bytes, and *value2* is storage in multiples of one million bytes. The *K* and *M* must follow *value1* or *value2*.

5.4.2 Rules for Coding

- REGION is an optional keyword parameter. It must be coded after positional parameters, regardless of whether it is coded on the JOB or the EXEC statements.

- If storage is specified in multiples of 1024 bytes (*K* format), then *value* can be up to 7 decimal digits long.

- If storage is specified in millions of bytes (*M* format), then *value* can be up to 4 decimal digits long.

- If REGION is specified in *K* format, then it should be specified as an even number. If it is not even, the system will automatically round it off.

- If REGION is specified in *M* format, then an even or odd number can be specified.

- If REGION is coded both on the JOB statement and the EXEC statements, the REGION specification on the JOB statement will override that on the EXEC statement.

- If this parameter is skipped, a default REGION is assigned.

- All available storage is assigned to the job or job step, if REGION is coded as 0K or 0M.

5.4.3 Some Examples

Example 1

```
//JOB1   JOB   (A123),'ALAN WHITE'
//STEP1 EXEC PGM=PROGRAM1,
//             REGION=96K
```

In this example, JOB1 is the name of the job, JOB is the operation, (A123) is the account number, ALAN WHITE is the programmer name. In the next statement, STEP1 is the name of the job step, the program

PROGRAM1 is executed, and the REGION parameter is coded on the EXEC statement, and is used to specify that this job step can utilize 96 thousand bytes of storage.

Example 2

```
//JOB2  JOB  (A123),'ALAN BLACK'
//STEP1 EXEC PGM=PROGRAM2,
//           REGION=87K
```

In this example, the REGION parameter is once again on the EXEC statement and set to 87K. The system will automatically assign 88 thousand bytes of storage for this job step. Because 87K is an odd number, the system rounds it off for you.

Example 3

```
//JOB3  JOB  (A123),'ALAN GRAY',
//           REGION=3M
//STEP1 EXEC PGM=PROGRAM3
```

In this example, REGION is coded on the JOB statement. The system will allocate 3 million bytes of storage for JOB3.

Example 4

```
//JOB4   JOB  (A123),'ALAN BROWN',
//            REGION=OM
//STEP1  EXEC PGM=PROGRAM4
```

In this example, all available storage will be assigned to JOB4.

Example 5

```
//JOB5   JOB  (A123),'ALAN GOLD',
//            REGION=40K
//STEP1  EXEC PGM=PROGRAM5,
//            REGION=10K
```

In this example, 40k bytes of storage will be allocated to each job step within JOB5, instead of 10k, as specified by the EXEC statement. The JOB statement specification overrides that of the EXEC statement.

We will now discuss the REGION parameter which has been coded on the JOB statement, and then REGION which has been coded on the EXEC statement.

5.5 REGION CODED ON THE JOB STATEMENT

Usually your installation will provide a default region size in which your job is to execute. However, you can override the assigned parameter by using the REGION parameter coded on the JOB statement. Keep in mind that you must specify enough storage for the job that is being submitted, otherwise your job will terminate abnormally.

5.5.1 Some Examples

Example 1

```
//JOB1     JOB   (A123),'MARY JOE',
//               REGION=100K
//STEP1    EXEC PGM=PROGRAM1
```

In this example, JOB1 is assigned 100K bytes of storage. All job steps within this job will be allowed to utilize 100k bytes of storage.
Thus, it is important that PROGRAM1 does not require more storage than this, or the job will terminate abnormally.

Example 2

```
//JOB2     JOB   (A123),'MARY ANN',
//               REGION=4M
//STEP1    EXEC PGM=PROGRAM2
```

In this example, 4 million bytes of storage are assigned to the job.

5.6 REGION Coded on the EXEC Statement

The REGION parameter coded on an EXEC statement requests storage only for that individual job step. If not enough storage is specified, then the job will abend abnormally.

5.6.1 Some Examples

Example 1

```
//JOB1     JOB   (A123),'BILLY DEE'
//STEP1    EXEC  PGM=PROGRAM1,
//               REGION=84K
```

In this example, STEP1 will be assigned 84K bytes of storage.

Example 2

```
//JOB2    JOB    (A123),'BILLY JOE'
//STEP2   EXEC   PGM=PROGRAM2,
//               REGION=1M
```

In this example, STEP2 will be assigned 1 million bytes of storage.

5.7 THE COND PARAMETER

Each step within a job sends a return code to the system upon completion. This is called a condition code. A condition code of 00 is returned upon successful completion of a job step. A condition code other than 0 is returned upon an unsuccessful execution of a job step. Sometimes, the execution of one job step depends upon the successful execution of a prior step. The COND parameter is used to control the execution of subsequent job steps, depending on the condition code that is returned for a prior step. The following example will help you understand this.

Suppose a job has two job steps. The first backs up a file, and the second deletes the source file after a successful backup. Obviously, if the file is not successfully backed up, it should not be deleted. The COND parameter can be used to control the execution of the second step, depending on the value returned by the first. Let's take a few minutes to discuss the condition code.

5.7.1 The Return/Condition Code

A return code is a number between 0 and 4095, and is issued by the system just before a program finishes executing. It is highly recommended that all executing programs issue meaningful return codes based on IBM-established conventions. In Table 5.2, we describe a few of the more common return codes. Refer to the appropriate manual for further information about established conventions.

We now describe the COND parameter as it applies to the JOB statement and the EXEC statement.

5.7.2 COND Coded in the JOB Statement

A COND parameter coded on the JOB statement applies to all job steps within that job, and it overrides COND parameters coded on the EXEC statement, if they exist.

Table 5.2 Some Common Condition Codes

Return Code	Explanation
0	Implies successful execution of job step.
4	Implies warning messages have been issued for the job step.
8	Implies serious error in job step.
16	Implies fatal error, execution of subsequent job steps is halted.

5.7.2.1 Syntax

The syntax of the COND parameter is as follows:

COND=(comparison-code,condition)

where *comparison-code* is a number between 0 and 4095, and condition specifies the type of comparison to be made between the *comparison-code* that has been coded, and the return code of the prior step. You can specify more than one condition code within sets of parentheses. Each condition is or'ed with the next. Example 3 illustrates this scenario. Table 5.3 lists valid operators and an explanation of each.

Table 5.3 Operators Coded on the COND parameter

Operator	Explanation
GT	Bypass current step if comparison-code is greater than return code.
GE	Bypass current step if comparison-code is greater than or equal to return code.
LT	Bypass current step if comparison-code is less than return code.
LE	Bypass current step if comparison-code is less than or equal to return code.
EQ	Bypass current step if comparison-code is equal to return code.
NE	Bypass current step if comparison-code is not equal to return code.

5.7.2.2 Some Examples

Example 1:

```
//JOB1      JOB    (A123),'GERRY PAPKE',
//                 COND=(4,LT)
//STEP1     EXEC   PGM=PROGRAM1
//STEP2     EXEC   PGM=PROGRAM2
//STEP3     EXEC   PGM=PROGRAM3
//
```

In this example, JOB1 consists of 3 job steps: STEP1, STEP2 and STEP3. The COND parameter looks like this:

```
COND=(4,LT)
```

Assume that STEP1 executes successfully. It will return a code of 0. Is the number 4 less than 0? No. Therefore, STEP2 will execute. Now suppose STEP2 returns a code of 004. Is 004 less than 004? No, it isn't. Therefore, STEP3 will also be executed. If a condition code greater than 4 was returned, then all subsequent steps would not have executed.

Example 2

```
//JOB2      JOB    (A123),'JERRY QUARRY',
//                 COND=(4,GT)
//STEP1     EXEC   PGM=PROGRAM1
//STEP2     EXEC   PGM=PROGRAM2
//
```

In this example we are specifying that if the number 4 is greater than the return code of STEP1, then STEP2 is to be bypassed. Elaborating further, if STEP1 is successful, it will return a 0. Since 0 is not greater than 4, STEP2 will not be executed.

Example 3

```
//JOB3      JOB    (A123),'JERRY HASADA'
//                 COND=((4,GE),(9,LT))
//STEP1     EXEC   PGM=PROGRAM1
//STEP2     EXEC   PGM=PROGRAM2
//
```

Take another look at the COND parameter:

```
COND=((4,GE),(9,LT))
```

As you can see, two conditions are specified:

(4,GE)

and

(9,LT)

Both conditions are enclosed within parentheses, separated from the next via a comma, and the entire expression is enclosed within brackets.

This condition code is specifying that if the number 4 is greater than the return code, or the number 9 is less than the return code, then the job will terminate.

5.7.3 COND Coded in the EXEC Statement

The COND parameter coded on the EXEC statement applies only to the job step that it is coded in. This job step is executed or bypassed, depending on the condition codes issued by one or more prior job steps.

5.7.3.1 Syntax

Here's the syntax:

COND=(comparison-code,condition)
or
COND=(comparison-code,condition,stepname,...)
or
COND=(comparison-code,condition,stepname,EVEN)
or
COND=(comparison-code,condition,stepname,ONLY)

The syntax of the COND statement coded on the EXEC statement is similar to that coded on the JOB statement, except for a few optional additional parameters. *Comparison-code*, as before, is a number between 0 and 4095. *Condition* specifies the type of comparison to be made between the comparison-code that has been coded, and the return code of the prior step. The designations for condition are the same as before, please refer to Table 5.2 if necesary. *Stepname* specifies the name of the preceding step whose return code is to be checked. If the test is true, then the job step that contains the COND parameter will be bypassed. If the test is not true, than the job step will be executed. The keyword *EVEN* is used to specify that the stepname specified is to execute, even if any prior steps terminate, abnormally. The keyword *ONLY* is used to specify that the stepname specified is to execute only if any prior steps terminate abnormally. The examples that follow illustrate the use of each of these parameters.

5.7.3.2 Some Examples

Example 1

```
//JOB1      JOB   (A123),'DAVID BECKER'
//STEP1     EXEC  PGM=PROGRAM1
//STEP2     EXEC  PGM=PROGRAM2,
//                COND=(8,EQ,STEP1)
//
```

In this example the COND parameter is used to specify that STEP2 should be bypassed if 8 is equal to the return code issued by STEP1.

Example 2

```
//JOB2      JOB   (A123),'DAVID CASSIDY'
//STEP1     EXEC  PGM=PROGRAM1
//STEP2     EXEC  PGM=PROGRAM2,
//                COND=(0,LT)
//
```

This example specifies that STEP2 should be bypassed if 0 is less than the return code issued by the prior step, which is STEP1. If you take a moment to think about this, you will realize that STEP2 will always execute, because return codes are never less than 0.

Example 3

```
//JOB3      JOB  (A123),'DAVID ZOWIE'
//STEP1     EXEC PGM=PROGRAM1
//STEP2     EXEC PGM=PROGRAM2
//STEP3     EXEC PGM=PROGRAM3,
//               COND=(8,GE),(80,LE STEP1)
//
```

In this example we are specifying that STEP3 is to be bypassed if 8 is greater than or equal to the return codes issued by any of the prior job steps. In addition to this, STEP2 is to be bypassed if 80 is less than or equal to the return code issued by STEP1. Thus, a return code less than 8 or greater than 80 will result in STEP3 being executed.

Example 4

```
//JOB4    JOB    (A123),'DAVID HU'
//STEP1   EXEC   PGM=PROGRAM1
//STEP2   EXEC   PGM=PROGRAM2,
//               COND=EVEN
//
```

In this example, the keyword EVEN is used to specify that STEP2 is to execute even if any previous steps terminate abnormally.

Example 5

```
//JOB5    JOB    (A123),'DAVID LIU'
//STEP1   EXEC   PGM=PROGRAM1
//STEP2   EXEC   PGM=PROGRAM2,
//               COND=ONLY
//
```

In this example, the keyword ONLY is used to specify that STEP2 is to execute only if STEP1 terminates abnormally.

Keep in mind that EVEN and ONLY are mutually exclusive. You can not code both of them for the same job step.

5.8 COND PARAMETER IN JOB AND EXEC STATEMENTS

The following are a few tips that should help you understand the relative benefits of coding the COND parameter in the JOB or EXEC statements.

- If the COND parameter is not coded in the JOB or EXEC statement, then all job steps will execute, regardless of return codes of the prior step. This could prove to be dangerous under some circumstances. As an example, consider a situation in which a backup is made of a file in step 1, and that the file is deleted in step 2. If the backup is unsuccessful, and the condition code of step 1 is not checked, the file will be deleted in step 2 anyway. It is recommended that you code the COND parameter to check the successful execution of a step.

- A successful test for the COND parameter coded on the JOB statement results in all subsequent steps being bypassed. A successful test for the COND parameter coded on the EXEC statement results only in that job step being bypassed. Often, you only want to bypass a step, as opposed to bypassing the entire job.

- If the COND parameter is coded on the JOB statement as well as the EXEC statement, then the specification on the JOB statement nullifies the specification on the EXEC statement.

5.9 THE TIME PARAMETER

This is an optional keyword parameter and is used to specify the amount of CPU time that a job or job step is permitted to utilize before it is terminated.   Please note that it specifies CPU time, not clock time, system time, or wait time.   CPU time is the time that a job takes to execute. System time is the same as clock time. Wait time is the time that a job waits for I/O devices in order to execute.

If this parameter is coded on the JOB statement, it specifies the amount of CPU time that the job is allowed to use. If it is defined on the EXEC statement, it specifies the amount of CPU time that the job step is allowed to use. The usefulness of the TIME parameter is evident in test environments, e.g., you wish to avoid wasting CPU time if the job, or job step, goes into an endless loop.

If the TIME parameter is not specified, then the installation defined TIME parameter is used.

When coding the time parameter, always estimate a little more time than you expect your job to take. A job that exceeds the specified time, regardless of whether the TIME parameter is coded on the JOB or EXEC statements, will result in its being terminated.

5.9.1 Syntax

Here's the syntax:

    TIME=minutes
or
    TIME=(minutes,seconds)
or
    TIME=(,seconds)

where *minutes* is a number from 1 to 1439 (that's 24 hours), and *seconds* is a number from 1 to 59.

If you code only the minutes field, seconds defaults to 0. If you code only the seconds field, minutes defaults to 0.

5.9.2 Some Examples

Example 1

```
//JOB1    JOB   (A123),'STEVE MARKOWITZ'
//STEP1   EXEC PGM=PROGRAM1,
//             TIME=25
```

In this example, 25 minutes of CPU time are assigned to STEP1. If STEP1 requires more than 25 minutes of CPU time, JOB1 will terminate abnormally.

Example 2

```
//JOB2    JOB   (A123),'STEVE BENOWITZ',
//             TIME=(45,30)
//STEP1   EXEC PGM=PROGRAM1
//STEP2   EXEC PGM=PROGRAM2
//STEP3   EXEC PGM=PROGRAM3
```

In this example, 45 minutes and 30 seconds of CPU time are assigned to the entire job. Thus, the collective CPU time that STEP1, STEP2, and STEP3 have to execute is 45 minutes and 30 seconds.

Example 3

```
//JOB3    JOB   (A123),'STEVE HOROWITZ',
//             TIME=0
//STEP3   EXEC PGM=PROGRAM3
```

In this example, TIME is set to 0. This results in unpredictable behavior, and it is recommended that you avoid coding it this way.

Example 4

```
//JOB4    JOB   (A123),'STEVE PERRY',
//             TIME=(,25)
//STEP4   EXEC PGM=PROGRAM4
```

In this example, the maximum amount of time that JOB4 is allowed to use is 25 seconds.

5.10 TIME Coded on Both JOB and EXEC Statements

If the TIME parameter is coded on both the JOB and EXEC statements, then the TIME parameter on the EXEC statement will override the TIME parameter on the JOB statement. If the job step exceeds the time specified in the EXEC statement, then the job will terminate abnormally. The following example illustrates what has just been said.

```
//JOB1    JOB  (A123),'LITTLE STEVIE',
//             TIME=12
//STEP1   EXEC PGM=PROGRAM1,TIME=4
//STEP2   EXEC PGM=PROGRAM2,TIME=4
//STEP3   EXEC PGM=PROGRAM3,TIME=4
//
```

In this example, JOB1 is allowed 12 minutes of CPU time. STEP1, STEP2, and STEP3 are allowed 4 minutes each. If any of these steps take more than 4 minutes of CPU time, the job will terminate abnormally.

If TIME on the job card is smaller than the time coded for one of its job steps, then the job will terminate, if the job takes longer to execute than its allocation.

5.11 Things That Can Go Wrong

Once again, we present a generalized correspondence between some common errors, and the error code and message that is generated from it. Please refer to Table 5.4 for these errors. Either refer to the JCL error code, or scan through *Probable Cause of Error*, to identify the cause of error in your JCL.

5.12 Review

In this chapter we discussed some additional parameters that can be coded on both the JOB and the EXEC statements. Table 5.5 summarizes the syntax and meanings of the parameters described.

Table 5.4 Some Common Errors

JCL Error Code	Description	Probable Cause of Error
IEF085I	Region unavailable	Specifying less storage in REGION than required for a job to execute
IEF450I		Specifying less time in TIME than required for a job to execute

Table 5.5 Mutual Parameters on the JOB and EXEC statements

JCL Parameter	Syntax and Description
REGION	REGION=value1K REGION=value2M where K is storage in multiples of 1024 bytes, and M is storage in multiples of one million bytes If an odd number is specified in K units, it will be rounded off to the nearest number by the system. REGION coded on the JOB statement overrides REGION parameter on the EXEC statement

COND	COND= (comparison-code, condition) COND= (comparison-code, condition, stepname, ONLY) COND= (comparison-code, condition, stepname, EVEN) where comparison-code is a number between 0 and 4095, condition is one or more of the following: GT, GE, LT, LE, EQ, NE stepname is the stepname which may or may not be executed, based on condition codes returned by prior steps EVEN is the execution of a step, even if prior steps did not execute successfully ONLY is the execution of a step only if the prior step did not execute successfully
TIME	TIME=minutes TIME=(minutes,seconds) TIME=(,seconds) where minutes is a number between 1 and 1439 and seconds is a number between 1 and 59

6

The DD (Data Definition) Statement

6.1 INTRODUCTION

The purpose of data processing is to take raw data, rearrange or modify it, and produce results in the form of output. Thus, every program requires some form of input, which is processed to produce output. The DD statement, (*Data Definition*), is used to identify the source of input and the placement of output information. This chapter will describe the DD statement in detail.

6.2 AN OVERVIEW

In order to process data, the following must be specified to the operating system.

- The statement that defines the DD statement must have a name, so that it can be identified by the system, and referenced as necessary.

- The source of the data that will be used must be identified. If this data is stored in a file, then the name of the file must be specified.

- Data may be created or stored in a file only for the duration of the job. Once the job is completed, it is deleted. The fact that a data set is temporary must be specified.

- The fact that data is not to be deleted upon job completion must be specified.

In other words,

- The data being processed may
  - be created during the job step
  - already exist
  - be modified during a job step
  - be shared between multiple users and jobs

- On successful execution of a job, the data can be:
  - deleted
  - kept
  - cataloged
  - sent to a subsequent job step
  - uncataloged

- On unsuccessful execution of a job, the data can be:
  - deleted
  - kept
  - cataloged
  - uncataloged

6.3 CORRESPONDING JCL

Table 6.1 indicates the JCL parameters used to specify the information listed in Section 6.2. If there is no corresponding parameter, then text is used to indicate how the information can be conveyed. If a specific subparameter within a parameter is used to convey the particular information, then the parameter (along with the relevant subparameter), is listed.

6.4 THE DD STATEMENT

As indicated in the introduction to this chapter, the DD statement is used to convey information about the data that will be read or written within the job.

//	Name	Operation	Operands	Comments
//	ddname	DD	operands <positional/ keyword params>	comments

Positional and/or keyword parameters are coded in the operands field. Positional parameters must precede keyword parameters, if both exist.

Table 6.1 JCL Parameters on the DD Statement

Function	Corresponding JCL Parameter and Subparameter
Specification of name for DD statement	ddname
Specification of name for data	DSN
Specification of temporary data set	&&name
Specification of permanent data set	data-set-name
Specification of the following actions on the data that will be processed: - create new data - use pre-existing data - create if it does not exist, add records at the end if it does exist - reserve for exclusive use - allow shared access	DISP Subparameters on DISP: NEW OLD MOD OLD SHR
Specification of the following actions to be implemented on data after successful execution of a job: - delete - don't delete - catalog - send to job step - uncatalog	DISP Subparameters on DISP: DELETE KEEP CATLG PASS UNCATLG
Specification of the following actions to be implemented on data if job does not execute successfully: - delete - don't delete - catalog - uncatalog	DISP Subparameters on DISP: DELETE KEEP CATLG UNCATLG

Now we'll look at each parameter and associated subparameter in detail.

6.5 Rules for Coding DD Statement

The following rules must be adhered to when coding this statement:

- The DD statement must immediately follow the EXEC statement.

- A valid name must be assigned to each data set used.

- A DD statement must exist for each data set used.

- Positional parameters may be coded in the operands field.   The following positional parameters may be coded:

  - *
  - DATA
  - DUMMY
  - DYNAM

- Keyword parameters may also be coded in the operands field. There are an abundant number of keyword parameters that can be coded here. The following are the most commonly used:

  - DSN
  - DISP
  - UNIT
  - SPACE
  - DCB
  - VOLUME

- Keyword parameters must follow positional parameters if both are coded.

In this chapter we will describe the *ddname*, DSN and DISP keyword parameters. Chapter 7 will describe the UNIT and VOLUME parameters. Chapter 8 will describe the SPACE and DCB parameters.   The keyword parameters will be described first because it is necessary for you to understand these before you can understand the positional parameters. But first, here's the syntax of the two parameters that will be described in this chapter.

```
//ddname    DD   DSN=data_set_name,
                 DISP=(status,
                 normal_disposition,
                 abnormal_disposition)
```

6.6 THE DDNAME

The *ddname* identifies the name of the *data definition* statement. As a job executes, the system performs device and space allocations for each ddname specified. Each ddname should be unique within the job step. If there are duplicate names, even though the system will make the allocations specified, it will direct all related messages to the first ddname.

6.6.1 Rules for Coding

- ddname must be 1 to 8 alphanumeric (A to Z, 0 to 9) or national characters (@, $, #). The first character must be alphabetic or national.

- The ddname must begin in Column 3, after the // in Columns 1 and 2.

- At least one blank must follow the name.

6.6.2 Some Examples

Example 1

```
//JOB1     JOB   A123,'MAE WEST'
//STEP1    EXEC  PGM=PROGRAM1
//NAME1    DD    DSN=DATA1
```

In this example, JOB1 is the name of the job, JOB is the operation, A123 is the account number, and MAE WEST is the programmer name. STEP1 is the stepname, and PROGRAM1 is being executed. The DD statement immediately follows the EXEC statement. NAME1 is the ddname, DD is coded in the operations field, and the data set name (DSN) is DATA1. The data set name will be explained later on in this chapter.

Example 2

```
//JOB2     JOB   A123,'MAE EAST'
//STEP2    EXEC  PGM=PROGRAM2
//@NAME2   DD    DSN=DATA2
```

In this example, the ddname starts with a national character.

6.6.3 ddnames Reserved for System Use

The following ddnames are reserved for system use and may not be used to define DD statements.

```
//JOBLIB        //SYSOUD
//JOBCAT        //SYSDBOUT
//SYSABEND
//SYSIN
//SYSCHK
//STEPLIB
//STEPCAT
//SYSUDUMP
//SYSOUT
```

6.7 THE DSN PARAMETER

The DSN parameter is a keyword parameter on the DD statement. It can also be coded as DSNAME. It is used to specify the name of the data set to the operating system.

6.7.1 Syntax

The syntax of the DSN parameter looks like this:

DSN=data-set-name

where *data-set-name* can be:

- Non-qualified

- Qualified

It is good practice to give meaningful names to your data set. Sections 6.7.2 and 6.7.3 describe these two categories in detail.

6.7.2 Non-qualified Names

Non-qualified names are comprised of 1 to 8 alphanumeric or national characters. The first character must be alphabetic or national. Here's an example:

```
DSN=FILE1
```

Non-qualified names are seldom used. It is impossible to catalog these data sets. We explain the reason for this in the next section.

6.7.3 Qualified Names

Qualified names consist of two or more non-qualified names, each separated from the next by a period. The first name is called the highest qualifier of that name.   When a qualified data set is referenced, the system determines if the highest qualifier is the alias given to a user catalog, and attempts to find its entry in the master catalog. If it is, then the system attempts to find the data set in that catalog. If there is no corresponding data set of that name, then the system attempts to create a new entry for it in the user catalog. The privilege to update the master catalogs is restricted to only one or a few users. Hence, the attempt to create a new entry will most probably fail. This is the reason why non-qualified names are seldom used.

Qualification results in the location of the data set being easily identified by its name. The maximum length of a data set name, including the periods, is 44 characters. Here are a couple of examples:

```
//JOB1    JOB   A123,'TOM L'
//STEP1   EXEC  PGM=PROGRAM1
//        DD    DSN=X.Y.Z
```

or

```
//JOB2    JOB   A123,'JERRY K'
//STEP2   EXEC  PGM=PROGRAM2
//        DD    DSN=PROJECT1.GROUP2.DATA(TEST1)
```

The first example was a simple concatenation of three letters, where each letter could have a special meaning. In the second example, we use the standard *ISPF* method of qualifying names. This consists of three levels, where the 1st level (PROJECT1) usually indicates the user ID, or project to which you may belong. The second level (GROUP2) specifies a location where similar data sets similar to the one being accessed, have been grouped together. The third level (DATA) indicates the type of data stored in that data set. The name inside the parentheses (TEST1) is the name of the data set being accessed. The advantage of qualifying data set names is that it gives you the ability to group data of similar types together.

6.7.4 Temporary Data Sets

Data sets can be temporary or permanent. A temporary data set is created during a job execution and deleted after a job completion. One reason for using temporary data sets would be to release storage utilized by the data set after termination of the job.

A temporary data set is recognized as such if the DSN parameter is omitted. In this case, the system assigns a unique name to it, and reference is made to it by referencing the stepname and ddname. This is called a referback. Referbacks will be explained in detail in the next chapter. For now, this simple example will suffice:

```
//JOB3    JOB   A123,'HARRY JOE'
//STEP1   EXEC  PGM=PROGRAM1
//DATA1   DD
//STEP2   EXEC  PGM=PROGRAM2
//DATA2   DD    *.STEP1.DATA1
```

In this example, JOB3 is the jobname. A123 is the accounting parameter and HARRY JOE is the programmer name. STEP1 executes PROGRAM1, and a data set DATA1 is created in the next statement. STEP2 executes PROGRAM2, and the temporary data set created in DATA1 is referenced via referback. It looks like this:

```
*.STEP1.DATA1
```

where * indicates a referback, and STEP1 and DATA1 are the stepname and ddname statements by which the temporary data set was created.

A temporary data set is also recognized by coding the DSN parameter, and naming the data set as follows:

- The name must start with two ampersands (&&) followed by 1 to 8 characters. The first character must be alphabetic or national. The remaining characters can be alphanumeric (A-Z or 0-9), national (@,$,#), hyphen(-) and or +0 (12-0 multipunch).
Here's an example that illustrates the use of this data set.

```
//JOB1    JOB   A123,'JOE HARRY'
//STEP1   EXEC  PGM=PROGRAM1
//DATA1   DD    DSN=&&TEMPDATA
```

In this example, a temporary data set called TEMPDATA is created. Notice that TEMPDATA is preceded by two ampersands.

6.7.5 Permanent Data Sets

A permanent data set is not deleted after a job completion and may be cataloged, if requested. It is coded by setting a DSN parameter that is equal to a qualified or nonqualified name. Here's an example that refers to a nonqualified data set name:

```
//JOB1     JOB   A123,'HARRY MOE'
//STEP1    EXEC  PGM=PROGRAM1
//DATA1    DD    DSN=DATAFILE
```

and here's an example that uses a qualified data set name:

```
//JOB1     JOB   A123,'MOE LARRY'
//STEP1    EXEC  PGM=PROGRAM1
//DATA1    DD    DSN=MIS.PROJECTA.COBOL(FILE1)
```

In this example the ddname is DATA1. The dataset name is qualified by project (MIS), group (PROJECTA), type (COBOL) and, finally, the name (FILE1). In IBM terminology, (FILE1) is called a member of a data set, and the data set itself is called a partitioned data set. Please note that the names of partitioned data sets must be enclosed in parentheses.

6.7.6 Accessing Qualified Permanent Data Sets

Permanent data sets can be accessed from the EDIT-ENTRY PANEL screen in the ISPF menu. (The ISPF menu was briefly described in Chapter 2, refer back to this menu if you need to refresh your memory.) In order for you to fully understand how data set names are qualified by the system, let's take a look at this screen, displayed in Figure 6.1.

At this time, it is not important that you understand each prompt on this screen. However, we do want you to take a moment to see where the user ID, group, project and member name are entered. Notice that the group can be further qualified by up to four levels.

We now describe the DISP parameter.

6.8 THE DISP PARAMETER

DISP is an keyword parameter. It is used to instruct the system as to the current status of a data set, and the steps to be taken with the data set upon successful or unsuccessful execution of the job. DISP is required, unless the data set is created and deleted within the same step.

```
------------------- EDIT - ENTRY PANEL ------------
-----------

COMMAND ===>

ISPF LIBRARY:
    PROJECT ===> Z100
    GROUP   ===> TEST    ===>     ===>     ===>
    TYPE    ===> JCLLIB
    MEMBER  ===> TESTJOB   (BLANK OR PATTERN FOR
MEMBER SELECTION LIST)

OTHER PARTITIONED OR SEQUENTIAL DATA SET:
    DATA SET NAME  ===>
    VOLUME SERIAL  ===>          (IF NOT CATALOGED)

DATA SET PASSWORD ===>        (IF PASSWORD PROTECTED)

PROFILE NAME       ===>       (BLANK DEFAULTS TO DATA
SET TYPE)

INITIAL MACRO      ===>        LMF LOCK  ===> YES
(YES, NO OR NEVER)

FORMAT NAME        ===>        MIXED MODE ===> NO (YES
OR NO)
```

Figure 6.1 The EDIT-ENTRY Screen in ISPF

6.8.1 Syntax

The syntax of the DISP parameter follows:

DISP=(status,normal-disposition,abnormal-disposition)

The status field indicates the current status of the data set, (i.e. whether it exists or has to be created), and, if the data set exists, mode of access to it (i.e. whether the data set will be used exclusively by the current executing job, or if it can be shared amongst other jobs that may need to access it at the same time).

The normal-disposition subparameter specifies how the data set is to be disposed upon normal execution of the job.

The abnormal-disposition subparameter specifies how the data set is to be disposed upon abnormal execution of the job.

Table 6.2 presents a synopsis of the values that each of the subparameters can contain. These subparameters can be mixed and matched.

Table 6.2 Parameters on the DISP Statement

Status	Normal Disposition	Abnormal Disposition
NEW	DELETE	DELETE
OLD	KEEP	KEEP
MOD	CATLG	UNCATLG
SHR	UNCATLG	CATLG
	PASS	

Subsequent sections in this chapter will explain each of the values listed in this table.

6.8.2 Rules for Coding

- One or more of the subparameters may be skipped. However, at least one subparameter must exist.

- The parentheses can be omitted if only the status field is coded, like this:

```
DISP=NEW
```

- If *normal-disposition* and/or *abnormal-disposition* fields are coded, and status is omitted, then a comma must be coded in its position, like this:

```
DISP=(,CATLG,DELETE)
```

- If the first and third sub-parameters are coded, then a comma must be coded in the location of the second subparameter, like this:

```
DISP=(OLD,,DELETE)
```

6.8.3 DISP Defaults

If the DISP parameter is not coded, the following happens:

- The *status* field defaults to NEW.

- The *normal-disposition* field defaults to DELETE, if the data set being accessed is new.

- The *normal-disposition* field defaults to KEEP, if the data set being accessed is old.

- The *abnormal-disposition* field defaults to the same value as the *normal-disposition* field.

The example below illustrates the default values if the DISP parameter is not coded:

    DISP=(NEW,DELETE,DELETE)

We now discuss the values that can exist in these subparameters.

6.9 THE STATUS FIELD

The STATUS field is used to indicate the status of the data set at the start of a job step. As indicated in Table 6.2, you can code NEW, OLD, MOD, or SHR in this field. A discussion of these subparameters follows.

6.9.1 The NEW Subparameter

Coding DISP=NEW indicates that a new data set is to be created. NEW is also the default, if nothing is coded in the status field.

If the data set resides on a direct access volume, such as disk or drum, then the UNIT and SPACE parameters must also be coded. This is an MVS requirement. Here are a couple of examples that illustrate the use of this parameter.

Example 1

```
//JOB1       JOB    A123,'LOU LOUIE'
//STEP1      EXEC   PGM=PROGRAM1
//DATANAME   DD     PROJECT1.GROUP1.JCL.TESTDATA,
//                  DISP=NEW
```

In this example, PROGRAM1 is executed and the data set (which, by the way, has a qualified name), PROJECT1.GROUP1.JCL.TESTDATA is accessed. The next statement utilizes the DISP parameter to inform the operating system that this is a new data set.

6.9.2 The OLD Subparameter

Coding the status field as OLD results in the operating system searching for an existing data set of the name specified. The data set becomes available exclusively to the step in which it is referenced. If this file is being written to, then its old data will be lost, and replaced by the new data.

The data set may or may not be cataloged. If it is not cataloged, then the VOLUME parameter must be coded. These parameters will be explained in detail in subsequent chapters. Here's an example:

```
//JOB1    JOB  A123,'SANDY HOOK'
//STEP1   EXEC PGM=PROGRAM1
//DATA1   DD   DSN=FINANCE.CAPITAL.COBOL.FILE1,
//             DISP=OLD
```

In this example, the file FINANCE.CAPITAL.COBOL.FILE1 is specified as preexisting.

6.9.3 The MOD Subparameter

The MOD subparameter is used to modify sequential data sets. Recall that sequential data set records can be processed in sequence only. These types of data sets can exist on magnetic tapes, card readers, and direct access storage devices. The MOD subparameter does different things under different circumstances. They are listed below.

- If the data set already exists, use of the MOD subparameter in the status field results in the reader/writer of the device positioning itself just after the last record, so that records can be added to it easily.

- If the sequential data set does not exist, then the system replaces MOD with NEW, and creates it.

- If the VOL parameter is coded on the DD statement in conjunction with the MOD subparameter, the system searches for the data set on the volume specified. If it is not found on this volume, the job is terminated with a non-zero condition code.

In addition to this, stick to these rules when you code this parameter:

- If the data set is created, make sure you code the appropriate parameters that are required when a new data set is created. For example, if the data set is being created on magnetic tape, the DCB and UNIT parameters must be coded.

- If an existing cataloged data set is being modified, make sure you code the CATLG parameter, so that additional volumes, if written to, may be recorded properly by the system.

An illustrative example follows:

```
//JOB1        JOB  A123,'SANDY BAY'
//STEP1       EXEC PGM=PROGRAM5
//DATANAME    DD   DSN=A.B.FILE,
//                 DISP=(MOD,CATLG)
```

In this example, two things can happen, depending upon successful or unsuccessful execution of the job. First, let's see what happens upon a successful execution of the job.

If an A.B.FILE already exists, it will be appended to, and the read/write mechanism will position itself to just after the last record in it. The CATLG parameter would result in the A.B.FILE being cataloged. If an A.B.FILE does not exist, then it will be created.

Now, an explanation of what happens upon abnormal termination of a job. If an A.B.FILE already exists, records may or may not be appended to it, depending on how far the job would have progressed before abending. If an A.B.FILE does not exist, it will not be created.

6.9.4 The SHR Subparameter

Setting DISP to SHR is identical to setting it to OLD except when OLD gives exclusive control of the data set to the user, whereas SHR allows multiple jobs to read the same data set.

For this reason, it is good practice to use the SHR parameter with data sets that will be read only, so that other users are not locked out. In a multiprogramming environment, data set sharing is necessary. One should not have exclusive control of the data set unless it is absolutely necessary.

An example follows:

Example 1

```
//JOB1    JOB   (A123),'SANDY BEACH'
//STEP1   EXEC  PGM=PROGRAM1
//INPUT1  DD    DSN=USER1.GROUP1.JCL.NAMEFILE,
//              DISP=SHR
```

In this example, multiple jobs can access the file called USER1.GROUP1.JCL.NAMEFILE, because DISP is set equal to SHR.

6.10 THE NORMAL-DISPOSITION FIELD

The *normal-disposition* field in the DISP parameter is used to indicate what to do with the data set upon normal termination of the job. We refresh your memory for its position in DISP:

DISP=(status,normal-disposition,abnormal-disposition)

and the subparameters that can be coded here are

```
DELETE
KEEP
CATLG
UNCATLG
PASS
```

A discussion of each of these parameters follows.

6.10.1 The DELETE Subparameter

The DELETE subparameter indicates that the data set being referenced is to be deleted after successful termination of the job, thereby releasing applicable resources for other users/jobs. The DELETE parameter behaves in different ways, based on where the data set resides:

- If the DELETE disposition is specified for a tape data set which has a retention period or expiration date subsequent to the current date, then it is deleted only after the retention period or expiration date on the tape. (The retention period on a tape is recorded at the time that it is allocated).

- If the DELETE disposition is specified for a tape data set, whose retention period or expiration date is not later than the current date, then the tape is rewound and the operator is instructed to dismount it.

■ If this disposition is specified for a disk data set, the system removes its entry from the system catalogs. The data is not actually removed until it is written over.

An example follows.

```
//DELETE1    JOB   D123,'STAN RICH'
//STEP1      EXEC  PGM=PROGRAM1
//DATA1      DD    DSN=TEMPFILE,
//                 DISP=(OLD,DELETE)
```

In this example, TEMPFILE is a pre-existing data set that is deleted upon the successful termination of the job DELETE1.

6.10.2 The KEEP Subparameter

The KEEP subparameter indicates that the data set is to be retained or *kept* upon successful execution of the job. This parameter should be used with permanent data sets. If it is used with a temporary data set, the system automatically changes it to PASS (which will be explained shortly). Here are a couple of examples.

Example 1

```
//KEEP1    JOB   (A123),'IVAN GORKY'
//STEP1    EXEC  PGM=PROGRAM1
//NAME1    DD    DSN=BOOKS,
//                DISP=(OLD,KEEP)
```

In this example, a permanent data set called BOOKS is retrieved, and kept after it has been read.

Example 2

```
//KEEP2    JOB   (B123),'IVAN PFEIFFER'
//STEP2    EXEC  PGM=PROGRAM2
//NAME2    DD    DSN=MANUAL,
//                DISP=(NEW,KEEP)
```

In this example, the NEW parameter is used in conjunction with KEEP, implying that a new permanent data set called MANUAL is created and retained upon successful termination of the job.

6.10.3 The CATLG Subparameter

The CATALG subparameter is used to specify that the data set is to be retained and recorded in the system catalogs after successful job termination. The data set name, unit, and volume are recorded. Like DELETE, it behaves in different ways, depending upon the status of the data set.

- If the data set spans multiple volumes, the additional volumes can be cataloged by coding CATLG in conjunction with MOD, like this:

```
DISP=(MOD,CATLG)
```

- If the data set is temporary, then it is deleted at the end of the job. For this reason, temporary data sets can never be cataloged, they can only be passed to the next step using the PASS subparameter. The CATLG subparameter cannot be used with temporary data sets.

6.10.4 The UNCATLG Subparameter

The UNCATLG subparameter is used to remove the entry of the data set from the system catalogs. The data itself is not deleted. Here's an example

```
//UNCATLOG   JOB   U123,'IVAN TORY'
//STEP1      EXEC  PGM=PROGRAM7
//DISK1      DD    DSN=DISK.OUTPUT,
//                 DISP=(OLD,UNCATLG)
```

In this example, the pre-existing data set, called DISK.OUTPUT, is removed from the system catalogs. If the data set is not found, then the job terminates abnormally.

6.10.5 The PASS Subparameter

Setting DISP to PASS specifies that the data set is to be passed to a subsequent job step within the same job. Use of this subparameter saves time, because the location of the data set and information with reference to the volume that it exists on, remains in memory for the duration of the execution of the job. Keep the following in mind while coding this parameter:

- The data set will continue to be passed to subsequent steps, if it is not utilized by any intervening job steps.

- The data set can be used by any subsequent step.

- Both temporary and permanent data sets can be passed to subsequent steps.

- Data from a prior step can be referenced by its name, or via the referback syntax, explained previously in this chapter.

- If this subparameter is used with tape data sets, then the tapes remain mounted between job steps.

Here are a few examples:

Example 1

```
//JOB1     JOB  (K123),'VICTOR VICKY'
//STEP1    EXEC PGM=PROGRAM1
//DATA1    DD   DSN=FILE1,
//              DISP=(NEW,PASS)
//STEP2    EXEC PGM=PROGRAM2
//DATA2    DD   DSN=FILE1,
//              DISP=(OLD,DELETE)
```

In this example, JOB1 consists of two steps. STEP1 executes PROGRAM1, which accesses a newly created data set called FILE1. The DISP parameter is used to pass it on to subsequent steps within that job.

In STEP2, PROGRAM2 is executed. The data set FILE1, which was passed from the prior step, is accessed. Notice the DISP parameter:

```
DISP=(OLD,DELETE)
```

As you can see, the system is informed that the data set already exists (it was created in STEP1), and upon successful termination of the job it will be deleted.

This example referenced the passed data set by its name. The next example uses the referback syntax to access the data.

Example 2

```
//JOB1     JOB  (L123),'VICTOR VICTORIA'
//STEP1    EXEC PGM=PROGRAM1
//DATA1    DD   DSN=FILE1,
//              DISP=(NEW,PASS)
//STEP2    EXEC PGM=PROGRAM2
```

```
//DATA2    DD    DSN=*.STEP1.DATA1,
//                DISP=(OLD,DELETE)
```

In this example, data passed from STEP1 is accessed in STEP2 via *referback*. Referback follows this syntax:

DSN=*.stepname.ddname

where * is required, *stepname* is the stepname, and *ddname* is the DD statement name.

Example 3

```
//JOB1     JOB   (L123),'VICKY LAWRENCE'
//STEP1    EXEC  PGM=PROGRAM1
//DATA1    DD    DSN=&&TEMP,
//                DISP=(NEW,PASS)
//STEP2    EXEC  PGM=PROGRAM2
//DATA2    DD    DSN=*.STEP1.DATA1,
//                DISP=(OLD,DELETE)
```

In this example, the referback method is used to access the temporary data set &&TEMP, which was created in STEP1.

6.11 THE ABNORMAL-DISPOSITION FIELD

The abnormal disposition field tells the system what to do with the data upon abnormal termination of the job. This subparameter is required only if the abnormal disposition is different from the normal disposition. The following subparameters can be used in this field:

```
DELETE
KEEP
UNCATLG
CATLG
```

A description of each subparameter follows.

6.11.1 The DELETE Subparameter

This subparameter is used to specify that the data set space on the volume is to be released if the job step terminates abnormally. This space is then available for use by other data sets. Keep in mind that the actual data is not removed until it is written over. Here's an example:

```
//JOB1      JOB   A123,'JOHN STERN'
//STEP1     EXEC  PGM=PROGRAM1
//DATA1     DD    DSN=FILE1,
//                DISP=(NEW,CATLG,DELETE)
```

In this example, the data set, called FILE1, is created. If the job terminates successfully, the system is informed that it should be cataloged. If the job terminates unsuccessfully, the system is instructed to delete it.

6.11.2 The KEEP Subparameter

This subparameter specifies that the data set is to be kept on the volume if the job step terminates abnormally. Here's an example:

```
//JOB2      JOB   J123,'MAGGIE SHORE'
//STEP1     EXEC  PGM=PROGRAM2
//DATA1     DD    DSN=FILE1,
//                DISP=(NEW,CATLG,KEEP)
```

In this example, a new data set, called FILE1, is created. If the job terminates successfully, the system is instructed to catalog it. Upon unsuccessful execution, the system is instructed to retain the data set, but not to catalog it.

6.11.3 The CATLG Subparameter

This subparameter specifies that the data set is to be kept, and placed as an entry in the system catalogs upon abnormal termination of the job. Here's an example:

```
//JOB3      JOB   L123,'JACK ROGERS'
//STEP1     EXEC  PGM=PROGRAM1
//DATA1     DD    DSN=FILE1,
//                DISP=(NEW,UNCATLG,CATLG)
```

In this example, the system is informed that FILE1 is a new data set. Upon successful termination of the job, this data set is to be uncataloged. Upon unsuccessful termination of the job, it is to be cataloged.

6.11.4 The UNCATLG Subparameter

This subparameter specifies that the data set is to be kept, but its entry must be removed from the system catalogs upon unsuccessful termination of the job. Here's an example:

```
//JOB4     JOB  K123,'SALLY STEPHENS'
//STEP1    EXEC PGM=PROGRAM1
//DATA1    DD   DSN=FILE1,
//              DISP=(OLD,CATLG,UNCATLG)
```

In this example the system is instructed to catalog the data set upon successful termination of the job. It is instructed to uncatalog it upon unsuccessful termination.

6.12 THINGS THAT CAN GO WRONG

Once again, we present a general correspondence between some common errors, and the error code and message that is generated from them. Either refer to the JCL error code or scan through *Probable Cause of Error* to identify the cause of error in your JCL. Please refer to Table 6.3

6.13 REVIEW

In this chapter we discussed the DSN and DISP parameters in detail. Table 6.4 presents a synopsis of the syntax and functions of these parameters.

Table 6.3 Some Common Errors on the DD Statement

JCL Error Code	Description	Probable Cause of Error
IEF647I	First character of name not alphabetic or not national on the DD statement	Coding an invalid DDname
IEF671I	Misplaced JOBCAT DD statement	Coding a reserved name for DDname, such as JOBCAT Similar messages will be displayed for other reserved names
IEF624I	Incorrect use of period in the DSNAME field	Coding two periods between a qualified name, instead of one
IEF643I	Unidentified positional parameter in the DISP field	Coding an invalid status in the DISP parameter
IEF617I	No name on first DD statement after EXEC statement	Skipping the DDname all together
IEF642I	Excessive parameter length in the DSNAME field	Coding an invalid temporary data set name

Table 6.4 DSN and DISP Parameters on the DD statement

JCL Parameter/Syntax	Function/Description
DD	Used to supply input and output information for the data sets being processed
DSN or DSNAME	Used to specify name of data set being processed Can consist of qualified or non-qualified names Data set being processed can be temporary, existing only for the duration of the job
DISP=(status,normal-disposition,abnormal-disposition)	Used to specify disposition of data set Instructs the system on what to do upon successful or unsuccessful execution of the job Status can be NEW, OLD, MOD or SHR Normal and abnormal disposition can be DELETE, KEEP, CATLG, UNCATLG, or PASS

The UNIT, VOL
and LABEL Parameters

7.1 INTRODUCTION

The DD statement is used to supply input and output information to the operating system. The UNIT parameter is coded on the DD statement to specify an input or output device that is to be accessed. The VOL parameter is also coded on the DD statement to identify specific disk tape volume(s). The LABEL parameter is used to specify information specific to tape data sets. This chapter describes the UNIT parameter in detail, and then the VOL and LABEL parameters.

7.2 THE UNIT PARAMETER, AN OVERVIEW

In an IBM mainframe environment, input and output devices can be categorized in different ways. The following characteristics can be used to identify them to the operating system:

- All devices have an address assigned to them at the time that they are added to the system. Devices can be referenced via this address.

- Devices can be distinguished by a number which indicates the numeric model type.

- Certain types of devices can be grouped together, and the group given a name. Devices can be referenced via group name.

- If a device is specified in one job step, then a subsequent step may request the same device by referencing the ddname of the DD statement in which the unit was originally specified.

In addition to identifying characteristics, the system can be instructed to take certain steps with certain types of devices. The following can be specified with tape data sets:

- Tape data sets have to be mounted in order to be accessed. However, a job can consist of multiple job steps, and it may be unnecessary to mount the tape until the step requiring it is executed. The system can be instructed to defer mounting of the tape until necessary.

7.3 CORRESPONDING JCL

Table 7.1 lists the JCL parameters used to specify the information listed in Section 7.2. If there is no corresponding parameter, then text is used to indicate how the information can be conveyed. If a specific subparameter within a parameter conveys the applicable information, then the parameter, along with the relevant subparameter, is listed.

Table 7.1 JCL Coded on the UNIT Parameter

Function	Corresponding JCL parameters and Subparameter
Specification of device via address	UNIT=device-address
Specification of device by model type	UNIT=device-type
Specification of device as part of a group	UNIT=group-name
Specification of device used by a previous job step	UNIT=AFF
Deferring the mounting of a tape device, until it is ready to be used	UNIT=(device,,DEFER)

We now discuss the UNIT parameter and its subparameters in detail.

7.4 THE UNIT PARAMETER

As indicated in the introduction to this chapter, the UNIT parameter conveys information about the input or output devices that will be used by the job. It is a keyword parameter on the DD statement. Thus, it must follow positional parameters, if any are coded. Its position within a JCL statement will be as follows:

//	Name	Operation	Operands	Comments
//	ddname	DD	UNIT=...	comments

7.5 SYNTAX

The general syntax for the UNIT parameter is:

    UNIT=device_address
or
    UNIT=device_type
or
    UNIT=device_group_name
or
    UNIT=AFF=prior_ddname
or
    UNIT=(device,,DEFER)

Each of these different specifications will be explained with examples.

7.6 SPECIFICATION OF DEVICE ADDRESS

Each I/O device attached to a computer is assigned a hardware address when a system is generated. Device addresses are expressed as three hexadecimal digits.

The authors do not recommend specification of a device via its hardware address and, in real life, this kind of specification is rarely used. The reason is that the device at that specific address could be off-line or busy at the time that the job is being run. MVS withholds processing of the job until the device becomes available. Other unit parameters are more generic, and permit the system to find any available unit, regardless of its address.

7.6.1 An Example

```
//JOB1   JOB   A123,'CAROL LEHN'
//STEP1  EXEC  PGM=PROGRAM1
//DATA1 DD    DSN=FILE1,
//            UNIT=S04
```

In this example JOB1 is submitted. PROGRAM1 is executed, and a dataset called FILE1, which resides on a device identified by its hardware address S04, is accessed.

7.7 SPECIFICATION OF DEVICE TYPE

A device type is identified by the model number assigned to that device by IBM. In order to code the device type on the UNIT parameter, you need to know what devices are being used by your installation. The use of a Device Type will permit the system to search for the specific device containing a file, or assign any available device of that type to receive output.

7.7.1 An Example

```
//JOB2   JOB   A123,'CAROL DELANEY'
//STEP1  EXEC  PGM=PROGRAM2
//DATA1  DD    DSN=FILE2,
//            UNIT=3380
```

In this example, JOB2 is submitted. PROGRAM2 is executed, and a dataset called FILE2, which resides on a 3380 disk unit, is accessed.

7.8 SPECIFICATION OF DEVICE GROUP

A device group name is a symbolic name which is assigned to a group of devices when the system is generated. Devices are often grouped together based on their function. For example, you can have all direct access storage devices assembled together under one grouping, temporary storage devices under another, permanent storage devices under another, and so on. Often, group names are based on conventions or traditions. For example, *SYSDA* is traditionally assigned to direct access storage devices, *TSTDA* is assigned to devices used in the testing environment only, and so on.

7.8.1 An Example

```
//JOB3    JOB   A123,'CAROL MILLER'
//STEP1   EXEC  PGM=PROGRAM3
//DATA1   DD    DSN=FILE3,
//              UNIT=SYSDA
```

In this example, JOB3 is submitted. PROGRAM3 is executed, which accesses FILE3. This file can reside on any of the devices which are grouped under the symbolic name SYSDA.

7.9 THE AFF SUBPARAMETER

In the prior sections, we have illustrated how the UNIT parameter is used to specify the device that will contain the data sets accessed by a job. The AFF subparameter can be used to reference a device specified in a prior DD statement. AFF stands for affinity. This kind of specification results in *unit affinity*, that is, the same unit is reused, thus forcing datasets onto the same device, and thereby conserving storage space on available I/O units. This is applicable to mountable media such as tapes and cartridges.

The syntax of the AFF subparameter, (in conjunction with the prior DD statement to which it relates to), looks like this:

```
//ddname1  DD  UNIT=TAPE
//ddname2  DD  UNIT=AFF=ddname1
```

where *ddname1* is the name of the DD statement in which the device for the UNIT parameter was originally specified, and *ddname2* is the name of the DD statement in which the AFF parameter is used to reference the prior DD statement (*ddname1*).

7.9.1 Rules for Coding

- The AFF subparameter must reference a unit previously specified on a DD statement within the same job step.

- The AFF subparameter can be used to reference mountable devices such as tapes.

7.9.2 Some Examples

Example 1

```
//JOB1   JOB   A123,'TOM LORENZO'
//STEP1  EXEC  PGM=PROGRAM1
//NAME1  DD    DSN=DATA1,
//             UNIT=CART
//NAME2  DD    DSN=DATA2,
//             UNIT=AFF=NAME1
```

In this example, JOB1 is submitted. STEP1 is the step name in which PROGRAM1 is executed. The DD statement called NAME1 specifies the data set called DATA1 which resides on a cartridge defined as CART. In the next statement, the AFF subparameter is used to specify that the data set called DATA2 must reside on the same unit as that specified in NAME1.

Example 2

```
//JOB1   JOB   B123,'JOHN CAMASTRA'
//STEP1  EXEC  PGM=PROGRAM2
//NAME1  DD    DSN=DATA1,
//             UNIT=TAPE
//NAME2  DD    DSN=DATA2,
//             UNIT=CART
//NAME3  DD    DSN=DATA3,
//             UNIT=AFF=NAME1
```

This example is the same as the prior one, except that an additional DD statement has been added. NAME3 uses the AFF subparameter to specify that DATA3 will exist on the same unit as that specified in the DD statement called NAME1. This example illustrates the fact that the AFF subparameter can be used to reference any prior DD statement, as long as it is within the same step. It is not necessary for the DD statement containing the AFF subparameter to immediately follow the DD statement containing the original UNIT specification.

7.10 THE DEFER SUBPARAMETER

The DEFER subparameter is coded on the UNIT parameter so that it may defer mounting of the volume that it references, until the data set that resides on it is opened. It prevents volumes from being mounted until they are actually needed, thereby freeing up resources for other jobs. If the DEFER parameter is encountered for a volume that is already mounted, then it is simply ignored.

The syntax of the DEFER parameter coded on the UNIT parameter looks like this:

//ddname   DD   UNIT=(device,,DEFER)

where *device* is any mounted device. The extra comma in the middle is used to specify the unit count subparameter. The unit count subparameter identifies the number of tapes required for the job.

7.10.1 An Example

```
//JOB1   JOB  C123,'MIKE CAZEAU'
//STEP1 EXEC PGM=PROGRAM1
//NAME1 DD   DSN=DATA1,
//           UNIT=(TAPE,,DEFER)
```

In this example JOB1 is submitted, and PROGRAM1 is executed in STEP1. The data set UNIT parameter, in conjunction with the DEFER subparameter, is used to specify that DATA1 resides on tape, and that the tape need not be mounted until the system specifically requests it. This request will be issued by the system at the time that JOB1 is executed and PROGRAM1 requires access to DATA1.

We now describe the VOL parameter in detail.

7.11 THE VOL PARAMETER, AN OVERVIEW

As indicated at the beginning of this chapter, the VOL parameter is also coded on the DD statement and is used to identify specific tape(s) or disk volume(s). In order to process the data which resides on multiple volumes, the following items are important.

- When a system is generated, devices are assigned identifying serial numbers. In order to access a specific device, its serial number must be specified to the operating system.

- Within the same job, a volume that has already been specified in a prior job step may be re-referenced in a subsequent step.

- Volumes may be made accessible to all users on the system.

- Volumes may be made accessible to only single users at one time.

■ Volumes may be required to remain mounted until the completion of the job. Usually, volumes may be dismounted upon completion of the job step in which they are referenced.

■ Data may exist on multiple volumes. Thus, volumes may be required to be mounted in a certain sequence.

7.12 CORRESPONDING JCL

Table 7.2 lists the JCL parameters used to specify the information listed in Section 7.11. If there is no corresponding parameter, then text is used to indicate how the information can be conveyed. If a specific subparameter within a parameter conveys the applicable information, then the parameter, along with the relevant subparameter, is listed.

Table 7.2 Paramaters Coded on the VOL Statement

Function	Corresponding JCL Sub-parameters Coded on the VOL Statement
Specification of serial number	SER
Referencing VOL specification from a prior step	REF
Allowing access to volume by all users	This is the default, unless coded otherwise
Allowing access to volume by single user	PRIVATE
Inhibiting dismounting of volume until end of job	RETAIN
Specification of sequence in which volumes are to be mounted	SEQ

We now discuss the VOLUME parameter and its subparameters in detail.

7.13 THE VOL (VOLUME) PARAMETER

VOL or VOLUME can be used interchangeably on the DD statement. This parameter is used to identify the volume serial number of the device on which a given data set is to be written, or on which a data set resides. The VOL parameter can be used with disk and tape data sets. Its position within a JCL statement is as follows:

//	Name	Operation	Operands	Comments
//	ddname	DD	VOL=...	comments

When a new data set is written to disk, the VOL parameter should be coded only if there is a real need to identify a specific disk volume. When it is not coded, then MVS determines an accessible disk volume with sufficient space and writes to it.

7.13.1 Types of Volumes

There can be two types of labels on a volume:

- *Volume label.* This contains the volume serial number, and is used for identification purposes by the system.

- *Data set label.* Data set labels are found at the beginning and the end of tape data sets. They consist of two 80 byte records that contain information for that data set. The data set labels found at the beginning of a tape are called *HDR1* and *HDR2,* respectively. The data set labels found at the end of the tape are called *EOF1* and *EOF2*, respectively.

Both types of labels reside on the volume itself as data.

If VOL is not coded, and data must be written to a specific volume, then a scratch tape (i.e. it has no specific label), is mounted by the operator and the data is written to it.

Volumes can also be classified by the type of access available to them. They can be categorized as follows:

- *Private.* These are accessible to a single user only. Tapes are accessible to only one user at a time, and therefore, are always private to the user who is accessing them at the time.

■ *Public.* These are accessible to all users.

A discussion follows of each subparameter listed in Table 7.2.

7.14 THE SER SUBPARAMETER

The SER subparameter coded on VOL in the DD statement is used to request specific volumes. Its syntax looks like this:

    VOL=SER=serial-number

or

    VOL=SER=(serial-number1,serial-number2,...)

7.14.1 Rules for Coding

■ No more than 255 serial numbers can be coded on one VOL statement.

■ The volume serial number must be 1 to 6 alphanumeric or national characters. A hyphen can be included, in addition to special characters such as blank, apostrophes, brackets, etc., as long as they are enclosed in apostrophes.

7.14.2 Some Examples

Example 1

```
//JOB1     JOB   D123,'BRIAN FOLEY'
//STEP1    EXEC  PGM=PROGRAM1
//NAME1    DD    DSN=DATA1,
//               VOL=SER=23456
```

In this example, JOB1 is submitted. PROGRAM1 is executed, DATA1 is accessed on a volume whose serial number is 23456.

Example 2

```
//JOB2     JOB   E123,'TERESA FOLEY'
//STEP1    EXEC  PGM=PROGRAM2
//NAME2    DD    DSN=DATA2,
//               VOL=SER=VOL001
```

In this example, a volume with serial number VOL001 is accessed.

Example 3

```
//JOB3      JOB   F123,'SCOTT FOLEY'
//STEP1     EXEC  PGM=PROGRAM3
//NAME3     DD    DSN=DATA3,
//                VOL=SER=(VOL1,VOL2,VOL3)
```

In this example the data set called DATA3 resides on 3 volumes whose serial numbers are VOL1, VOL2, and VOL3, respectively. The operating system will request that all volumes be mounted at the same time.

7.15 THE REF SUBPARAMETER

The REF subparameter is a shortcut method used to specify a volume which has been previously defined within the same job, but not in the current step. Instead, it has been defined in a prior step. Its syntax looks like this:

```
VOL=REF=*.referback
```

where *referback* specifies the name of the prior DD statement in which the VOL parameter was originally defined.

7.15.1 Rules for Coding

- The data set name cannot contain any special characters.

- The data set name being referenced must have been defined in a prior step.

7.15.2 Some Examples

Example 1

```
//JOB1      JOB   (F123),'MOLLY HATCHET'
//STEP1     EXEC  PGM=PROGRAM1
//DD1       DD    DSN=DATA1,
//                VOL=SER=VOL1
//DD2       DD    DSN=DATA2,
//                VOL=REF=*.STEP1.DD1
```

In this example, Molly Hatchet submits a job called JOB1. PROGRAM1 is executed. In the DD statement called DD1, the data set named DATA1 is accessed from the volume whose serial number is VOL1. Reference is once again made to the same volume (VOL1) in DD2, via the REF subparameter coded on VOL.

In order for this example to work, the data set called DATA1 must have been cataloged in the system catalogs.

Example 2

```
//JOB2      JOB   (G123),'MOLLY MOE'
//STEP1     EXEC  PGM=PROGRAM1
//DD1       DD    DSN=INFILE,
//                VOL=SER=VOL1,
//                DISP=(NEW,PASS)
//STEP2     EXEC  PGM=PROGRAM2
//DD2       DD    DSN=INFILE2,
//                DISP=(NEW,CATLG)
//                VOL=REF=*.STEP1.DD1
```

In this example, JOB2 is submitted. PROGRAM1 is executed. In DD1, the data set called INFILE residing on VOL1 is accessed. Notice the DISP statement that follows the VOL statement:

```
//                DISP=(NEW,PASS)
```

The DISP statement indicates that the dataset INFILE is new, and that it will be passed on to the next step.

Next, STEP2 executes PROGRAM2. This program accesses dataset INFILE2. The REF subparameter is used to indicate that this dataset resides on the same volume specified in the DD statement, DD1.

Referbacks are not encouraged, particularly if there is an error during execution of the step that is being referred. The subsquent step containing the referback will not execute either.

7.16 THE PRIVATE SUBPARAMETER

Coding PRIVATE on the VOL parameter results in exclusive use of the volume for the data set specified in the job step. Once the job is completed, the system requests that the private volume be dismounted to free up resources for other jobs. This does not mean that other jobs are not allowed to access this data set. This simply means that only one job can access it at a time. Here's the syntax:

VOL=PRIVATE

or

VOL=(PRIVATE,...)

Tape data sets are private by default, since only one user can access them at a time. Hence, coding PRIVATE for tape data sets really makes no sense.

Also, this parameter would be of no use with non-removable disk volumes, because the system requests removal of the data set deemed private, after it has been used. Hence, do not use this parameter with non-removable volumes. If you do, the system will simply ignore this specification.

7.16.1 Rules for Coding

■ The PRIVATE subparameter is positional. Hence, it must precede all keyword parameters coded on VOL. If other positional parameters are coded, and this one is not, then its absence must be indicated via a comma.

7.16.2 An Example

```
//JOB1     JOB   H123,'SUE PATRICK'
//STEP1    EXEC  PGM=PROGRAM1
//DD1      DD    DSN=FILE1,
//               VOL=(PRIVATE,SER=VOL1)
```

In this example, a job is submitted by Sue Patrick. PROGRAM1 is executed, and FILE1, which exists on VOL1, is accessed privately.

7.17 THE RETAIN SUBPARAMETER

The RETAIN subparameter is used to indicate that the volume is not to be dismounted after completion of the job step that it is coded in. The volume remains mounted until the entire job is completed. Like PRIVATE, this subparameter is applicable only to removable device types, such as magnetic tapes. It is a positional parameter. Here's the syntax:

```
    VOL=(,RETAIN)
```
or
```
    VOL=(,RETAIN,...)
```

where the first comma indicates the absence of the first positional parameter, which is PRIVATE, and the three dots indicate the position of keyword parameters, if they exist.

7.17.1 An Example

```
//JOB1     JOB   K123,'CHRIS KLINE'
//STEP1    EXEC  PGM=PROGRAM1
//DD1      DD    FILE1,
//               VOL=(,RETAIN,SER=TAPE1)
//STEP2    EXEC  PGM=PROGRAM2
//DD2      DD    FILE2,
//               VOL=(,,SER=TAPE1)
```

In this example Chris Kline submits a job consisting of two job steps. In the first step (STEP1), PROGRAM1 is executed, which accesses a data set called FILE1, which resides on a volume whose serial number reads TAPE1. The system is advised to tell the operator to refrain from dismounting this volume after completion of STEP1, via the RETAIN subparameter.

In STEP2, PROGRAM2 is executed, and the data set called FILE2 is accessed. This data set resides on the same volume as FILE1 (Serial number is TAPE1). The operator was advised not to dismount TAPE1, since this same tape was being accessed by a subsequent step within the same job. Notice that the operator will be free to dismount TAPE1 after the successful execution of STEP2, since the RETAIN subparameter is not coded.

By the way, the last statement in the above example:

```
//DD2          DD    FILE2,
//                   VOL=(,,SER=TAPE1)
```

could just as well have been coded like this:

```
//DD2          DD    FILE2,
//                   VOL=SER-TAPE1
```

7.18 THE SEQ (SEQUENCE) SUBPARAMETER

As indicated previously, data can exist on multiple volumes. The system catalogs the serial numbers of all volumes that relate to each other in this way. The SEQ subparameter is used to specify the sequence number of the volume that is to be mounted for a particular step. Like PRIVATE and RETAIN, it is a positional parameter.

Omission of this subparameter results in processing starting at volume number 1.

Here's the syntax:

```
VOL=(,,sequence-number)
```
or
```
VOL=(,,sequence-number,..)
```

where the first two commas indicate the absence of the two positional parameters PRIVATE and RETAIN, and the '...' indicate the presence of keyword parameters, if any exist.

7.18.1 Rules for Coding

- The SEQ subparameter can be used only with cataloged data sets.

- The sequence number must be between 1 and 255. The number can be no greater than 59 for SMS-managed data sets. (For now, don't worry about these data sets, just ask your system administrator what the maximum number is at your installation.)

7.18.2 An Example

Example 1

```
//JOB1    JOB    K123,'TIM BERGEN'
//STEP1   EXEC   PGM=PROGRAM1
//DD1     DSN    FILE1,
//               VOL=(,,,,SER=HUGE)
//STEP2   EXEC   PGM=PROGRAM2
//DD2     DSN    VOL=(,,5,,SER=HUGE)
```

In this example JOB1 is submitted. STEP1 executes PROGRAM1, and the dataset called FILE1 is accessed on the volume whose serial number is HUGE. Since no value is supplied in the third position, processing starts at volume 1 .

In STEP2, PROGRAM2 is executed. This time the VOL parameter is used to specify that processing should start at volume number 5 of the volume whose serial number is HUGE. Notice the two commas that precede the number 5. They must exist, since they indicate the absence of the positional parameters PRIVATE and RETAIN. The comma that follows the number 5 is for another positional parameter, which also relates the volume sequence number, indicating the total number of volumes that the data set spans.

7.19 UNIT AND VOL PARAMETERS TOGETHER

In this section, we will describe various situations in which different combinations of subparameters are coded on the UNIT and VOL parameters in order to obtain the desired result.

Example 1

Assume that you are running a job that consists of 50 steps, and it accesses data from a data set that resides on a tape unit. Now, suppose that data needs to be accessed from this unit for the first 25 steps only. However, you do not wish to have the tape dismounted until the end of the job, because you may need that tape unit for another job that will be executed later. The following will be coded on UNIT and VOL parameters:

```
//JOB1     JOB  A123,'KAREN B'
//STEP1    EXEC PGM=PROGRAM1
//NAME1    DD   DSN=DATA1,
//              UNIT=(TAPE,,DEFER),
//              VOL=(,RETAIN)
```

In this example, DEFER coded on the UNIT parameter defers the mounting of the tape volume until the data set that resides on it is opened. Notice the extra comma before the DEFER subparameter, which indicates the position of the optional unit count subparameter.

RETAIN coded on the VOL parameter specifies that the volume is not to be dismounted until the completion of the entire job.

Example 2

Assume that you are running a job that requires 100 cylinders of primary space and 50 cylinders of secondary space, and you don't wish to take a chance on space running out and the job terminating abnormally. The following will be coded on the UNIT and VOL parameters:

```
//JOB2     JOB  A123,'KAREN C'
//STEP1    EXEC PGM=PROGRAM2
//NAME1    DD   DSN=DATA1,
//              UNIT=UNIT1,
//              VOL=PACK01,PACK02,PACK03
```

In this example, PACK01, PACK02, and PACK03 will be mounted simultaneously. If space runs out on one pack, then the system will immediately attempt to find space on the next one. If enough packs are not specified, then the job will terminate abnormally.

Example 3

Assume that you wish to access a particular volume that was referenced in a prior step, and you do not want this volume to be dismounted until the end of the job. The following will be coded on the UNIT and VOL parameters:

```
//JOB3      JOB  A123,'KAREN F'
//STEP1     EXEC PGM=PROGRAM3
//DD1       DD   DSN=DATA1,
//               UNIT=TAPE1,
//               VOL=SER=VOL1,
//               DISP=(NEW,PASS)
//STEP2     EXEC PGM=PROGRAM4
//DD2            DSN=INFILE2,
//               VOL=REF=*.STEP1,RETAIN
```

In this example, the system is notified of a data set called DATA1, which resides on unit TAPE1, and volume VOL1. All of this is done in STEP1. In STEP2, PROGRAM4 is executed, and dataset INFILE2 is accessed. REF coded on the VOL parameter indicates that the volume for this data set is the same as that specified in STEP1. The RETAIN subparameter is used to indicate that you wish to have this volume dismounted upon termination of the job, instead of after termination of that particular step.

7.20 THE LABEL PARAMETER, AN OVERVIEW

Tape data sets have characteristics that uniquely identify them from other types of data sets:

- Tape data sets can be identified by their sequence number on a volume.

- Tape data sets can have different types of labels.

- Tape data sets can be password protected.

- The system has to be notified as to whether the tape data set is being opened for input or output.

- Tape data sets can have an expiration or a retention period date.

7.21 CORRESPONDING JCL

Table 7.3 lists the JCL parameters used to specify the information listed in Section 7.20. If there is no corresponding parameter, then text is used to indicate how the information can be conveyed. If a specific subparameter within a parameter conveys the applicable information, then the parameter, along with the relevant subparameter, is listed.

7.22 SYNTAX

The general syntax of the LABEL parameter is:

    LABEL=sequence-number
or
    LABEL=sequence-number,type-of-label
or
    LABEL=sequence-number,type-of-label,pw
or
    LABEL=sequence-number,type-of-label,pw,i/o
or
    LABEL=sequence-number,type-of-label,pw,i/o,EXPDT=yyddd
or

    LABEL=sequence-number,type-of-label,pw,i/o,RETPD=nnnn

pw is the password specification, and can be PASSWORD or NOPWREAD. *i/o* is used to specify if the data set will be used for input or output. Valid values in this parameter are IN or OUT. *EXPDT* is coded to specify the expiration date of the tape, yy is coded to specify a 2 digit year and ddd is used to specify a 3 digit day. *RETPD* is coded to specify retention period, and *nnnn* is a 4 digit number. Keep in mind that the first parameters are positional, and if they are omitted, their absence must be specified via a comma.

EXPDT and RETPD are keyword parameters. For this reason, if these are the only parameters that will be coded, the preceding commas need not be coded. Thus, the LABEL parameter would look like this:

    LABEL=EXPDT=yyddd

or

    LABEL=RETPD=nnnn

Table 7.3 JCL Parameters Coded on the LABEL Statement

Function	Corresponding JCL Parameters and Subparameters
Specification of sequence number	LABEL=sequence-number
Specification of type of label	LABEL=(,type-of-label) Initial , is required, for the sequence-number, since both parameters are positional
Specification of password	LABEL=(,,PASSWORD) or LABEL=(,,NOPWREAD) This is also a positional parameter
Specification of whether tape data set is being opened for input or output	LABEL=(,,,IN) or LABEL=(,,,OUT) This is also a positional parameter
Specification of expiration date or retention period	LABEL=(RETPD=nnnn) or LABEL=(EXPDT=yyddd) Both parameters function to achieve the same result. However, EXPDT provides a more convenient method of specifying expiration date.

7.23 SEQUENCE NUMBER

The sequence-number is a four digit number, and describes the data set's position (or sequence) relative to other data sets that may exist on the volume. This number can range from 1 to 9999, where number 1 indicates the first data set on the tape. If this parameter is not coded, it defaults to 1. If a 0 is coded in its position, this also defaults to 1.

The sequence number is coded for tape data sets only; it would be a meaningless parameter for disk data sets.

7.23.1 An Example

```
//JOB1    JOB  A123,'SINBAD'
//STEP1   EXEC PGM=PROGRAM1
//DATA1   DD   DSN=FILE3,
//             UNIT=TAPE1,
//             VOL=SER=0001,
//             LABEL=3
```

In this example, PROGRAM1 is executed. DATA1 DD statement specifies that a data set called FILE3 will be accessed. This data set exists on a unit identified as TAPE1. This serial number of the tape unit is 0001, and the data set sequence number on this volume is 3, i.e., it is the third file on the tape.

7.24 TYPES OF LABELS

Magnetic data tapes can contain:

- Volume labels

- Data set labels

- ASCII labels

Volume and data set labels can be standard, as established by IBM, non-standard, or a combination of both. Table 7.4 lists the valid labels that can be coded for this subparameter, and their meaning.

Table 7.4 Values Coded on the type-of-label Subparameter

Label	Meaning
SL	Standard IBM label. This is the default. Tape data sets default to SL. This is a commonly used specification.
NSL	NonStandard Label This specification is used to specify that the data set has a user defined label. This is a commonly used specification.
SUL	Standard and user Label This is used to specify that the data set has both IBM standard and user-defined labels. This specification is rarely used.
BLP	Bypass Label Processing This is used to specify that the system should bypass label processing altogether. The tape is positioned to the specified file without any kind of volume or data set label checking. This specification is commonly used.
NL	No Label This is used to specify that the data set has no label. This specification is frequently used for tape data sets that are processed at different installations which do not have SL capabilities. This specification is rarely used.
AL	American National Standard Label This is used to specify that the data set label is recorded in the ASCII code, as opposed to the more commonly used EBCDIC code. This specification is rarely used.

LTM	Leading Tape Mark
	This is used to specify that no labels are used. Instead, the tape volume starts with a tape mark.

7.24.1 An Example

```
//JOB2    JOB  A123,'SINBAD'
//STEP1   EXEC PGM=PROGRAM2
//DATA1   DD   DSN=FILE1,
//             UNIT=TAPE1,
//             VOL=SER=0001,
//             LABEL=,SL
```

In this example, the data set FILE1 is specified as having standard labels. Notice the leading comma, coded for the positional sequence number parameter. The first data set on the volume will be accessed.

7.25 PASSWORD SPECIFICATION

This is the third positional parameter on the LABEL statement. You can code PASSWORD or NOPWREAD here. Coding PASSWORD specifies that the data set cannot be read, changed, written to, or deleted, until a correct password is supplied by the operator or user. Coding NOPWREAD specifies that the data set can be read without a password. However, it cannot be modified or deleted without specification of the correct password by the operator.

7.26 SPECIFICATION OF I/O USE OF TAPE UNIT

The fourth positional parameter on the LABEL statement is used to specify whether the tape data set will be used for input only, using Basic Sequential Access Method (BSAM). It is beyond the scope of this book to explain BSAM, and this parameter is rarely used. We have included it in our discussion so that you are aware of its existence. Please consult the appropriate IBM manual if you require further explanation for this.

7.27 SPECIFICATION OF EXPIRATION DATE

EXPDT is coded to specify the expiration date of the tape unit. The first two digits are used to specify the year, and the next three digits are used to specify the julian date. The julian date can range from 1 to 365, or from 1 to 366. Together, they indicate the date until which time the data set will not be deleted or over-written.

Expiration dates are used almost exclusively for tape data sets only. They help determine when a volume becomes *scratch*, and thereby becomes available for rewriting or updating.

If this parameter is not coded, it defaults to 00000.

7.27.1 An Example

```
//JOB4    JOB   A123,'SINBAD'
//STEP1   EXEC  PGM=PROGRAM4
//DATA1   DD    DSN=FILE1,
//              UNIT=TAPE1,
//              VOL=SER=0001,
//              LABEL=EXPDT=94031
```

In this example, the tape data set will expire on the 31st of January, 1994.

7.28 SPECIFICATION OF RETENTION PERIOD

RETPD is coded to specify the retention period of a tape unit. The retention period is specified in number of days. The number of days can range from 1 to 9999.

If this parameter is not coded, it defaults to 0.

7.28.1 An Example

```
//JOB5    JOB   A123,'SINBAD'
//STEP1   EXEC  PGM=PROGRAM5
//DATA1   DD    DSN=FILE1,
//              UNIT=TAPE1,
//              VOL=SER=0001,
//              LABEL=RETPD=20
```

In this example, the data set will be available for deletion after 20 days of its creation. It can also be written over after these 20 days.

7.29 Things That Can Go Wrong

Table 7.3 contains a generalized correspondence for some common errors, and the error code and message that is generated from it. Either refer to the JCL error code, or scan through *Probable Cause of Error* to identify the cause of error in your JCL.

Table 7.3 Some Common Errors

JCL Error Code	Description	Probable Cause of Error
IEF272I	Invalid Unit Name	Specifying an incorrect name for the UNIT parameter
IEF642I	Excessive parameter length in the UNIT field	Coding one comma, instead of two, where two commas are required, such as UNIT=(TAPE,DEFER), instead of UNIT=(TAPE,,DEFER)

7.30 Review

In this chapter we discussed the UNIT, VOL and LABEL parameters which are coded on the DD statement. Table 7.4 summarizes the syntax and meanings of the parameters described.

Table 7.4 UNIT, VOLUME and LABEL Parameters on the DD Statement

JCL Parameter	Syntax and Description
UNIT	Used to specify input or output devices to be accessed within a job
UNIT=device-address	device-address is a 3 hexadecimal digit address assigned to device
UNIT=device-type	device-type is the model number assigned to the device
UNIT=device-group-name	device-group is a symbolic name assigned to a group of devices categorized in a specific way
UNIT=AFF=ddname1	Used to specify the use of the same device as specified in a prior DD statement ddname1 is the name of the DD statement which originally specified the device
UNIT=(device,,DEFER)	Used to prevent mountable volumes from being dismounted after termination of the job step

VOL or VOLUME	Used to specify specific or multiple tape or disk volumes Volumes can have two types of labels: volume and data
VOL=SER=serial-number VOL=SER=(serial-number1, serial-number2,...) VOL=REF=ddname VOL=REF=*.referback VOL=PRIVATE	serial-number is the serial number assigned to a device when the system is generated ddname is the name of the DD statement in which the volume was originally defined referback is the ddname of those data sets which are not cataloged by the system, and are passed from a prior step PRIVATE implies single user access to a volume PUBLIC is the default
VOL=(,RETAIN)	Specifies that the volume is not to be dismounted after completion of the job step, or that the volume must continue to be mounted until the termination of the job
VOL=(,,SEQ)	Specifies the sequence number of the volume that is to be mounted. Is useful for specifying the correct volume for data sets that span multiple volumes
LABEL=(sequence-number)	Specifies sequential number of data sets on tape unit
LABEL=(,type-of-label)	Specifies type of label on tape data set Following can be coded: SL, NSL, SUL, BLP, NL, AL, LTM

LABEL=(,,PASSWORD)	Specifies tape data set cannot be read/modified/deleted without a password
LABEL=(,,NOPWREAD)	Specifies tape data set can be read without password, but it cannot be modified or deleted
LABEL=(,,,IN) or LABEL=(,,,OUT)	Specifies whether tape data set is for input or output only
LABEL=(EXPDT=yyddd)	Specifies expiration date of tape data set
LABEL=(RETPD=nnnn)	Specifies retention period of tape data set

The SPACE and DCB Parameters

8.1 INTRODUCTION

The SPACE and DCB parameters are also coded on the DD statement. The *SPACE* parameter is used to allocate storage for new data sets on direct access storage devices. The *DCB* parameter is used to customize the way data is stored on devices. This chapter first describes the SPACE parameter in detail, then the DCB parameter.

8.2 THE SPACE PARAMETER, AN OVERVIEW

The following storage requirements can be specified to the operating system:

- Space can be requested in *tracks*. A track is a fixed amount of storage space on a disk or drum, which will always have the capability of containing the same amount of data. Tracks exist as concentric circles on each disk, and disks are layered on top of each other.

- Space can be requested in *cylinders*. A cylinder is an area of data storage on a disk, and consists of multiple concentric tracks.

- Space can also be requested in *blocks*. A block is a specific number of bytes of storage on the direct access storage device.

- A specific amount of storage space can be allocated when a data set is created.

- An additional amount of storage space can be allocated if the original amount of space specified is inadequate.

- Space will also have to be allocated to record the name and location of partitioned data sets within the applicable directory.

- The operating system may be instructed to release the space previously allocated after the successful or unsuccessful execution of the job.

- Space can be requested in contiguous blocks.

- Space can be requested in the largest area of contiguous space available on the direct access storage device.

- Entire cylinders can be requested for storage, instead of portions of it.

8.3 CORRESPONDING JCL

Table 8.1 lists the JCL parameters used to specify the information listed in Section 8.2. If there is no corresponding parameter, then text is used to indicate how the information can be conveyed. If a specific subparameter within a parameter conveys the applicable information, then the parameter along with the relevant subparameter is listed.

8.4 THE SPACE PARAMETER

The SPACE parameter is an optional keyword parameter on the DD statement. Its position within a JCL statement will be as follows:

//	Name	Operation	Operands	Comments
//	ddname	DD	SPACE=...	comments

Table 8.1 JCL Parameters which allocate SPACE

Function	Corresponding JCL parameters and Subparameter
Requesting space in tracks	TRK
Requesting space in cylinders	CYL
Requesting space in blocks	A number corresponding to the number of blocks required is coded
Specification of specific storage space at the time that a data set is created	PRIMARY
Specification of additional storage space if amount originally specified is insufficient	SECONDARY
Specification of storage space for recording of name and location of partitioned data sets	DIRECTORY
Request for release of space previously allocated	RLSE
Request for contiguous space	CONTIG
Request for largest area of contiguous space	MXIG
Request for entire cylinder for storage of data set	ROUND

As mentioned earlier in the chapter, the SPACE parameter is used to specify storage requirements on direct access devices. On each direct access device, a *Volume Table of Contents* (called *VTOC*) is maintained. The VTOC records the name of the data sets on that volume, and the amount of free space available on that volume. At the time that storage is requested on a particular volume, its VTOC is scanned for space availability. If space is available, the system attempts to fulfill the request using adjacent tracks on the volume. If adjacent tracks are unavailable, then the system attempts to allocate space on non-contiguous tracks on that device, the name *extent* is given to non-contiguous tracks. If more than fifteen non-contiguous tracks are required, then space will be sought on other similar volumes.

If none of these conditions are met, then the job is abended.

8.5 SYNTAX OF THE SPACE PARAMETER

The general syntax for the SPACE parameter, using all of the options listed in Table 8.1, is:

SPACE=(CYL,(primary,secondary,directory),
    RLSE,CONTIG,MXIG,ROUND)

CYL indicates request of storage space in cylinders. CYL can be replaced by *TRK*, or by *blk*, which is a number. Thus, any of the following variations to the syntax just presented are valid:

SPACE=(TRK,(primary,secondary,directory),RLSE,CONTIG,MXIG, ROUND)

or

SPACE=(blk,(primary,secondary,directory),RLSE,CONTIG,MXIG, ROUND)

primary is a number indicating the amount of primary storage space requested. If the programmer is certain that the amount of the primary allocation will be sufficient, or wants to limit the size of the output file, then *secondary*, which is another number indicating the amount of secondary space allocation, can be skipped. Thus, the following variation to the syntax just presented is also valid:

SPACE=(TRK,(primary,,directory),RLSE,CONTIG,MXIG,ROUND)

Notice the extra comma between *primary* and *directory*. This is required, since all subparameters on the SPACE parameter are positional.
    If space is being allocated for a non-partitioned data set, then the *directory* subparameter can be skipped. Thus, the following variation to the syntax presented is also valid:

SPACE=(blk,PRIMARY,RLSE,CONTIG,MXIG,ROUND)

Notice the absence of the inner set of brackets.
    RLSE, MXIG, CONTIG and *ROUND* are all optional subparameters, and can be skipped if necessary. The SPACE parameter can be reduced to this:

SPACE=(TRK,PRIMARY)

Each of these different specifications will be explained with examples. But first, an explanation of the TRK subparameter.

8.6 THE TRK SUBPARAMETER

The TRK subparameter is used to allocate small data sets. Small data sets are often used in a test environment, where it is unnecessary to test programs with large data sets.

Usually, one track consists of 56,664 bytes on a 3390 disk. Exactly how many tracks are actually allocated by the system depends on the values specified in LRECL and BLKSIZE parameters for the data set. These parameters will be explained later on in this chapter, and you really don't need to think about them for now.

However, something that you should make a note of is that TRK is device-dependent, i.e. the number of bytes actually allocated depends on the type of device on which the data set will be stored. Thus, the amount of storage space that you request using the TRK parameter will vary for different device types. It is beyond the scope of this book to go into details on how to compute this figure; we advise you to seek out more advanced books on the subject, should you require more information. Let's continue with an example.

8.6.1 An Example

```
//JOB1   JOB    A123,'GEETHA ABRAHAM'
//STEP1  EXEC   PGM=PROGRAM1
//DATA1 DD      DSN=FILE1,
//              UNIT=3390,
//              SPACE=(TRK,4)
```

Geetha Abraham submits JOB1. PROGRAM1 is executed in STEP1. The dataset called FILE1 is created on a 3390 disk. Space in the amount of four tracks is requested for this data set. Thus, the system will attempt to allocate 226,656 (56,664 x 4) bytes of storage space for this data set.

8.7 THE CYL SUBPARAMETER

The CYL subparameter is used to allocate large data sets. Like the TRK parameter, the number of bytes actually allocated is device dependent. Thus, the number of bytes allocated for one cylinder on a 3390 disk will be different from one cylinder allocated on a 3380 disk.

Storing data on cylinders will result in a faster access time than if it were placed on tracks. This is because more time is required to position the read/write head (the mechanism by which devices are read) on a specific track within a cylinder, than to position it on a cylinder itself.

8.7.1 AN EXAMPLE

```
//JOB2    JOB  (B123),'MINNIE ABRAHAM'
//STEP1   EXEC PGM=PROGRAM1
//DATA1   DD   DSN=FILE1,
//             UNIT=3390,
//             SPACE=(CYL,10)
```

In this example, ten cylinders of storage space are requested on a 3390 disk for the dataset called FILE1. Remember, the total number of bytes actually allocated varies with the device type being used.

8.8 REQUESTING SPACE IN BLOCKS

Space can also be requested in blocks. Unlike TRK and CYL, blocksize is independent of device type. Thus, the same number of bytes will be allocated, regardless of which device they are requested on.

Exactly how many bytes are assigned to one block is determined by the value stored in the DCB=BLKSIZE subparameter. This parameter will be discussed in the latter half of this chapter.

Space for blocks will be allocated in tracks, based on the number of blocks that will completely fit on a track. That is, if a track can hold ten 1000 byte blocks, and a request is issued for 15 1000 byte blocks, then two tracks will be allocated. (15 x 1000 = 15,000 bytes, one track holds 10000 bytes, thus two tracks will be required to hold 15,000 bytes of data.) The space actually allocated will always be rounded to a whole number of tracks.

8.8.1 An Example

```
//JOB3    JOB  C123,'USHA ABRAHAM'
//STEP1   EXEC PGM=PROGRAM1
//DATA1   DD   DSN=FILE1,
//             UNIT=3390,
//             SPACE=(20,1000)
```

In this example, Usha Abraham executes PROGRAM1 and requests

1000 records having an average block length of 20 bytes on a 3390 disk.

8.9 PRIMARY SPACE ALLOCATION

At the time that space is allocated, you can request a *primary* amount of storage. This is the number of bytes that you expect the data set will require for storage. All examples presented so far request primary space. Then, as a safety measure, you can also request *secondary* space. We discuss this next.

8.10 SECONDARY SPACE ALLOCATION

Secondary space allocation is used to specify additional tracks, cylinders or blocks to be allocated if the primary specification is insufficient for the job. Secondary space, when allocated, does not have to be contiguous with the location of the primary allocation. Instead, the system may utilize *extents* for this kind of allocation. (Extents were explained earlier in this chapter). Up to 15 extents may be allocated on a volume. If secondary allocation requires more than 15 extents, than a second volume of the same type will be sought by the system.

Secondary space allocation has its benefits and drawbacks. The benefit is that space is automatically allocated. If the amount of primary space specified is insufficient, the job does not abend. The drawback is that space is allocated in extents, which results in data being fragmented over the device, increasing the time required to access this data set.

8.10.1 Some Examples

Example 1

```
//JOB1     JOB    A123,'GEORGE STERN'
//STEP1    EXEC   PGM=PROGRAM1
//DATA1    DD     DSN=FILE1,
//                UNIT=3390,
//                SPACE=(TRK,(50,25))
```

In this example PROGRAM1 is executed, 50 tracks are assigned as primary space, and 25*15 as secondary space for FILE1 on a 3390 disk. If 50 tracks are insufficient for FILE1, then additional space will be allocated automatically by the system.

Example 2

```
//JOB2    JOB    B123,'PAUL MCGRAW'
//STEP1   EXEC   PGM=PROGRAM2
//DATA1   DD     DSN=FILE2,
//               UNIT=3390,
//               SPACE=(CYL,(20,5))
```

In this example, 20 cylinders are requested as primary space and 5 additional cylinders as secondary space.

Example 3

```
//JOB3    JOB    C123,'JOHN MICHAEL'
//STEP1   EXEC   PGM=PROGRAM3
//DATA1   DD     DSN=FILE3,
//               UNIT=3390,
//               SPACE=(1000,(500,250))
```

In this example, 500 blocks of 1000 bytes each are requested as primary space. An additional 250*15 blocks (of 1000 bytes each) are requested if the original specification is found to be inadequate.

8.11 THE DIRECTORY SUBPARAMETER

The DIRECTORY subparameter, as mentioned previously, is used when defining partitioned data sets. This storage space is used to record the names and locations of the members created within the partitioned data set. If storage space for a partitioned data set is requested, and this parameter is not specified, the job will abend.

One directory block contains 256 bytes. Generally speaking, you can store information for up to six partitioned data sets in a directory block. To be on the safe side, the authors recommend that you calculate the amount of directory space required to be four members per block. Thus, if the name and location of five partitioned data sets has to be recorded, you should specify two directory blocks for that information. The directory subparameter follows the primary and secondary space subparameters.

8.11.1 Some Examples

Example 1

```
//JOB1    JOB   A50,'JEEWAN KAPOOR'
//STEP1   EXEC  PGM=PROGRAM1
//DATA1   DD    DSN=FILE1,
//              UNIT=3390,
//              SPACE=(TRK,(200,50,10))
```

In this example 200 tracks are allocated as primary space, and 50 tracks are allocated as secondary space. Ten tracks are requested for storing name and location information for members that will reside in the partitioned data set.

Example 2

```
//JOB2    JOB   B60,'CHANDER KAPOOR'
//STEP1   EXEC  PGM=PROGRAM2
//DATA1   DD    DSN=FILE2,
//              UNIT=3390,
//              SPACE=(CYL,(30,,10))
```

In this example 30 cylinders are requested as primary space, and 10 cylinders are requested for information pertaining to members that will reside on this partitioned data set. Notice the extra comma between the two specifications. This is required, since the SECONDARY space parameter is skipped, and this is a positional parameter.

8.12 THE RLSE SUBPARAMETER

The RLSE subparameter is used to specify the request that space originally allocated to an output data set be released when the data set is closed. A data set is considered to be closed after the successful implementation of an operation on it, such as a write. For example, if 20 tracks are assigned to a data set, and only 15 are used by it, then the remaining 5 tracks are released after the data set has been created and written to. The RLSE parameter also frees up unused extents, if they are only partially used. The RLSE parameter helps free up resources for other jobs.

One drawback associated with the RLSE parameter is that it utilizes I/O time to release the space. Thus, the time required to execute a job which contains the RLSE parameter is more than that for a job that does not use this parameter. Furthermore, if the data set is to be appended, then the additional data will be stored in extents (given that the secondary allocation parameter was specified), and this will further add to the access time required to write the data set and then access it.

8.12.1 Some Examples

Example 1

```
//JOB1     JOB  D70,'JAN RANADE'
//STEP1    EXEC PGM=PROGRAM1
//DATA1    DD   DSN=FILE100,
//              UNIT=3380,
//              SPACE=(TRK,(100,50),RLSE)
```

In this example, JOB1 is executed. 100 tracks of primary storage space and additional tracks of secondary storage space are requested for FILE100. If FILE100 actually occupies less space, then the remaining tracks will be released after FILE100 has been written and closed.

Example 2

```
//JOB2     JOB  E80,'HIRDAY RANADE'
//STEP1    EXEC PGM=PROGRAM1
//DATA1    DD   DSN=FILE200,
//              UNIT=3380,
//              SPACE=(CYL,4,RLSE)
```

In this example JOB2 is executed. Four cylinders of primary space are allocated to FILE200. Secondary space is not specified. If only three cylinders are actually required, then one cylinder will be released after FILE200 has been written to disk and the data set has been closed.

8.13 THE CONTIG SUBPARAMETER

The CONTIG subparameter is used to specify that only contiguous space should be allocated to the data set. This parameter applies only to primary space allocations. Use of this parameter results in decreased data set access time, since the entire space is contiguous. However, the use of this parameter has a primary drawback, which is that the job will terminate abnormally if the requested space is not found contiguously. This parameter is rarely used.

8.13.1 An Example

```
//JOB1    JOB    F100,'ANNA MARIA'
//STEP1   EXEC   PGM=PROGRAM1
//DATA1   DD     DSN=FILE300,
//               UNIT=3390,
//               SPACE=(TRK,600,,CONTIG)
```

In this example, 600 contiguous tracks are requested on a 3390 disk. Notice the extra comma between the primary specification and the CONTIG parameter. This is required to account for the absence of the RLSE parameter, which is positional.

8.14 THE MXIG SUBPARAMETER

The MXIG subparameter is used to specify that space requested should be allocated to the largest contiguous area of space available on the volume. Like the CONTIG parameter, MXIG applies to primary space allocation only. Space will be allocated in areas which are as large, or larger than, the request. Like the CONTIG parameter, MXIG is also rarely used. If this parameter must be used, it is a good idea to use it in conjunction with the RLSE parameter, so that unused space can be released as necessary.

8.14.1 An Example

```
//JOB1    JOB   G200,'MARIA ANNE'
//STEP1   EXEC  PGM=PROGRAM1
//DATA1   DD    DSN=FILE400,
//              UNIT=3390,
//              SPACE=(TRK,700,RLSE,MXIG)
```

In this example, 700 tracks of primary space are requested on a 3390 disk, in an area where 700 or more tracks of contiguous space are available. If the data set occupies less than 700 tracks, say 500, then the unused space will be released, as per the RLSE subparameter.

8.15 THE ROUND SUBPARAMETER

The use of this subparameter results in space being allocated on the entire cylinder instead of just portions of it. The system computes the amount of storage required, rounds it off to the nearest cylinder, and allocates that number of cylinders to the request. The advantage associated with the use of this parameter is that data will reside, starting with the first track of the cylinder, and end on the last track. Thus, all data is stored starting at the cylinder boundary, and access time is decreased. The disadvantage is that if a whole cylinder is not available, the job will abend.

8.15.1 An Example

```
//JOB1    JOB   H400,'ANNA MAE'
//STEP1   EXEC  PGM=PROGRAM1
//DATA1   DD    DSN=FILE500,
//              UNIT=3390,
//              SPACE=(500,50,,,ROUND)
```

In this example, 50 blocks of 500 bytes are requested as storage space for FILE500. Use of the ROUND subparameter results in space being allocated to be rounded to the nearest cylinder.

8.16 THE DCB PARAMETER, AN OVERVIEW

The DCB (*Data Control Block*) is used to supply information to the system that allows it to manage the data sets that are created as jobs are submitted. As indicated at the beginning of the chapter, it helps customize the way data is stored on devices. When a new data set is created, the following has to be specified to the operating system:

- Records within a data set can have different types of formats. For example, they can be of a fixed or variable length, data can be stored in them in different ways, etc. Specifications such as these must be conveyed to the system.

- The number of bytes of a record within the data set must be specified.

- Multiple records can be logically grouped together inside what is called a *block*. The block size helps establish the efficiency with which records within the data set can be accessed. An appropriate block size must be determined and specified according to the operating system.

- Access time of a data set can be speeded up by specifying an extra amount of virtual storage for it. Virtual storage can be visualized as the amount of space that is reserved in memory for reading/writing data sets. Data sets are swapped into this space from the I/O device, and then swapped out again as different I/O requests are implemented by the operating system. Virtual storage space may be classified into buffers, where one buffer space equals a certain amount of memory. A specific number of buffers for a data set may be specified to the operating system, depending on the speed of access time required.

8.17 CORRESPONDING JCL

Table 8.2 lists the JCL parameters that are used to convey the information listed in Section 8.16.

Table 8.2 JCL Parameters Coded to Allocate DCB

Function	Corresponding JCL Sub-parameters Coded on the DCB Parameter
Specifcation of record format	RECFM
Specification of record length	LRECL
Specification of block size	BLKSIZE
Specification of buffers	BUFNO

We will now discuss the DCB parameter and its subparameters in detail.

8.18 THE DCB PARAMETER

The DCB parameter is a keyword parameter that is coded on the DD statement. This parameter is required if a new data set is created. Its position within a JCL statement is as follows:

//	Name	Operation	Operands	Comments
//	ddname	DD	DCB=...	comments

8.19 SYNTAX OF DCB PARAMETER

The syntax of the DCB parameter looks like this:

DCB=(RECFM=format,LRECL=record-length,BLKSIZE=block-size)

8.20 THE RECFM PARAMETER

The RECFM parameter coded on the the DCB statement is used to specify to the operating system the record format of the data set being created. Record format can be of a fixed length, variable length, or undefined length. But first, here's the syntax:

8.21 SYNTAX

The syntax of the RECFM parameter looks like this:

    RECFM=F
or
    RECFM=FB
or
    RECFM=V
or
    RECFM=VB
or
    RECFM=U

Each of these different types of formats will now be explained.

8.22 SPECIFICATION OF FIXED LENGTH FORMAT

Coding an F or FB (*F* for *Fixed*, and *FB* for *Fixed Block*, both are interchangeable) for the RECFM subparameter results in the operating system creating fixed length records for the specified data set.   All records in this data set will be of the same length.

8.22.1 An Example

```
//JOB1     JOB    123,'DANNY'
//STEP1    EXEC   PGM=DCB1
//DATA1    DD     DSN=FILE1,
//                UNIT-3390,
//                DCB=(RECFM=F)
```

In this example, a job is submitted by Danny. DCB1 is executed, and a data set called FILE1 is created on a 3390 disk. An F is coded in the DCB parameter, indicating that this file will have fixed length records. Coding an FB instead of an F would have produced the same results.

8.23 SPECIFICATION OF VARIABLE LENGTH FORMAT

Coding a V for the RECFM subparameter results in the operating system allowing records of a variable length to be created for the specified data set. A file containing the names and addresses of people is an example of variable length records, since names and addresses of people can be of varying lengths.

8.23.1 An Example

```
//JOB2    JOB    456,'MANNY'
//STEP1   EXEC   PGM=DCB2
//DATA1   DD     DSN=FILE2,
//               UNIT-3390,
//               DCB=(RECFM=VB)
```

In this example, JOB2 is submitted. DCB2 is executed, and FILE2 is created on a 3390 disk. A VB is coded for RECFM resulting in variable length records being created for the data set. Coding a V would have produced the same results.

8.24 SPECIFICATION OF UNDEFINED LENGTH

Coding a U in the RECFM subparameter results in the operating system allowing records of undefined length to be created for the data set specified. What this means is that the decision (whether a record should be of fixed or variable length) is left to the operating system. A load module data set is an example in which RECFM should be specified as U.

8.24.1 An Example

```
//JOB3    JOB   789,'VINNY'
//STEP1   EXEC  PGM=DCB3
//DD1     DD    DSN=FILE3,
//              UNIT=3390,
//              DCB=(RECFM=U)
```

In this example, a data set called FILE3 is created. The record format of this file is undefined. The operating system will determine what kind of record format it should have, based on the kind of data that will be stored in it.

8.25 Relationship of RECFM to COBOL Program

In a COBOL program, RECFM is defined in the FILE SECTION. Here's an example that shows part of the COBOL code and the JCL that will correspond to this code. First, the COBOL program:

```
IDENTIFICATION DIVISION.
PROGRAM=ID.  PROGRAM1.
**
ENVIRONMENT DIVISION.
CONFIGURATION SECTION.
SOURCE-COMPUTER.
 IBM-370.
INPUT-OUTPUT SECTION.
FILE-CONTROL.
 SELECT FILE1 ASSIGN TO INPUT1.
**
DATA DIVISION.
FILE SECTION.
FD  FILE1
    RECORDING MODE IS F
**
** REST OF THE PROGRAM GOES HERE...
```

Now take a look at the corresponding JCL:

```
//JOB1    JOB    123,'DANNY'
//STEP1   EXEC   PGM=DCB1
//DATA1   DD     DSN=FILE1,
//               UNIT-3390,
//               DCB=(RECFM=F)
```

The COBOL statement

```
    RECORDING MODE IS F
```

relates to the following JCL statement:

```
//               DCB=(RECFM=F)
```

RECORDING MODE could have been set to V for variable length records, or U for undefined length. The JCL coded for RECFM would be changed to V or U, respectively.

8.26 THE LRECL PARAMETER

The LRECL parameter (*Logical Record Length*) is used to specify the length of the record, in bytes, for fixed or variable length records. For fixed length records, LRECL is set equal to the record length. For variable length records, LRECL is set equal to the size of the largest record, plus four bytes, which is used by the system to specify the actual length of the record that follows.

This parameter is used to save storage space on the computer. For example, suppose a file had variable length records, the smallest record being 20 bytes long, and the largest one being 150 bytes. If we were unable to specify variable length records, then all records would have to be of the same length. Thus, a fixed length of 150 bytes would have to be allocated for each record, resulting in a lot of wasted space.

8.26.1 Syntax

The syntax of the LRECL subparameter coded on the DCB parameter looks like this:

    LRECL=number

where *number* is the appropriate length in decimal digits.

8.26.2 Some Examples

Example 1

```
//JOB1      JOB    890,HONEY
//STEP1     EXEC   PGM=LRECL1
//DD1       DD     DSN=FILE1,
//                 UNIT=3390,
//                 DCB=(RECFM=F,LRECL=40)
```

In this example, the program LRECL1 is executed. A data set called FILE1 is created on a 3390 disk. This file is specified as having fixed length records, and each record is allocated a size of 40 bytes.

Example 2

```
//JOB2      JOB    780,CONEY
//STEP1     EXEC   PGM=LRECL2
//DD1       DD     DSN=FILE2,
```

```
//                 UNIT=3390,
//                 DCB=(RECFM=V,LRECL=164)
```

In this example, a file of variable length records is created. Specifying LRECL as 164 bytes indicates that the length of the largest record in the file is 160 bytes. Four bytes are added to the largest record size; these bytes will contain the actual length of each variable length record in the file.

8.27 RELATIONSHIP TO COBOL PROGRAM

In a COBOL program, like the record format, the logical record length is also specified in the FILE SECTION. Here's an example that relates the COBOL code with its corresponding JCL. First, the COBOL:

```
IDENTIFICATION DIVISION.
PROGRAM=ID.    PROGRAM2.
**
ENVIRONMENT DIVISION.
CONFIGURATION SECTION.
SOURCE-COMPUTER.
  IBM-370.
INPUT-OUTPUT SECTION.
FILE-CONTROL.
  SELECT FILE1 ASSIGN TO INPUT1.
**
DATA DIVISION.
FILE SECTION.
FD   FILE1
     RECORD CONTAINS 40 CHARACTERS
     RECORDING MODE IS FB
**
```

The corresponding JCL for this program will be:

```
//JOB1    JOB    123,'FANNY'
//STEP1   EXEC   PGM=DCB1
//DATA1   DD     DSN=FILE1,
//               UNIT-3390,
//               DCB=(RECFM=FB,LRECL=40)
```

The COBOL statement

```
RECORD CONTAINS 40 CHARACTERS
```

relates to the following JCL statement:

```
//                    DCB=(RECFM=FB,LRECL=40)
```

8.28 THE BLKSIZE PARAMETER

BLKSIZE refers to block size. This parameter is used to specify the block size of a data set in bytes. It can be as small as a few bytes, and as large as 32,760 bytes. It must be specified as a multiple of the record length for fixed length records. Space will be wasted if it is not. It must be set equal to at least the record length plus four bytes for variable length records. Block size must be set equal to the size of the largest block for undefined length records. Also, please note that block size can not be larger than the track size of the direct access volume on which the data set will reside.

Access time for data sets that are created using the BLKSIZE parameter is much faster than those data sets in which this parameter is not specified.

8.28.1 Syntax

The syntax of the BLKSIZE subparameter coded on the DCB parameter looks like this:

```
BLKSIZE=number
```

where *number* is the appropriate length in decimal digits.

8.28.2 Relationship of BLKSIZE to COBOL Program

Like the record format and logical record length, the BLKSIZE of a data set is also specified in the FILE SECTION of a COBOL program. Here's an example that relates the COBOL code with its corresponding JCL. First, the COBOL:

```
IDENTIFICATION DIVISION.
PROGRAM=ID.   PROGRAM3.
**
ENVIRONMENT DIVISION.
CONFIGURATION SECTION.
SOURCE-COMPUTER.
  IBM-370.
INPUT-OUTPUT SECTION.
```

```
FILE-CONTROL.
  SELECT FILE1 ASSIGN TO INPUT1.
**
DATA DIVISION.
FILE SECTION.
FD   FILE1
     RECORD CONTAINS 40 CHARACTERS
     RECORDING MODE IS FB
     BLOCK CONTAINS 0 RECORDS
**
```

The corresponding JCL will be as follows:

```
//JOB1    JOB    123,'FANNY'
//STEP1   EXEC   PGM=DCB1
//DATA1   DD     DSN=FILE1,
//               UNIT-3390,
//               DCB=(RECFM=FB,LRECL=40,BLKSIZE=1600)
```

The COBOL statement

```
    BLOCK CONTAINS 0 RECORDS
```

relates to the following JCL statement:

```
//               DCB=(RECFM=FB,LRECL=40,BLKSIZE=1600)
```

In a COBOL program, the BLOCK CONTAINS 0 RECORDS statement should be specified. If it is not, then the default block size is a
value which is quite inefficient in terms of its overall access to these
records.

Specifying the BLOCK statement in the COBOL program as we did
allows us to code any block size in the corresponding JCL. It is not
good practice to hardcode a block size in a COBOL program, since each
time the block size is changed in the JCL, it will also have to be changed
in the program.

8.29 THE BUFNO PARAMETER

The BUFNO parameter is used to specify the number of buffers to be
allocated to virtual storage for the data set. As indicated earlier in this
chapter, a large number of buffers can improve I/O performance.

If this parameter is not coded, the default is five buffers. A maximum
number of 255 buffers can be specified.

8.29.1 Syntax

The syntax of the BUFNO subparameter coded on the DCB parameter looks like this:

BUFNO=number

where *number* is the appropriate length in decimal digits.

8.29.2 An Example

```
//JOB1      JOB    999,'LENNY'
//STEP1     EXEC   PGM=BUFNO1
//DD1       DD     DSN=FILE1,
//                 UNIT=3390,
//                 DCB=(LRECL=80,
//                 RECFM=FB,
//                 BLKSIZE=800,
//                 BUFNO=40)
```

In this example, Lenny submits JOB1. BUFNO1 is executed and FILE1 is created on a 3390 disk. The DCB parameter specifies that this file is to have a logical record length of 80 bytes, it will have a fixed block record format, and the blocking factor is established at 800 bytes. (800 is a multiple of 80). The BUFNO parameter is set to 40, indicating that up to 40 buffers may be utilized in virtual storage for this data set. This specification will result in faster access time for this data set, since the number 40 is greater than 5, which would have been the default allocation. Please note that the SPACE and DISP parameters must be specified to create this file.

8.30 THINGS THAT CAN GO WRONG

We now list the error messages and descriptions of things that can go wrong while coding the SPACE or DCB parameters. Either refer to the JCL error code, or scan through *Probable Cause of Error* to identify the cause of the error in your JCL. Please refer to Table 8.2.

8.31 REVIEW

In this chapter we discussed the SPACE and DCB parameters which are coded on the DD statement. Tables 8.3 and 8.4 summarize the syntax and meanings of the parameters described.

Table 8.2 Some Common Errors

JCL Error Code	Description	Probable Cause of Error
ABEND B-37		Coding less space than required on the SPACE parameter
IEF630I	Unidentified keyword TRK	Coding CYL and TRK parameters on one line, instead of two

Table 8.3 SPACE Parameter Coded on the DD Statement

JCL Parameter	Syntax and Description
SPACE	SPACE is an optional keyword parameter on the DD statement Used to specify storage requirements of data sets that reside on direct access devices such as disks. Tapes do not require the SPACE parameter
SPACE=(TRK,#)	# is a number specifying total number of tracks to be allocated Actual number of bytes allocated is device dependent
SPACE=(CYL,#)	# is a number specifying total number of cylinders to be allocated Actual number of bytes allocated is device dependent
SPACE=(#)	# is the number of blocks to be allocated This kind of allocation is not device dependent

SPACE=(primary,secondary)	primary is the number of bytes that you expect the data set will require for storage
	secondary is the amount of additional storage that can be requested if primary storage is insufficient
SPACE=(,,directory)	,, is required, as place holders for the primary and secondary parameters, which are positional
	directory is a required positional parameter when partitioned data sets are created
SPACE=(type,RLSE)	type is the kind of storage requested.
	RLSE is used to release any unused space after storage allocation
SPACE=(type,,,CONTIG)	type is the kind of storage requested.
	CONTIG is used to request contiguous storage for the data set
SPACE=(type,,,MXIG)	type is the kind of storage requested.
	MXIG is used to request largest contiguous space available on the data set
SPACE=(type,,,ROUND)	type is the kind of storage requested.
	ROUND is used to request the entire cylinder for the data set, instead of portions of it

Table 8.4 The DCB Parameter Coded on the DD Statement

JCL Parameter	Syntax and Description
DCB	DCB is a keyword parameter coded on the DD statement It is used to supply information to the system with reference to the organization of data in a data set
RECFM=format	RECFM is used to specify the record format of the data set. format can be F or FB for fixed length V or VB for variable length U for undefined
LRECL LRECL=number	LRECL is used to specify length, in bytes, of fixed or variable length records number is equal to record length for fixed length records number is equal to largest record size + 4 bytes for variable length records
BLKSIZE BLKSIZE=number	Used to specify block size in bytes of data set number is the number of bytes. Highest number can be 32,760 bytes
BUFNO BUFNO=number	Used to specify number of buffers to be allocated to virtual storage for the data set number is the number of buffers. Up to 255 buffers can be specified The larger the number of buffers, the faster the access time

Coding Data Sets,
and I/O
on the DD Statement

9.1 INTRODUCTION

We continue our discussion of the DD statement. In this chapter we will discuss the different types of data sets that can be specified, such as dummy and concatenated. We also include a discussion on special DD statements, such as SYSOUT, SYSUDUMP, and the SYSABEND.

9.2 SPECIAL DD STATEMENTS, AN OVERVIEW

The following becomes significant when different types of processing are required on data sets:

■ There may be a need to test the execution of a program without actually resorting to the reading and/or writing to data sets in the process. Situations such as these are typical in a test environment, when only the flow of a program needs to be tested, and actual processing of data is to be bypassed. If a *dummy* data set is to be processed, then the operating system needs to be informed.

■ In an MVS environment you have the capability to read several input data sets in sequence, as though they were only one. These data sets must reside on similar device types, but they do not have to reside on the same volume. Access time for these data sets will be faster, because they will be concatenated together for the duration of the request.

Situations in which data sets need to be concatenated together can be specified to the system.

- The system can be requested to supply information with reference to the source of any errors that may occur during the execution of a specific job step within a job.

- The system can be requested to supply information relating to its nucleus, in addition to the miscellaneous information relating to the job step, if errors should occur during the execution of a job step within a job.

- Information can be directly input to a data set, at the time that the job step is executed.

- The end of input must be specified to the system.

- Output can be directed to a specific pre-defined class.

- Output can be printed to a specific device in a different or remote location.

- Output can be held over until further notice.

- Output can be limited to a specific number of lines.

9.3 CORRESPONDING JCL

Table 9.1 lists the JCL parameters used to specify the information listed in Section 9.2. If there is no corresponding parameter, then text is used to indicate how the information can be conveyed. If a specific subparameter with a parameter conveys the applicable information, then the parameter, along with the relevant subparameter, is listed.

9.4 THE DUMMY PARAMETER

The DUMMY parameter is coded on the DD statement to test the execution of a program without actually reading or writing to a data set. It causes the operating system to simulate the presence of a file, without it actually being there. Its position within a JCL statement is as follows:

//	Name	Operation	Operands	Comments
//	ddname	DD	DUMMY	comments

Table 9.1 JCL Parameters related to DD Parameter

Function	Corresponding JCL parameters and Subparameter
Specification of dummy data sets	DUMMY or DSN=NULLFILE
Concatenating data sets	Data set names are coded one after the other, all DD statements appear in the sequence that the data sets are to be concatenated
Requesting information relating to errors during execution of job step	SYSUDUMP
Requesting information relating to system nucleus, in addition to that which is generated by a regular job step error	SYSABEND
Inputting information to a data set during execution of job step	SYSIN DATA or SYSIN *
Specifying end of input following SYSIN parameter	DLM
Directing system output to a predefined output class	SYSOUT
Directing output to a specific device in a remote location	DEST
Holding output for later	HOLD
Limiting output to a specific number of lines	OUTLIM

The same results can be obtained by coding NULLFILE for the DSN parameter, like this:

//	Name	Operation	Operands	Comments
//	ddname	DD	DSN=NULLFILE	comments

If a DUMMY or NULLFILE is read, then the operating system passes an *end-of-file* indicator to the program that is being executed. This results in the program continuing to execute, based on its logic, without having read any data set. If write requests are issued to these imaginary files, they are simply ignored.

DUMMY is a very commonly used parameter, since it provides a safe way to eliminate input/output activity when it is not required.

9.4.1 Some Examples

Example 1

```
//JOB1    JOB   A1,DELIA
//STEP1   EXEC  PGM=DUMMY1
//DATA1   DD    DUMMY
```

In this example, Delia submits JOB1. The program DUMMY1 is executed and a dummy data set is accessed.

Example 2

```
//JOB2    JOB   B1,CELIA
//STEP1   EXEC  PGM=DUMMY2
//DATA1   DD    DSN=NULLFILE
```

This example is similar to example 1 in that a dummy data set is accessed. However, the method used here is via the DSN parameter coded to NULLFILE, instead of specifying DUMMY directly on the DD statement.

Example 3

```
//JOB3    JOB   C1,AMELIA
//STEP1   EXEC  PGM=DUMMY2
//DATA1   DD    DUMMY,
//              DSN=FILE1,
//              UNIT=3390,
//              SPACE=(CYL(1,1,RLSE),
//              DCB=(RECFM=FB,
```

```
//              LRECL=80,
//              BLKSIZE=6160)
```

In this example, Amelia submits JOB3. The program called DUMMY2 is executed. A dummy data set is used. However, all of the parameters used to create and write to a real data set are also coded. This example illustrates how the DUMMY data set can be used to test real code without affecting any data sets. Take another look at the SPACE parameter:

```
//              SPACE=(CYL(1,1,RLSE),
```

There is a syntax error in this statement, a missing bracket after the secondary space allocation. This is how the statement should actually have been coded:

```
//              SPACE=(CYL(1,1),RLSE),
```

When JOB3 is submitted, this syntax error will be caught and the programmer will be able to correct this error before the job is submitted with a real data set. Once all bugs have been cleared, then all that needs to be done is to change the DUMMY specification to the name of a real data set. The original DD statement

```
//DATA1   DD    DUMMY,
```

would be modified as follows:

```
//DATA1   DD    DSN=FILE1,
```

and the programmer would be assured that there will be no errors at the time that the job is submitted, since all bugs had been cleared while testing with the DUMMY data set.

9.5 CONCATENATING DATA SETS

A data set can be concatenated together and perceived as one file by the operating system by coding each applicable data set name one after the other.

9.5.1 Rules for Coding

- Up to 255 sequential data sets can be concatenated together.

- Up to 16 partitioned data sets can be concatenated together.

- All data sets concatenated together must have the same type of record format. (The RECFM specification should be the same.)

- All data sets concatenated together must exist on the same type of device. For example, if five data sets are being concatenated together, and if three of them reside on a disk device, and the other two reside on tape devices, then the access to them will be disallowed. It is not necessary for all data sets to exist on the same volume.

- All data sets concatenated together must be of the same type. For example, partitioned data sets can be concatenated only with partitioned data sets, sequential data sets can be concatenated only with sequential data sets, and so on.

- If tape data sets are concatenated together, then the block size of the first data set must be larger than, or equal to, that of the subsequent data set.

- It is not OK to concatenate fixed length records with variable length records.

9.5.2 An Example

```
//JOB1     JOB   0001,AL
//STEP1    EXEC  PGM=CONCAT1
//DATA1    DD    DSN=FILE1
//         DD    DSN=FILE2
//         DD    DSN=FILE3
```

In this example, three files called FILE1, FILE2, and FILE3 are concatenated together. Notice how the DD statements are coded one after another.

9.6 THE SYSUDUMP DD STATEMENT

The SYSUDUMP is coded in the name field of the DD statement. Its position in a JCL statement looks like this:

//	Name	Operation	Operands	Comments
//	SYSUDUMP	DD	...	comments

It is used to obtain a dump of the contents of various registers and variables in case of abnormal termination of the job. This dump is in hexadecimal. Information about various subroutines called within the job and data sets accessed is also provided.

9.6.1 An Example

```
//JOB2       JOB   0002,ED
//STEP1      EXEC  PGM=PROGRAM2
//SYSUDUMP   DD    DSN=DUMPFILE,
//                 UNIT=3390,
//                 SPACE=(CYL,(1,1),RLSE)
```

In this example, Ed submits JOB2, and PROGRAM2 is executed. If this job terminates abnormally, a dump of the contents of various registers, variables, subroutine trace-backs, and data sets accessed will be written to the data set called DUMPFILE. This data set will reside on a 3390 disk. one cylinder of primary space and up to 15 *extents* of one cylinder each of secondary space will be allocated to this data set, and any unused space after the data set that has been written to (if it is written at all!) will be released. An extent is the term given to secondary allocations of space.

9.7 THE SYSABEND DD STATEMENT

The SYSABEND is coded in the name field of the DD statement. Its position in a JCL statement looks like this:

//	Name	Operation	Operands	Comments
//	SYSABEND	DD	...	comments

Like SYSUDUMP, it is used to obtain a dump of the contents of various registers and variables in case of abnormal termination of the job. The dump is in hexadecimal, and information about various subroutines called within the job, and data sets accessed is provided. In addition to this, the system nucleus at the time of termination of a job is also listed to the output device or data set.

A storage dump requires quite a lot of paper to print, and presence of mind to analyze. Given that you are a novice JCL user, we recommend that you stick with the SYSUDUMP statement and avoid the SYSABEND. This parameter is useful mainly for system programmers.

9.7.1 An Example

```
//JOB3       JOB  0003,DI
//STEP1      EXEC PGM=PROGRAM3
//SYSABEND   DD   SYSOUT=A
```

In this example, if the job terminates abnormally, a dump of the contents of various registers, variables, subroutine trace-backs, and data sets accessed will be written to the output device. On top of all of this, the system nucleus at the time of abnormal termination will also be written to the output data set.

9.8 SYSIN - Input Stream Data

SYSIN is not a parameter. It is the conventional ddname assigned to input data streams. An input data stream is data that is entered at the time that the job is submitted. Its position in a JCL statement looks like this:

//	Name	Operation	Operands	Comments
//	SYSIN	DD	* <data follows> /*	comments

Notice the single asterisk in the operands field. When the operating system detects an asterisk in the operands field, it pauses for input which can be entered in the form of keystrokes on the keyboard, or coded. It considers all data that follows to be input data. The /* indicates the end of the input data stream. You may code several SYSIN statements within the same job or job step.

The keyword DATA may replace the *, as follows:

//	Name	Operation	Operands	Comments
//	SYSIN	DD	DATA <data statements> /*	comments

Both statements produce the same result. The only difference is that when you code the asterisk in the operand field, you cannot code a statement containing the special characters // or /* in the data statements that follow. However, there is no restriction such as this when you code DATA on the DD statement; these special characters are considered part of the input stream.

9.8.1 Rules for Coding

- The * or DATA parameters are positional, and must precede all keyword parameters.

- If you code * in the operands field, then you cannot code // or /* in Columns 1 or 2 of the input data stream.

- If you code DATA in the operands field, then you may code // or /* in Columns 1 or 2 of the input data stream.

- Input data must immediately follow the * or DATA parameters.

- The * or DATA parameters cannot be coded in cataloged procedures.

9.8.2 Some Examples

Example 1

```
//JOB1      JOB  A100,JOHN
//STEP1     EXEC PGM=PROGRAM1
//SYSIN     DD   *
  <lines of data>
/*
```

In this example, when the system encounters the asterisk in the DD statement, it pauses for input. Input is supplied at this point. When there is no further input required, a /* is entered. When the system encounters these control characters, it continues with the completion of the job.

The /* marks the end of the input data set.

Example 2

```
//JOB2     JOB  B100,PAUL
//STEP1    EXEC PGM=PROGRAM2
//SYSIN    DD   DATA
  <lines of data>
/*
```

This example illustrates the use of the keyword DATA used to specify the input of a data stream.

9.9 THE DLM PARAMETER

The DLM parameter is related to coding * or DATA in the operands portion of a JCL statement. In the prior section, we stated that coding DATA in the operands field allows us to code the special characters // and /* in the first two columns of the input data. These two special characters must appear in the input data stream that follows the * as well, but only if the DLM parameter is used to specify the two characters that will delimit the input data stream instead of /*. Thus, the DLM parameter can be used both with the * and DATA statements to specify the two delimiting characters that will be used to specify the end of the input stream.

Here's the position of the DLM parameter in a JCL statement:

//	Name	Operation	Operands	Comments
//	SYSIN	DD	*,DLM='xx' <input data> xx	comments

or

//	Name	Operation	Operands	Comments
//	SYSIN	DD	DATA,DLM='xx' <input data> xx	comments

In both cases, the characters enclosed within the single quotes ('xx') will be used to terminate the input stream.

9.9.1 An Example

```
//JOB1      JOB   D100,JACK
//STEP1     EXEC  PGM=PROGRAM4
//SYSIN     DD    *,DLM='AZ'
  <lines of text>
/*'INPUT'
AZ
```

In this example, input stream is specified via the asterisk in the operands field. The DLM parameter is used to indicate that the letters 'AZ' will be used to indicate the end of the input stream. It was necessary to use the DLM parameter in this instance, because the statement

```
/*                  'INPUT'
```

is part of the input stream, and contains the special characters /*.

9.10 SYSOUT - SPECIFYING OUTPUT CLASS

The SYSOUT parameter is used to direct the output that is generated during the execution of a job to an output device. As indicated earlier in this book, at the time that a system is generated, a set of devices may be grouped together under a specific class name. Thus, the SYSOUT parameter is used to direct output to an output class. This results in relevant output being sent to any of the devices belonging to that class. The position of the SYSOUT parameter in a JCL statement is as follows:

//	Name	Operation	Operands	Comments
//	ddname	DD	SYSOUT=class	comments

where *class* is the predesignated output class, containing any single alphanumeric character. When a system encounters a SYSOUT statement, it writes the output to some direct access volume such as a disk. Then, depending on the priorities assigned to the different classes, the system writes the output from the direct access device to the specified output device.

Traditionally, class *A* has been the designation for the printer.

You can also code an asterisk in the SYSOUT parameter. This results in the same class being designated to SYSOUT as the assignment to the MSGCLASS parameter. The MSGCLASS parameter was explained earlier in this book, (see chapter 3 if you need to refresh your memory).

Multiple SYSOUT statements can be coded within a job. Each data set will be output in the sequence in which it appears, and directed to the appropriate output class.

9.10.1 Some Examples

Example 1

```
//JOB1    JOB    F100,'MARK'
//STEP1   EXEC   PGM=PROGRAM1
//DATA1   DD     SYSOUT=A
```

In this example, PROGRAM1 is executed, and all output generated by the job step and the program, is directed to the class designated by the letter A. As mentioned earlier, this is the line printer.

Example 2

```
//JOB2    JOB    G100,'ANTHONY',
//               MSGCLASS=K
//STEP1   EXEC   PGM=PROGRAM2
//DATA1   DD     SYSOUT=*
```

In this example, an asterisk is assigned to the SYSOUT parameter, implying that the class assigned to the MSGCLASS parameter will also be used for SYSOUT. Thus, SYSOUT is assigned the class K.

Example 3

```
//JOB3    JOB    H100,'MICHAEL'
//STEP1   EXEC   PGM=PROGRAM3
//DATA1   DD     DSN=FILE1,
//               SYSOUT=A
//DATA2   DD     DSN=FILE2,
//               SYSOUT=B
//DATA3   DD     DSN=FILE3,
//               SYSOUT=C
```

In this example, three DD statements are coded, and the three data sets called FILE1, FILE2, and FILE3 are sent to three different output classes, *A*, *B*, and *C,* respectively.

9.11 THE DEST PARAMETER

The DEST parameter is used to route output to a specific destination, which may or may not be in a remote location. DEST is coded in the operands field of a JCL statement as follows:

//	Name	Operation	Operands	Comments
//	ddname	DD	DEST	comments

9.11.1 Syntax

The syntax of the DEST parameter depends on the job entry subsystem that you are using. If you are working in a JES2 environment, then the syntax looks like this:

    DEST=RMTxxxx
or
    DEST=RMxxxx
or
    DEST=Rxxxx
or
    DEST=Uhhh
or
    DEST=Nxxxx
or
    DEST=NnnnRyyy
or
    DEST=LOCAL
or
    DEST=name

RMT, *RM* and *R* stand for *ReMote Terminal*. *U* specifies a local terminal. *N* specifies a node. For the following syntax:

    DEST=NnnnRyyy

N specifies a node, and *R* specifies a remote workstation connected to the node.

    xxxx are 1 to 4 alphanumeric or national characters. The range of numbers that can be coded in this field are 0 to 4000. *hhhh* are hexadecimal digits. *nnn* is a 1 to 3 digit number. *yyy* is a number from 1 to 999 designating a remote node. *LOCAL* indicates a local destination. *name* can be 1 to 8 character alphanumeric or national characters used to specify the destination device name.

    In a JES3 environment, the syntax of the DEST parameter looks like this:

        DEST=ANYLOCAL
or
        DEST=LOCAL
or
        DEST=device_name
or
        DEST=address
or
        DEST=group_name
or
        DEST=node_name

ANYLOCAL is used to route output to a local device. *device_name* is the name of the destination device comprised of one to eight alphanumeric or national characters. *address* is the device address. It can be one to three characters long, and specifies the physical address that was assigned to a device at the time that the system was generated. The name of the output device to which output is directed to is *group_name*. The name of the remote node is *node_name*.

9.12 SOME EXAMPLES

JES2 Subsystem

Example 1

```
//JOB1    JOB    J1,'AGATHA'
//STEP1   EXEC   PGM=NODE1
//DATA1   DD     DSN=FILE1,
//               SYSOUT=A,
//               DEST=RMT1190
```

In this example, output is directed to the line printer. The location of this printer is designated by the code RMT1190. Designations for remote and local locations are made at the time that the system is generated.

Example 2

```
//JOB2    JOB    J2,'AGATHA'
//STEP1   EXEC   PGM=NODE2
//DATA1   DD     DSN=FILE1,
//               SYSOUT=A,
//               DEST=R2244
```

In this example, output is directed to the location designated as R2244.

Example 3

```
//JOB3      JOB  J3,'AGATHA'
//STEP1     EXEC PGM=NODE3
//DATA1     DD   DSN=FILE1,
//               SYSOUT=A,
//               DEST=UF01
```

In this example, output is routed to the device whose address is F01.

Example 4

```
//JOB4      JOB  J4,'CHRIS'
//STEP1     EXEC PGM=NODE4
//DATA1     DD   DSN=FILE1,
//               SYSOUT=A,
//               DEST=N123
```

In this example, output is routed to node 123.

Example 5

```
//JOB5      JOB  J5,'CHRIS'
//STEP1     EXEC PGM=NODE5
//DATA1     DD   DSN=FILE1,
//               SYSOUT=A,
//               DEST=N8R10
```

In this example, output is routed to remote station 10 (R10) on node 8 (N8).

Example 6

```
//JOB6      JOB  J6,'CHRIS'
//STEP1     EXEC PGM=NODE6
//DATA1     DD   DSN=FILE1,
//               SYSOUT=A,
//               DEST=LOCAL
```

In this example, output is routed to the printer. This printer is local.

JES3 Subsystem

Example 1

```
//JOB1      JOB  K1,CHRISTY
//STEP1     EXEC PGM=NODE1
//DATA1     DD   DSN=FILE1,
//               SYSOUT=A,
//               DEST=ANYLOCAL
```

In this example, output is routed to any local device.

Example 2

```
//JOB2      JOB  K2,CHRISTY
//STEP1     EXEC PGM=NODE2
//DATA1     DD   DSN=FILE1,
//               SYSOUT=A,
//               DEST=BRONX
```

In this example, output is routed to a device associated with the remote node called BRONX. Recall that a device name can be one to eight alphanumeric or national characters. Device names are installation defined.

Example 3

```
//JOB3      JOB  K3,CHRISTY
//STEP1     EXEC PGM=NODE3
//DATA1     DD   DSN=FILE1,
//               SYSOUT=A,
//               DEST=H41
```

Output is routed to the device whose address is H41. Device address can be one to three hexadecimal characters. Devices are assigned addresses at the time that a system is generated.

Example 4

```
//JOB4      JOB  K4,CHRISTY
//STEP1     EXEC PGM=NODE4
//DATA1     DD   DSN=FILE1,
//               SYSOUT=A,
//               DEST=NY50
```

In this example, output is routed to a device which belongs to the group called NY50. Group names can be one to eight alphanumeric or national characters.

Example 5

```
//JOB5      JOB  K5,CHRISTY
//STEP1     EXEC PGM=NODE5
//DATA1     DD   DSN=FILE1,
//               SYSOUT=A,
//               DEST=MEXICO
```

In this example, output is routed to a remote node called MEXICO.

9.13 THE HOLD PARAMETER

The HOLD parameter is coded on the DD statement and is used to specify whether the output is to be printed immediately, or held until further notice. Here's the position of the HOLD parameter in a JCL statement:

//	Name	Operation	Operands	Comments
//	ddname	DD	HOLD	comments

9.13.1 Syntax

The syntax of the HOLD parameter looks like this:

    HOLD=YES

or

    HOLD=NO

If the HOLD parameter is not coded, then it automatically defaults to NO.

9.13.2 An Example

```
//JOB1      JOB   L100,KENNY
//STEP1     EXEC  PGM=HOLD1
//DATA1     DD    DSN=FILE1,
//                SYSOUT=A,
//                HOLD=YES
```

In this example, output will be held until it is released by the operator. The RELEASE parameter is used to release output which has been held.

9.14 THE OUTLIM PARAMETER

The OUTLIM parameter is coded on the DD statement and is used to limit the number of lines that are output to the destination specified in SYSOUT. This parameter is usually used to avoid printing excessive amounts of data in a print environment. Here's the position of the OUTLIM parameter in a JCL statement:

//	Name	Operation	Operands	Comments
//	ddname	DD	OUTLIM	comments

A number between 1 and 16,777,215 can be specified for the OUTLIM parameter. If this parameter is not coded, and you work in a JES2 environment, then there is no limit to the number of lines that will be printed. (Of course, if the device to which output is being routed becomes full, it's a different matter.) If you work in a JES3 environment, then the number of lines that will be output will be limited to the installation-defined default. You may code OUTLIM to a number lower than the default.

9.14.1 An Example

```
//JOB1      JOB   A1,HELEN
//STEP1     EXEC  PGM=OUT1
//DATA1     DD    DSN=FILE1,
//                SYSOUT=A,
//                OUTLIM=1000
```

In this example, the amount of output that will be routed to the printer is limited to 1000 lines.

9.15 THINGS THAT CAN GO WRONG

Once again, we present a general correspondence between some common errors, and the error code and message that are generated from them. Please refer to Table 9.1.

9.16 REVIEW

In this chapter we discussed how different types of data sets are coded on the DD statement. We also described how data can be inputted at the time that a job is executed, and how the output can be routed to various devices. Special DD statements, such as SYSOUT, SYSDUMP, and SYSABEND were also discussed. Table 9.3 summarizes the syntax and meanings of the parameters described.

Table 9.2 Common Errors on the DD Statement

JCL Error Code	Description	Probable Cause of Error
IEC020I	DCB EROPT=ABE or an invalid code, and/or no SYNAD exit specified	Attempting to concatenate data sets with different record formats Attempting to concatenate a partitioned data set with a sequential data set
IEF640I	Excessive number of positional parameters on the DD statement	Coding ** in the operands field for SYSIN, instead of *
IEF605I	Unidentified operation field	Coding a // in the first two columns of the input stream that follows the SYSIN statement
IEF480I	Invalid destination requested	Coding a non-existent destination on the DEST parameter

Table 9.3 Additional Parameters on the DD Statement

JCL Parameter/Statement	Syntax and Description
DUMMY or DSN=NULLFILE	Creates a dummy data set that is never read or written to Allows programs to be tested for errors without reading/writing data to files
SYSUDUMP statement	Dumps contents of various registers and variables upon abnormal termination of job step
SYSABEND statement	Dumps contents of various registers and variables upon abnormal termination of job step Also dumps the system nucleus

SYSIN DD * or SYSIN DD DATA	SYSIN is the conventional ddname assigned to input data streams Allows on-line input of data Data input starts when system encounters a * DATA parameter in operands field Data input terminates when system encounters a /* or delimiting character in the operand field
DLM='xx'	Specifies characters that will delimit input Used if the special characters /* or // are part of the input
SYSOUT=class	Used to direct output to a class SYSOUT=A is traditionally used to route output to printer
DEST	Used to route output to a specific local or remote destination
HOLD	Used to specify that output is to be held over until further notice
OUTLIM	Used to limit the number of output lines that are routed to the output device Is useful in a test environment, to avoid excessive printing of data

In-Stream and Cataloged Procedures and Symbolic Parameters

10.1 INTRODUCTION

Coding JCL is probably not the most exciting thing that you have ever done. Not only does it look a lot like Greek (for those of you who don't know Greek), but it is prone to a lot of errors while coding (due to the simple reason that it looks a lot like Greek!) Thus, the art of producing a completely bug-free collection of JCL statements can turn into a rather tiring, nerve-wracking task.

For those of you who can relate to some of the irksome negatives of JCL just listed, you will be happy to know that commonly used JCL statements can be grouped together into procedures. Then, these procedures can be made available for general use, and executed simply by executing the name given to the procedure. This chapter describes how these kinds of procedures are created and executed.

10.2 PROCEDURES, AN OVERVIEW

The following items become significant when we start to deal with multiple JCL statements grouped together into procedures:

- Often, in a working environment, the same JCL can be utilized by several users. For example, if a common data set is to be accessed by several users, then the JCL that they will code to open and read this data set will be similar.

- Groups of commonly used JCL statements can be categorized into procedures that are given names. The system has to be notified when these kinds of procedures are being created and/or accessed.

- The names of the procedures comprised of groups of JCL statements can be recorded by the system and stored just like any other members of partitioned data sets. The system has to be notified each time these kinds of procedures are to be recorded and/or accessed.

- Before a group of statements can be recorded under a procedure name by the system, they should be tested. Thus, the group of JCL statements comprising the procedure become a part of the input stream of the job itself. The system has to be notified if a group of JCL statements are grouped together in this way.

- Sometimes, the same JCL can be utilized by different users, but with different parameters. In these cases, JCL provides us with a useful feature that allows us to override one parameter with another. If a parameter has the capability of being overriden in this way, then the system has to be notified.

10.3 CORRESPONDING JCL

Table 10.1 lists the term given to the each of the features listed in the prior section.

Table 10.1 JCL Procedures

Function	Corresponding JCL Term
Grouping JCL statements together and giving them a name	Procedure or PROC
Grouping JCL statements together, giving them a name, and recording the name as a partitioned data set	Cataloged Procedure
Grouping JCL statements together and making them a part of the JCL input stream	In-Stream Procedure
Overriding parameters	Symbolic Parameters

The remainder of this chapter will describe each one of these concepts in detail.

10.4 A PROCEDURE OR PROC

The use of procedures helps minimize duplication of code and probability of error. This is because a procedure should consist of pre-tested statements. Each time a procedure is invoked, there is no need to retest its functionality, since it is pre-tested. A procedure is initiated with the keyword PROC. The system is notified about the end of the procedure with the keyword PEND. The position of these keywords in a JCL statement look like this:

//	Name	Operation	Operands	Comments
//	name	PROC		
<group of JCL statements>				
//		PEND		

10.4.1 Creating and Executing a Procedure

First, take a look at the JCL that we will group together under a procedure name:

```
//STEP1    EXEC PGM=PROGRAM1
//DD1      DD   DSN=FILE1,
//              DISP=SHR
//STEP2    EXEC PGM=PROGRAM2
//DD2      DD   DSN=FILE2,
//              DISP=SHR
```

Next, we place these statements into a procedure, like this:

```
//PROC1    PROC
//STEP1    EXEC PGM=PROGRAM1
//DD1      DD   DSN=FILE1,
//              DISP=SHR
//STEP2    EXEC PGM=PROGRAM2
//DD2      DD   DSN=FILE2,
//              DISP=SHR
//         PEND
```

Notice that the original first statement in the JCL now becomes the second. The new first statement identifies the beginning of a procedure:

```
//PROC1    PROC
```

Also, the PEND statement is added at the end of the JCL:

```
//        PEND
```

This statement is used to identify the end of the procedure to the system.

The segment of JCL that will execute this procedure is:

```
//JOB1     JOB   A123,LORENZO
//BATCH    EXEC  PROC1
```

The remaining JCL within the job would presumably have something to do with the data sets FILE1 and FILE2, since these data sets were identified in the procedure. Meanwhile, another user can invoke the same procedure, perhaps like this:

```
//JOB2     JOB   B456,CAMASTRA
//STEP4    EXEC  PROC1
```

As you can see, duplication of pre-tested code is avoided, and probability of error in coding is minimized.

10.4.2 Rules for Coding Procedures

- A procedure name can be one to eight alphanumeric or national characters. The first character must be alphabetic or national.

- No more than 255 job steps can be coded in one procedure.

- The following JCL statements cannot be included within the procedure:

  - JOB
  - EXEC, under special circumstances, which are described below
  - DD * or DD DATA
  - JOBLIB DD
  - JES2 or JES3 control statements

Please note that the EXEC statement can be coded in a PROC if it is being used to execute a program (the PGM parameter will be used).

10.5 CATALOGED PROCEDURES

A *cataloged procedure* is a set of job control statements that are grouped together, given a name, and then recorded as a member of a partitioned data set. IBM supplies a utility program called IEBUPDTE; this program places cataloged procedures into partitioned data sets. Traditionally, these procedures are placed inside a system library called SYS1.PROCLIB.

A cataloged procedure is executed like a regular procedure. That is, by coding an EXEC statement for that procedure name.

10.5.1 Rules for Coding

■ All rules listed in Section 10.3 apply to cataloged procedures as well.

■ The procedure name must be unique within the procedure library that it is placed in.

■ The PEND statement is not required.

10.5.2 An Example

Here's the JCL comprising the procedure that will be cataloged:

```
//CATLOG1    PROC
//STEP1      EXEC   PGM=PROGRAM1
//DD1        DD     DSN=FILE1,
//                  DISP=SHR
//STEP2      EXEC   PGM=PROGRAM2
//DD2        DD     DSN=FILE2,
//                  DISP=SHR
```

Once the procedure has been created and tested, it can be cataloged and placed inside a *system* or *user-defined* library. A system or user-defined library is simply an area in the system which is used to store cataloged procedures. These libraries reside as partitioned data sets within the system. IBM supplies a system library called SYS1.PROCLIB. This procedure can be placed in this library, or it can be placed inside a user-defined library. We will be storing this procedure inside a user-defined library called USER.TEST.PROCLIB.

The IBM-supplied utility called IEBUPDTE is used to catalog this procedure and add it to the aforementioned library.

Once the procedure has been cataloged, it is executed as follows:

```
//JOB1     JOB    G700,MATLING
//PROCLIB  DD     DSN=USER.TEST.PROCLIB,
//                DISP=SHR
//JOBLIB   DD     DSN=USER.TEST.JOBLIB,
//                DISP=SHR
//DATA2    EXEC   CATLOG1
```

The first DD statement defines the location of the cataloged procedure, which is USER.TEST.PROCLIB. The disposition of any data sets residing here is shared (SHR), meaning that multiple users may access the same data set at the same time.

The next statement

```
//DATA2    EXEC   CATLOG1
```

executes the cataloged procedure called CATLOG1.

10.6 IN-STREAM PROCEDURES

In-stream procedures are similar to cataloged procedures, except that they are not members of partitioned data sets. They are included in the input stream of the job itself. The same in-stream procedure can be invoked more than once from within a job. In-stream procedures provide a convenient method for pretesting procedures that will ultimately be cataloged, and short-cutting the coding process where the same JCL must be coded multiple times within the same job.

Before continuing with the rules for coding in-stream procedures, we will now describe what happens when a PROC statement is detected.

When a job is executed, and the system detects a PROC immediately following the JOB statement, the system goes through a special routine that reads and saves all the statements that follow, until the PEND statement. This saved JCL is then assigned a name, just like cataloged procedures. Then, each time an EXEC statement followed by this predefined name is detected, the group of saved JCL statements are executed.

10.6.1 Rules for Coding

- In-stream procedures must begin with the PROC statement.

- In-stream procedures must end with the PEND statement.

- If in-stream procedures are defined within a job, then they must be coded immediately after the JOB statement, and before the first EXEC statement.

- No more than 15 in-stream procedures can be coded in a job.

10.6.2 An Example

```
//JOB1      JOB     (A123),DAVID
//INSTREAM  PROC
//STEP1     EXEC    PGM=PROGRAM1
//DD1       DD      DSN=FILE1,
//                  DISP=SHR
//STEP2     DD      DSN=PROGRAM2
//DD2       DD      DSN=FILE2,
//                  DISP=SHR
//          PEND
//STEP3     EXEC    INSTREAM
```

In this example, JOB1 is submitted by David. Immediately following the JOB statement is the PROC statement, which defines the start of an in-stream procedure. The name INSTREAM is given to this procedure. Within the procedure, PROGRAM1 is executed in STEP1, and PROGRAM2 is executed in STEP2. Also, two data sets called FILE1 and FILE2 are declared. The PEND statement identifies the end of the in-stream procedure. STEP3 executes the procedure previously identified as INSTREAM.

10.7 COMPARING CATALOGED AND IN-STREAM PROCEDURES

Cataloged procedures are identical to in-stream procedures, with the following exceptions:

- Cataloged procedures are members of partitioned data sets and remain there until they are deleted. In-stream procedures are not members of partitioned data sets, and exist only for the duration of the job.

- The PROC statement is mandatory in cataloged procedures. It is also mandatory in in-stream procedures.

- The PEND statement cannot be coded in cataloged procedures. It must be coded in in-stream procedures.

10.8 OVERRIDING PARAMETERS IN PROCEDURES

Sometimes there may be a need to override one or more parameters in procedures. For example, suppose you wish to use the JCL coded in a procedure which accesses a specific data set, for a different file name. Instead of having to rewrite the procedure for the new data set name, you can easily override this parameter in the DD statement, without actually changing the contents of the original procedure.

As you read through the next section, keep in mind that the modified contents of a procedure which has overrides in it are activated only for the duration of the job in which they exist; the original contents remain intact.

10.8.1 Syntax

The syntax for overriding existing parameters in a procedure is as follows:

```
//name            EXEC  procedure_name
//procstep.ddname DD    modified_parameter,modified_parameter...
```

where *name* is the stepname in the job that the procedure will be executed from; *procedure_name* is the name of the procedure whose parameters will be overridden; *procstep* is the step name in the procedure whose parameters will be overridden; and *ddname* is the ddname of the DD statements containing those parameters. One or more modified parameters can follow the DD operation field.

10.8.2 An Example

Here's the JCL for a procedure called PROC1. This procedure exists in USER.TEST.LIB1:

```
//PROC1    PROC
//STEP1    EXEC  PGM=PROGRAM1
//DD1      DD    DSN=FILE1,DISP=SHR
//STEP2    EXEC  PGM=PROGRAM2
//DD2      DD    DSN=FILE2,DISP=SHR
//         PEND
```

Suppose we wish to execute this procedure, but modify the disposition of FILE1 from SHR to OLD, and modify the data set name FILE2 to NEWFILE. This is how we want the JCL to look:

```
//DD1       DD      DSN=FILE1,DISP=OLD
```

and

```
//DD2       DD      DSN=NEWFILE,DISP=SHR
```

Here's the JCL that will modify the contents of a procedure at the time that it is executed:

```
//JOB1       JOB      A123,'H BLAKELY'
//PROCLIB    DD       DSN=USER.TEST.LIB1,
//                    DISP=SHR
//EXEC1       EXEC     PROC1
//STEP1.DD1  DD       DSN=FILE1,DISP=OLD
//STEP2.DD2  DD       DSN=NEWFILE,DISP=SHR
//
```

PROC1 is executed. Immediately after the EXEC statement are the two statements that are intended to replace existing parameters in PROC1. STEP1 is the stepname, and PROCLIB is the DDname of the statement in which the DISP parameter is to be modified. STEP2 is the stepname, and DD2 is the DDname of the statement in which FILE2 is to be modified to NEWFILE. Remember, the modifications come into effect only when the JCL is executed; they are not rewritten to the procedure.

10.9 OVERRIDING PARAMETERS, CONCATENATED DATA SETS

Concatenated data sets are coded on DD statements which appear in the sequence that the data set is to be concatenated in. If data sets are concatenated in a procedure, and you wish to override parameters in one or more of these statements, then you have to code each DD statement over. The following example will help you understand what has just been said.

10.9.1 An Example

Here's a procedure which concatenates data sets together. This procedure resides in USER.TEST.LIB1:

```
//PROC2      PROC
//STEP1      EXEC     PGM=PROGRAM2
//DD1        DD       DSN=TEST.FILE1,DISP=SHR
//           DD       DSN=TEST.FILE2,DISP=OLD
//           DD       DSN=TEST.FILE3,DISP=MOD
//           DD       DSN=TEST.FILE4,DISP=OLD
//           PEND
```

Now, suppose we wish to override TEST.FILE2 and TEST.FILE4, with PROD.FILE2 and PROD.FILE4, respectively. Here's the JCL that will override these parameters:

```
//JOB1       JOB    A123,'H BLAKELY'
//PROCLIB    DD     DSN=USER.TEST.LIB1,
//                  DISP=SHR
//EXEC1      EXEC   PROC2
//STEP1.DD1  DD
//           DD     DSN=PROD.FILE2,DISP=OLD,
//           DD
//           DD     DSN=PROD.FILE4,DISP=OLD
//
```

Notice that the DD statements for those data set names which are not being overridden are left blank. The DD operand, however, must be coded for each data set name included in the concatenation.

10.10 SYMBOLIC PARAMETERS

Symbolic parameters are used to override parameters on the DD statement. They can be used in both cataloged and in-stream procedures. Frequently, the same JCL can be used by different programmers to implement common tasks, such as the opening, reading, and writing of data sets. The only difference is in the parameters required to access different data sets. Symbolic parameters provide a convenient means of assigning different parameters to commonly used JCL procedures.

A symbolic parameter on a DD statement is coded by preceding the parameter that will be assigned a value with an ampersand (&). The value that will be assigned to a symbolic parameter is coded in the PROC statement of the cataloged or in-stream procedure. Symbolic parameters can be used with parameters, subparameters, and even hard-coded values.

Here's the position of symbolic parameters in a JCL statement:

//	Name	Operation	Operands	Comments
//	ddname	DD	symbolic parameters	comments

10.10.1 Rules for Coding

■ A symbolic parameter can consist of one to eight alphanumeric or national characters (including the ampersand). The first character must be an ampersand (&). The next character must be alphabetic or national. Subsequent characters can be alphanumeric or national.

■ They must be coded in the operands field only.

■ They cannot be coded for the keywords on the EXEC statement. An example of some keywords on the EXEC statement are PGM, COND, TIME, and PARM. However, they may be coded for the values associated with a keyword.

■ A value assigned to a symbolic parameter may be overridden by yet another value, as long as the redefinition is within the same job. If it is not overridden, then the same value will be assigned to it each time it is called.

■ There is no restriction on the length of the value assigned to a symbolic parameter. However, the assignment must fit on the same line; it cannot continue on the next line.

■ If positional parameters are coded as symbolic, then a period should be inserted between them. This period is in addition to any periods that would be required for the correct syntax of the statement that is being coded.

■ Symbolic parameters cannot be concatenated with other symbolic parameters, to produce yet another symbolic parameter. However, they can be concatenated with each other, each retaining the value originally assigned to it.

■ Symbolic parameters cannot be concatenated with regular parameters, or portions of regular parameters, in order to produce other symbolic parameters. They can be concatenated with other parameters, or portions of them, as long as they retain the value originally assigned to them.

■ Concatenated symbolic and/or regular parameters must not exceed 120 characters.

■ If a symbolic parameter is defined, then it must be assigned a value and used within the procedure that defines that parameter.

- Special characters listed in Table 10.1 can be coded as is, if they are assigned to symbolic parameters.

- Any other kind of special characters must be enclosed within apostrophes. An apostrophe must be preceded by another apostrophe, if it is a part of the value assigned to a symbolic parameter.

Table 10.2 Special Characters as they appear in Symbolic Parameters

Special Character	Represented as
blank comma period slash apostrophe braces and sign asterisk plus minus equal	, . / ' ( ) & * + - =

10.10.2 Assigning Values to Symbolic Parameters

Values can be assigned to symbolic parameters in either or both of the following statements:

- PROC statement

- EXEC statement

Values are assigned in the operands field for both the PROC and EXEC statements, in the following way:

//	Name	Operation	Operands	Comments
//	name	PROC	value assigned to symbolic parameters	comments

and/or

//	Name	Operation	Operands	Comments
//	name	EXEC	value assignment to symbolic parameters	comments

If the same symbolic parameter is assigned in the PROC and EXEC statement, then the definitions on the EXEC statement will override those on the PROC statement.

10.10.3 Some Examples

Example 1

```
//JOB1      JOB    Y1,DONNA
//ASSIGN    PROC   FILE1=DATAFILE
//STEP1     EXEC   PGM=SYMBOL1
//DATA1     DD     DSN=&FILE1
```

In this example, JOB1 is submitted. The next statement is a PROC, where DATAFILE is assigned to FILE1. The statement after that executes a program called SYMBOL1, and the last statement accesses a data set whose name is defined as the symbolic parameter &FILE1. If you take another look at the ASSIGN statement, you will see that the name DATAFILE is assigned to this symbolic parameter. Hence, the statement that is actually executed looks like this:

```
//DATA1      DD      DSN=DATAFILE
```

&FILE is substituted with DATAFILE.

Example 2

```
//JOB1      JOB    Y1,BETTY
//ASSIGN    PROC   FILE1=NEWFILE,
//                 DISPO=SHR,
//                 DEVICE=CYL,
//                 FORMAT=FB
//STEP1     EXEC   PGM=SYMBOL1
//DATA1     DD     DSN=&FILE1,
//                 UNIT=3390,
//                 DISP=&DISPO,
```

```
//                      SPACE=(&DEVICE(1,1)),
//                      DCB=(RECFM=&FORMAT),
//                      SYSOUT=A,
//                      DEST=LOCAL
```

In this example, four symbolic parameters are defined. Each symbolic parameter is substituted when the job is submitted. The DATA1 statement that is executed will look like this:

```
//DATA1      DD       DSN=NEWFILE,
//                      UNIT=3390,
//                      DISP=SHR,
//                      SPACE=(CYL(1,1)),
//                      DCB=(RECFM=FB),
//                      SYSOUT=A,
//                      DEST=LOCAL
```

This example illustrates the versatility that can be obtained from the same code, simply by substituting the symbolic parameters as necessary.

Example 3

```
//JOB1       JOB      Y1,RON
//ASSIGN     PROC     PARMX='01-01-93'
//STEP1      EXEC     PGM=SYMBOL1,PARM=&PARMX
//DATA1      DD       DSN=FILE2
```

This example illustrates how data containing special characters is assigned to variables that will be used as symbolic parameters. Notice the use of apostrophes around the assignment of the data:

```
'01-01-93'
```

After the substitution, the statement whose name is STEP1 will look like this:

```
//STEP1      EXEC        PGM=SYMBOL1,PARM=01-01-93
```

Example 4

```
//JOB1       JOB      Y1,WALT
//ASSIGN     PROC     PDS1=USER,
//                      PDS2=TEST,
//                      PDS3=FILE1
//STEP1      EXEC     PGM=SYMBOL1
//DATA1      DD       DSN=&PDS1..&PDS2..&PDS3
```

This example illustrates the use of symbolic parameters used in the place of positional parameters. The last statement in this example is substituted as follows:

```
//DATA1    DD    DSN=USER.TEST.FILE1
```

This example illustrates how symbolic parameters can be coded to specify the names of partitioned data sets.

10.11 THINGS THAT CAN GO WRONG

Once again, we present a general correspondence between some common errors, and the error code and message that is generated from them. Either refer to the JCL error code, or scan through the section titled *Probable Cause of Error*, to identify the cause of error in your JCL.

Table 10.3 Some Common Errors

JCL Error Code	Description	Probable Cause of Error
IEF612I	Procedure xxx was not found	Executing a non-existent procedure
IEF647I	First character of name not alphabetic or not national	Coding a procedure name whose first character is not alphabetic or national
IEF607I	Job has no steps	Coding a PROC for an in-stream procedure, but without the PEND

10.12 REVIEW

In this chapter we discussed the in-stream and cataloged procedures, and symbolic parameters. Table 10.4 summarizes the syntax and meanings of the concepts and parameters presented in this chapter.

Table 10.4 In-Stream & Cataloged Procedures & Symbolic Parameters

JCL Parameter, Concept	Syntax and Description
PROC <group of JCL statement> PEND	Consists of groups of commonly used JCL statements Help minimize code duplication and probability of error End with the PEND statement Are executed by coding their name in the EXEC statement
Cataloged Procedures	Consists of procedures whose names are cataloged (recorded) by the system Are stored as members of partitioned data sets in system or user-defined libraries Do not require a terminating PEND statement Are executed by coding their names in the EXEC statement
In-Stream Procedures	Are similar to cataloged procedures, except they are not members of partitioned data sets Are included in the input stream of the job itself Provide a convenient way to pre-test procedures which will ultimately be cataloged

Symbolic Parameters &parameter	Are used to override parameters on the DD statement Are also used in cataloged and in-stream procedures Provide a convenient means of assigning values to commonly used JCI parameters Are assigned values in the PROC or EXEC statements

Generation Data Groups (GDG)

11.1 INTRODUCTION

The concept of *Generation Data Groups* has to do with the chronological and functional relationships between data sets. That is, Generation Data Groups or GDGs are a group of data sets which are related to each other chronologically and functionally.

Many data processing applications are cyclical in nature. They consist of new input which is stored inside a file. Then, at a later date, this existing data is updated with new data, to produce a new file. If you can think of the original file as the older generation, then the new updated file can be considered a new generation.

Generations can continue until a specified limit is reached. This limit specifies the total number of generations that can exist at one time. Once this limit is reached, the oldest generation can be deleted. Thus, the cyclical nature of adding new generations, and deleting the oldest one each time the limit is reached, would continue. MVS provides the GDG feature that supports this cyclical process. This chapter is devoted to describing this feature.

11.2 GDGs, AN OVERVIEW

In order for Generation Data Groups to work, the following have to be taken into consideration:

- Generation Data Groups have to be created before data sets that are to be included in them can be made a part of them.

- In order to create a GDG, the following must be specified to the operating system:

  - The name of the GDG
  - The number of generations that are to be retained
  - Whether or not the oldest generation is to be uncataloged once the limit for the number of generations that are to be retained is reached
  - Whether or not all generations are to be uncataloged once the limit for the number of generations that are to be retained is reached
  - Whether or not an entry for a data set that is deleted from a GDG is to be uncataloged and physically deleted from the volume that it resides on
  - Whether or not an entry for a data set that is deleted from a GDG is to only be uncataloged (and not physically deleted) from the volume that it resides on

- When a GDG is created, it will not have any data set belonging to it initially. However, each data set that is added to it must be of the same type. That is, all data sets belonging to a GDG must have the same specifications for their DCB subparameters. They will have the same record format, blocksize, record length, and so on. Thus, a model containing parameter information, which includes all the data sets added to a GDG, must be specified to the system.

- Once a model for a GDG has been established, the system must be informed each time a data set is to be added to it.

- The system must be able to specify the generation number of each data set within a GDG.

- The system must be informed if a data set within a GDG is to be deleted.

- The system must be informed if a data set within a GDG is to be deleted, even if its retention period has not expired.

- The system must be informed if only the index of a GDG is to be deleted.

- The system must be informed if the entire GDG is to be deleted; this includes the index and all related data sets.

11.3 CORRESPONDING JCL

Table 11.1 lists the JCl parameters or subparameters that are used to specify the information listed in Section 11.2 to the operating system.

Table 11.1 JCL Parameters and Subparameters used to Create GDGs.

Function	Corresponding JCL parameters and/or Subparameter and/or IBM Supplied Utility Program
Creation of Generation Data Groups (GDGs)	Before a GDG can be created, its index is created and cataloged. The index conveys information relating to the next seven features. The DEFINE GDG satement in the IDCAMS utility is used to create the index of a GDG
Specifying name of GDG	NAME coded on the DEFINE GDG statement
Specifying number of generations to be retained	LIMIT coded on the DEFINE GDG statement
Uncataloging oldest generation of a GDG once the limit is reached	NOEMPTY coded on the DEFINE GDG statement
Uncataloging all generations of a GDG once the limit is reached	EMPTY coded on the DEFINE GDG statement
Physically deleting the entry of a GDG from the volume that it resides on	SCRATCH coded on the DEFINE GDG statement
Uncataloging the entry of a GDG from the volume that it resides on, without physically deleting it	NOSCRATCH coded on the DEFINE GDG statement
Defining a model for the GDG, which will specify the format of all applicable parameters for data sets that are added to the GDG	Defining DCB parameters in a DSCB model, which is an installation defined data set, or Creating a user-defined model

Adding a data set to a GDG	Data set is created in usual way, the name of the model containing the GDG DCB parameters is coded in the DCB parameter on the DD statement
Specifying a generation number for a data set within a GDG	Generation number is specified within brackets, preceded by plus or minus sign.
Deleting a data set within a GDG	DELETE, coded on the DISP parameter in the DD statement
Deleting a data set within a GDG, even though its retention period has not expired	PURGE coded on the DD statement for that GDG
Deleting the GDG index only	IBM supplied IDCAMS utility is used to delete index only
Deleting entire GDG, index and data sets inclusive	FORCE coded on the DD statement for that GDG

11.4 RULES FOR CODING GDGS

■ No more than 255 data sets can exist within one GDG.

■ All rules that apply to coding data sets apply equally to data sets within GDGs. The only difference is that a generation number must be coded within brackets for the data set name, in the DSN parameter.

■ GDGs must be cataloged.

■ GDGs must reside on tape or direct access devices.

■ The DSN and UNIT parameters must be coded for all new generation data sets.

■ The DISP parameter must be set to CATLG for all new generation data sets.

11.5 FEATURES OF GDGs

Generation Data Groups are characterized by the following:

- All data sets within a GDG will have the same name.

- The generation number of a data set within a GDG is automatically assigned by the operating system when it is created.
  The syntax of this number is recorded by the system as follows:

    GaaaaVnn

    where G is for Generation, *aaaa* is the absolute sequence number of the generation, V is for Version, and nn is the version number. The absolute generation number can range from 0000 to 9999, and version number can range from 00 to 99. Version number will always automatically default to 00.

- Data sets within a GDG can be referenced by their relative generation number or the actual data set name, as assigned by the operating system.

- Generation 0 always references the current generation.

- Generation -1 always references the generation just before the current one.

- Generation +1 will always reference the next generation after the current one.

11.6 ADVANTAGES OF GDGs

The record keeping (as to what generation number should be assigned to new data sets, and which data set goes if the limit is reached), is the responsibility of the operating system, not the application programmer. Furthermore, GDGs provide a convenient method of relating data sets together, and automatically discarding those data sets which are outdated.

11.7 A CONCEPTUAL EXAMPLE

Assume that inventory information is stored in a master file. This file is processed each month. Assume that the current month is July. If this information was to be stored in data sets that were part of a Generation Data Group, then the file for the month of July would be the current or 0 generation. The inventory file for the month of June would be generation -1, and for May would be -2. If the file is updated in August, the data set for the month of August would become the new current generation. All generations before it would be updated by being decremented by 1.

Figure 11.1 illustrates the generation number before and after the updates.

The remainder of this chapter will describe how GDGs are created, updated, deleted, and so on.

Before August Update	After August Update
July, generation 0	August, generation 0
June, generation -1	July, generation -1
May, generation -2	June, generation -2
	May, generation -3

Figure 11.1 GDGs Before and After Udpates

11.8 CREATING AN INDEX FOR A GDG

Before a GDG is created, an index which defines its name along with other features must be created and cataloged. In current versions of the MVS/XA and MVS/ESA systems, the IDCAMS utility is used to create this index. This is an IBM- supplied all purpose utility, and will be described in detail later on in the book. In older systems, the IEHPROGM utility was used for this purpose. We will illustrate the creation of an index via the IDCAMS utility.

The DEFINE GDG statement is used to convey information to the IDCAMS utility relating to the index.

The following subparameters on the GDG statement are used to convey information about the index to the IDCAMS utility:

- NAME

- LIMIT

- EMPTY/NOEMPTY

- SCRATCH/NOSCRATCH

11.8.1 The NAME Subparameter

This subparameter is coded on the DEFINE GDG statement and is used to specify the name of the data set that is to be created. Its syntax looks like this:

NAME(name)

where *name* can range from 1 to 35 characters.

11.8.2 The LIMIT Subparameter

The LIMIT subparameter is coded on the DEFINE GDG statement and is used to specify the total number of generations that the GDG may contain. Its syntax looks like this:

LIMIT(number)

where *number* can range from 1 to 255.
    LIMIT cannot be changed once the GDG is established.

11.8.3 The EMPTY/NOEMPTY Subparameter

The EMPTY and NOEMPTY subparameters are mutually exclusive. EMPTY specifies that all existing generations of the GDG are to be uncataloged once the limit of possible generations within the GDG has been reached. NOEMPTY specifies that only the oldest generation of the GDG is to be uncataloged if the limit is reached.

11.8.4 The SCRATCH/NOSCRATCH Subparameter

The SCRATCH and NOSCRATCH subparameters are also mutually exclusive. SCRATCH specifies that if the entry of a data set in a GDG is removed from the index, (either due to user request, or because it is the generation whose time has come), then its entry should be physically deleted from the volume that it resides on. NOSCRATCH indicates that the entry of the data set should only be uncataloged, not physically deleted from the volume.

11.8.5 An Example

```
//JOB1    JOB     (A123),'C. KENNEDY'
//STEP1   EXEC    PGM=IDCAMS
//SYSIN   DD      *
  DEFINE GDG(NAME(FINANCES.MONTHLY)  -
  LIMIT(5)                           -
  NOEMPTY                            -
  SCRATCH)
/*
//
```

In this example the IDCAMS utility is used to create an index for a GDG called FINANCES.MONTHLY. The number of generations that can exist in this GDG is limited to five. Once this limit is reached, the system is instructed to uncatalog the oldest generation data set within the GDG. Also, the index entry of that generation data set is to be physically deleted from the volume that it used to reside on, thereby allowing other users to utilize these resources, if necessary. The SCRATCH parameter allows us to specify this.

Before we proceed to the next section, take another look at the JCL, and notice the hyphen (-) at the end of each statement that follows the SYSIN statement. Also notice the absence of the hyphen after the SCRATCH parameter. The hyphen is a continuation character used in *Access Method Services* (AMS) commands. It is used to indicate that the AMS command on that line is not yet complete, and will be continued onto the next line. The absence of the hyphen on the last line indicates the end of the particular AMS command. If the hyphen is skipped between lines, then the AMS command will terminate unsuccessfully.

11.9 A GDG MODEL

Once the index has been created for a GDG, a model prototype data set must be created. This model prototype will contain the specifications for the DCB subparameters for all data sets that will belong to that GDG. This model should reside on the same volume as its related index. Each time a data set belonging to a GDG is created, it will use the DCB subparameters specified in the model protototype.

Most installations supply a special cataloged data set called DSCB which can be used to hold the DCB attributes of a GDG data set. Generally speaking, this is an empty data set. Whenever a programmer needs to create a GDG, the programmer can specify the DCB subparameters which are applicable to the application, thereby overriding any subparameters that may exist in this prototype.

11.9.1 Creating Your Own Model

If your installation does not provide a model DSCB, you can create your own to serve as a GDG model. Here's the JCL that will do just that. We re-display the JCL used to create a GDG index from the prior section and expand on it.

```
//JOB1    JOB   (A123),'C. KENNEDY'
//STEP1   EXEC PGM=IDCAMS
//SYSIN   DD    *
  DEFINE GDG(NAME(FINANCES.MONTHLY)  -
  LIMIT(5)                           -
  NOEMPTY                            -
  SCRATCH)
//STEP2   EXEC PGM=IEFBR14
//MODEL1 DD    DSN=FINANCES.MONTHLY,
//              DISP=(NEW,KEEP,DELETE),
//              UNIT=SYSDA,
//              SPACE=(TRK,0),
//              DCB=(LRECL=80,RECFM=FB,BLKSIZE=800)
```

The following JCL creates the index for the GDG:

```
//SYSIN   DD    *
  DEFINE GDG(NAME(FINANCES.MONTHLY)  -
  LIMIT(5)                           -
  NOEMPTY                            -
  SCRATCH)
```

and this JCL creates the model:

```
//STEP2   EXEC PGM=IEFBR14
//MODEL1 DD    DSN=FINANCES.MONTHLY,
//              DISP=(NEW,KEEP,DELETE),
//              UNIT=SYSDA,
//              SPACE=(TRK,0),
//              DCB=(LRECL=80,RECFM=FB,BLKSIZE=800)
```

The model data set is called FINANCES.MONTHLY. The system is instructed that this is a new data set, which must be kept after it has been created. Note that if the job terminates abnormally, it will be deleted. The model must be created on a direct access storage device (SYSDA is the group name traditionally assigned to devices of this type). Zero tracks of space are to be allocated to it. Take another look at the JCL statement which contains the specifications for the DCB subparameters:

```
//               DCB=(LRECL=80,RECFM=FB,BLKSIZE=800)
```

The system is instructed to create the data set FINANCES.MONTHLY with a logical record length of 80 bytes, and a block size of 800 bytes.

The reason we gave special emphasis to this statement is because all data sets that will be created for the GDG called FINANCES.MONTHLY will have the same DCB subparameters as the model data set.

In the next section we will create a generation data set for FINANCES.MONTHLY, using an installation defined model DSCB.

11.9.2 Creating a Generation Data Set

We continue to expand the JCL presented in the prior two sections and illustrate the creation of a generation data set.

Example 1

```
//STEP3      EXEC    PGM=GDG1
//FILE1      DD      DSN=FINANCES.MONTHLY(+1),
//                   DISP=(NEW,CATLG,DELETE),
//                   UNIT=SYSDA,
//                   SPACE=(TRK,(20,10),RLSE),
//                   DCB=(MODEL.DCB,
//                   RECFM=FB,
//                   LRECL=80,
//                   BLKSIZE-800)
```

The program GDG1 is executed. A new generation data set belonging to the GDG FINANCES.MONTHLY is created via the statement:

```
//FILE1      DD      DSN=FINANCES.MONTHLY(+1),
```

The syntax (+1) creates a new generation relative to the current generation, which is referenced as generation 0. All existing generations are pushed down by one level at the end of the job. The generation numbers will not be updated until the end of the job.

The disposition of all new generations must be cataloged. Hence, the DISP parameter will always be

```
DISP=(NEW,CATLG,DELETE)
```

for all new generations.

The generation data set is created on SYSDA, which happens to be the same device as where the GDG index and model prototype reside. Please note that the GDG data set does not have to be created on the same device; it could have been created on any valid device.

20 tracks of primary space are allocated to this data set, in addition to secondary space. If any space is left unused, then the system is instructed to release it.

Finally, the system is instructed to reference the DCB subparameters specified for the data set called MODEL.DCB. Thus, the statement

```
//              DCB=(MODEL.DCB,
//              RECFM=FB,
//              LRECL=80,
//              BLKSIZE-800)
```

results in a new generation being created using an installation-defined model called MODEL.DCB.

Before we conclude our explanation of this example, remember the following:

■ The DEFINE GDG statement names the generation data group.

■ A model data set is created using the same name. You can also use an installation defined model prototype.

■ A new generation data set is created with the same name as the one referenced in the DEFINE GDG statement.

■ The DCB parameter must have a GDG model prototype, along with its other parameters.

11.10 MODIFYING FEATURES OF A GDG

The features of an existing GDG can be modified via the ALTER command. The ALTER command is coded on the SYSIN statement. Here's the syntax:

```
//SYSIN    DD   *
  ALTER    gdg_name   parameter,parameter..
/*
```

where *gdg_name* is the name of the GDG that is to be altered, and parameter is the modified parameter.

The ALTER command is explained in detail in Chapter 18 (Additional VSAM Commands). We describe it briefly in the context of GDGs in this chapter. We will use the same example that was described in Section 11.9.

Here's the JCL that creates a GDG index:

```
//JOB1     JOB     (A123),'C. KENNEDY'
//STEP1    EXEC    PGM=IDCAMS
//SYSIN    DD      *
  DEFINE GDG(NAME(FINANCES.MONTHLY)  -
  LIMIT(5)                           -
  NOEMPTY                            -
  SCRATCH)
```

Notice that this GDG is created with the NOEMPTY and SCRATCH features. Suppose we wish to modify these features to EMPTY and NOSCRATCH, repectively. Here's the JCL that will do this:

```
//JOB1     JOB    A123,'R. KENNEDY'
//STEP1    EXEC   PGM=IDCAMS
//SYSPRINT DD     SYSOUT=A
//SYSIN    DD     *
  ALTER    FINANCES.MONTHLY NOSCRATCH EMPTY
/*
//
```

In this example, the ALTER statement is used to modify the features of the GDG called FINANCES.MONTHLY. Any generations that may exist for that GDG will now contain the modified features as well. Any new generations that are created for this GDG will now be created based on these new features.

11.11 DELETING A GENERATION DATA SET

Individual generation data sets can be deleted by coding a DELETE on the DISP parameter in the DD statement for that generation data set. The following example illustrates its usage.

11.11.1 An Example

```
//JOB3      JOB    (A123),'C. KENNEDY'
//STEP1     EXEC   PGM=IEFBR14
//DEL1      DD     DSN=FINANCES.MONTHLY(O),
//                 DISP=(OLD,DELETE,DELETE)
```

In this example, the program IEFBR14 is executed. The current generation data set for FINANCES.MONTHLY is deleted via the DISP parameter. The JCL statement

```
//                 DISP=(OLD,DELETE,DELETE)
```

specifies the current status of this data set; since it pre-exists, it must be deleted, regardless of the normal or abnormal termination of jobstep STEP1.

11.12 DELETING GENERATION DATA GROUP INDEX

The GDG index can be deleted using the DELETE parameter in the IBM supplied IDCAMS utility. Deletion of the index will result in references to any generation data sets of the same name generating an error, thus resulting in abnormal termination of the job or job step.

11.12.1 An Example

```
//JOB4      JOB    (A123),'C KENNEDY'
//STEP1     EXEC   PGM=IDCAMS
//SYSIN     DD     *
   DELETE(FINANCES.MONTHLY)GDG
/*
```

In this example, the IDCAMS utility is executed to delete the index for the Generation Data Group called FINANCES.MONTHLY.

11.13 PURGE CODED ON DELETE STATEMENT

The PURGE parameter can be coded in conjunction with the DELETE statement to delete the GDG index, even if its retention period has not expired. When a data set is created, a retention period is automatically recorded for it. When this period is up, the system automatically deletes the data set from the system. The PURGE parameter can be used to override this retention period.

11.13.1 An Example

```
//JOB5      JOB    (A123),'C KENNEDY'
//STEP1     EXEC   PGM=IDCAMS
//SYSIN     DD     *
   DELETE(FINANCES.MONTHLY)GDG PURGE
/*
```

In this example, the index for FINANCES.MONTHLY will be deleted from the system catalogs (even if the command is issued before the retention period recorded for this data set).

11.14 FORCE CODED ON DELETE STATEMENT

The FORCE parameter can be coded on the DELETE statement to delete the GDG index, the model, and all related generation data sets, if they exist.

11.14.1 An Example

```
//JOB6      JOB    (A123),'C KENNEDY'
//STEP1     EXEC   PGM=IDCAMS
//SYSIN     DD     *
   DELETE(FINANCES.MONTHLY)GDG FORCE
/*
```

All traces of the GDG called FINANCES.MONTHLY will be removed from the system catalogs upon successful execution of this job step.

11.15 CONCATENATING GENERATIONS OF A GDG

Sometimes it may be necessary to concatenate all of the generations of a GDG into a master file. For example, suppose a daily production job creates a new generation data set each day, and that these files have to be processed as one master file at the end of the month. Here's the JCL that will concatenate the GDGs together.

```
//JOB1      JOB    A123,'C KENNEDY'
//STEP1     EXEC   PGM=PROGRAM1
//DD1       DD     DSN=FINANCES.MONTHLY,
//                 DISP=SHR
//DD2       DD     DSN=FINANCES.MASTER,
//                 DISP=(NEW,CATLG,DELETE),
//                 UNIT=SYSDA,
//                 SPACE=(CYL,(10,2),RLSE),
```

```
//                    DCB=(RECFM=FB,
//                    LRECL=80,BLKSIZE=23440)
//
```

In this example, since FINANCES.MONTHLY is a GDG file, all generations that belong to it are concatenated together into FINANCES.MASTER. The remaining parameters coded on DD2 specify features for FINANCES.MASTER.

11.16 RECREATING A CORRUPTED GENERATION

Sometimes the data in a generation data set can get corrupted. This can be a potentially dangerous situation, especially if new generations are to be created from previous ones. JCL can be coded to recreate a corrupt generation, thereby alleviating the possibility of corrupt new generations.

11.16.1 An Example

Suppose the following generations exist:

FINANCES.MONTHLY.G0001V00
FINANCES.MONTHLY.G0002V00
FINANCES.MONTHLY.G0003V00
FINANCES.MONTHLY.G0004V00

Now, suppose the data in FINANCES.MONTLY.G0004V00 is corrupted. This data in this data set can be rectified as follows:

- Delete corrupt generations by executing the IEFBR14 utility, and coding DELETE on the DISP parameter, like this:

```
//JOB1      JOB    A123,'C KENNEDY'
//STEP1     EXEC   PGM=IEFBR14
//DD1       DD     DSN=FINANCES.MONTHLY.G0004V00,
//                 DISP=(OLD,DELETE,DELETE)
//
```

The DISP statement specifies that FINANCES.MONTLY.G0004V00 is a pre-existing data set, and that it is to be deleted.

- Recreate, using the usual method, as follows:

```
//JOB1      JOB    A123,'C KENNEDY'
//STEP1     EXEC   PGM=GDG1
```

```
//DD1       DD      DSN=FINANCES.MONTHLY(+1),
//                  DISP=(NEW,CATLG,DELETE),
//                  UNIT=SYSDA,
//                  SPACE=(CYL,(1,1),RLSE),
//                  DCB=(MODEL.DCB,
//                  RECFM=FB,
//                  LRECL=80,
//                  BLKSIZE=800)
//
```

Executing this program will result in the correct GDG being recreated.

11.17 THINGS THAT CAN GO WRONG

In Table 11.4, we present a general correspondence between some common errors and the error codes and messages that are generated from them. Either refer to the JCL error code or scan through the column titled *Probable Cause of Error*, to identify the cause of error in your JCL.

Table 11.4 Some Common Errors while Coding GDGs

JCL Error Code	Description	Probable Cause of Error
IEF212I	Data set not found	Attempt to access a GDG which does not exist Attempt to access a GDG which is not cataloged

11.18 REVIEW

This chapter described the concept of Generation Data Groups, how they are coded, how they are deleted, and so on. Table 11.5 summarizes the syntax and meanings of the parameters described.

Table 11.5 Coding GDGs

JCL Parameter/Concept	Syntax and/or Description
GDG	These are groups of data sets which are related to each other chronologically and functionally
GDG Index	Contains information pertaining to the following: - Name - Number of generations to be retained - Steps to be taken once limit of number of generations is reached
GDG Model	Used as a prototype for all data sets that will be created for a GDG New data sets added to the GDG are created using the DCB parameter specifications as this model
IDCAMS utility	Used to create GDG index
DEFINE GDG(...)	Defines the GDG index
NAME coded on DEFINE GDG statement	Names the GDG
LIMIT coded on DEFINE GDG statement	Specifies number of generations belonging to GDG
NOEMPTY/EMPTY coded on DEFINE GDG statement	Specifies whether or not existing generations are to be uncataloged once the limit of generations is reached
SCRATCH/NOSCRATCH coded on DEFINE GDG statement	Specifies whether or not existing generations are to be physically removed once the limit of generations is reached
DSCB model	Used as a model generation data set This is usually an empty data set whose DCB parameters can be customized as necessary

User Defined model	May be created, if a DSCB model is unavailable Must be kept, after it is created Must be created on a direct access storage device
DELETE subparameter in DISP parameter coded on DD statement	Can be used to delete a data set belonging to the GDG
DELETE coded on DD statement followed by GDG name, in the IDCAMS utility	Deletes the GDG index
PURGE coded on DELETE statement in IDCAMS utility	Deletes the GDG data set, even if retention period has not expired
FORCE coded on DELETE statement in IDCAMS utility	Deletes the GDG index, model, and all related subparameters

Utilities

Utility
Programs

12.1 INTRODUCTION

A *utility* is exactly what its name implies, a useful tool that helps expedite a task. MVS provides a number of pre-written utility programs that can be used by analysts, system programmers, and application programmers to assist them in maintaining and organizing data.

Many of the utilities provided by IBM are outdated, and as a result are practically obsolete. Others still provide a variety of useful functions. This chapter discusses some of those utilities which are still used in the JCL community.

12.2 UTILITY PROGRAMS, AN OVERVIEW

Some functions that are frequently required by application programmers that work in an MVS/JCL environment are the following.

- Copy sequential files.

- Copy partitioned data sets.

- Catalog data sets.

- Uncatalog data sets.

- Rename data sets.

- Compress partitioned data sets.

- Include members of partitioned data sets when a copy transaction is implemented.

- Exclude members of partitioned data sets when a copy transaction is implemented.

- Compare sequential data sets.

- Compare partitioned data sets.

- Create or delete data sets, allocate or deallocate space on data sets, or code other functions on the DD statement, without having to execute a program.

- Create Generation Data Groups.

12.3 CORRESPONDING JCL

Table 12.1 lists the utility programs that are available for implementing the functions listed in Section 12.2.

Table 12.1 Some Common Utilities

Function	Corresponding Utility Name
Copy sequential files	IEBGENER
Copy partitioned data sets	IEBCOPY
Catalog data sets	IEHPROGM
Uncatalog data sets	IEHPROGM
Rename data sets	IEHPROGM
Compress partitioned data sets	IEBCOPY
Include members of partitioned data sets when implementing a copy command	SELECT statement coded in the COPY command of the IEBCOPY utility
Exclude members of partitioned data sets when implementing a copy command	EXCLUDE statement coded in the COPY command of the IEBCOPY utility

Compare sequential data sets	IEBCOMPR
Compare partitioned data sets	IEBCOMPR
Code functions available on the DD statement without executing a program	IEFBR14
Create Generation Data Groups	IEHPROGM

These utilities will be discussed in detail later on in this chapter. But first, we want you to see the general pattern of the JCL statements that are required to execute these utilities.

12.4 JCL REQUIRED TO EXECUTE UTILITIES

The JCL statements which are required to execute utility programs follow one general pattern. Once you have a group of statements that successfully execute a utility program, you need to make only minor changes in order to execute another utility program. The following is the JCL in pseudo-code that executes a utility program.

```
//jobname     JOB  (accounting-information),
//                 programmer-name
//stepname    EXEC PGM=utility-name,
//                 PARM=parm-value
//printname   DD   SYSOUT=print-device-class
//inputfile   DD   input-file-features
//outputfile  DD   output-file-features
//workfile    DD   work-file-features
//inputdata   DD   *
  <data statements specific to utility follow>
/*
//
```

The first statement, as always, identifies the name of the job being submitted to the operating system. This statement also usually contains accounting information and programmer name.

The EXEC statement follows the JOB statement, and identifies the name of the utility that is to be executed.

The PARM parameter coded on the EXEC statement is required by some utilities to specify additional information about the data set that will be processed by that utility.

The next statement

```
//printname    DD     SYSOUT=print-device-class
```

specifies the output class to which output will be directed. Keep in mind that output is generated by the operating system throughout the run, and also by the utility program that is being executed.

The next two statements

```
//inputfile   DD     input-file-features
//outputfile  DD     output-file-features
```

specify the characteristics of the input and output data sets (if both exist). These characteristics are coded on the DD statement.

The next statement

```
//workfile    DD     work-file-features
```

may be coded if temporary or work files are required by the utility that is being executed. These work files are created at the start of the job, and deleted when it ends.

The next group of statements

```
//inputdata  DD     *
  <data statements specific to utility follow>
/*
```

are used to specify whatever else is required by the utility in order for it to execute successfully. This group of statements could also have been coded using the DATA statement, as follows:

```
//inputdata  DATA
  <data statements specific to utility follow>
```

This is the general pattern of the JCL required to execute a utility program. In the pseudo-code just presented, we have used DDnames that will help convey the function of its corresponding DD statement. Traditionally, the DDname SYSPRINT is coded for the SYSOUT statement, and SYSUT, (e.g. SYSUT1, SYSUT2, and so on), is coded on the DD statements that specify features of the input, output, and work files. For the remainder of the chapter we will adhere to this convention when naming DD statements.

A discussion of each utility follows.

12.5 IEBGENER

IEBGENER is perhaps one of the most commonly used utility programs. It is used to copy one sequential file to another.

12.5.1 Rules for Coding

- Original data set name must be specified.

- Destination data set name must be specified.

- Attributes of both data sets (such as record format and logical record length), must be the same.

12.5.2 JCL Required to Execute IEBGENER

The following JCL executes the IEBGENER program:

```
//IEBGENR1   JOB   A123,'L. BLAIR'
//STEP1      EXEC  PGM=IEBGENER
//SYSPRINT   DD    SYSOUT=A
//SYSUT1     DD    DSN=FILE1.ORIGINAL,
//                 DISP=SHR
//SYSUT2     DD    DSN=FILE2.DUPLICATE,
//                 DISP=(NEW,CATLG,KEEP),
//                 UNIT=DISK1,
//                 SPACE=(TRK,(20,10),RLSE),
//                 DCB=(RECFM=FB,
//                      LRECL=80,BLKSIZE=800)
//SYSIN      DD    DUMMY
//
```

The utility IEBGENER is executed and the output is directed to the device designated by A. Traditionally, this is the line printer.

SYSUT1 identifies the features of the input file to IEBGENER. The name of the file to be copied is FILE1.ORIGINAL. It can be shared among users.

SYSUT2 identifies the characteristics of the output file, which will be a copy of the file identified in SYSUT1. This file is called FILE2.DUPLICATE. Its disposition is identified as NEW, (obviously, it is a new file). Once created, it should be cataloged and kept. This file will be created on the unit device identified as DISK1. 20 tracks of primary space are allocated to it, and 10 tracks of secondary space. Any unused space should be released. The DCB features of this file are that it should be fixed block, and that it must have a logical record length of 80 bytes, and a blocksize of 800 bytes. The SYSIN statement is used as a dummy data set since there are no control statements. When IEBGENER encounters this SYSIN statement, it immediately gives an end-of-file indication.

12.6 IEBCOPY

IEBCOPY provides the following functions:

- *Copy* partitioned data sets.

A partitioned data set can be copied to another partitioned data set, or a sequential data set. This is known as unloading.

Partitioned data sets are usually backed up on tape. IEBCOPY can be used to restore partitioned data sets to direct access devices. This is known as loading.

- *Compress* partitioned data sets.

When existing members of partitioned data sets are updated, gaps of unused space can be created between them inadvertently.

For this reason, members of partitioned data sets are compressed periodically. Any unused space between records is eliminated.

- *Include* members of partitioned data sets within a copy transaction.

- *Exclude* members of partitioned data set within a copy transaction.

The JCL required to execute the IEBCOPY utility for the cases just listed is shown below.

12.6.1 Unloading Data Sets

As stated previously, unloading consists of copying one partitioned data set into another partitioned or sequential data set. In order to do so, the COPY statement is coded. The syntax of the COPY statement is as follows:

```
COPY INDD=input-ddname,
     OUTDD=output-ddname
```

where *input-ddname* is the DDname of the statement that defines the characteristics of the input file name, and *output-ddname* is the DDname of the statement that defines the characteristics of the file into which the input file will be copied. Now take a look at the JCL:

```
//IEBCOPY1   JOB   A123,'J. FOSTER'
//STEP1      EXEC  PGM=IEBCOPY
//SYSPRINT   DD    SYSOUT=A
//SYSUT1     DD    DSN=COBOL.FILE1,
//                 DISP=SHR
//SYSUT2     DD    DSN=COBOL.FILE2,
//                 DISP=(NEW,KEEP),
//                 UNIT=TAPE1,
//                 VOL=SER=9999
//SYSIN      DD    *
  COPY INDD=SYSUT1,
  OUTDD=SYSUT2
/*
//
```

In this example, the program IEBCOPY is executed. Output is directed to the line printer.

Next, the characteristics of the two data sets that are involved in the transaction are defined.

The first data set is defined in the SYSUT1 statement. The name of this file is COBOL.FILE1, and it can be shared among users.

The characteristics of the second data set is defined in the SYSUT2 statement. The file is called COBOL.FILE2; it is a new file, and the system is advised to retain the file after the termination of the job. This file will reside on the unit designated as TAPE1, and the volume number for this tape unit is 9999.

Next comes the SYSIN statement. This contains the COPY statement specifying which file will be copied into what. Take another look at the COPY statement:

```
//SYSIN      DD    *
            COPY  INDD=SYSUT1,
                  OUTDD=SYSUT2
/*
```

This statement specifies that the data set defined in SYSUT1 will be the input data set, while that defined in SYSUT2 will be the output data set. COBOL.FILE1 will be copied into COBOL.FILE2. After successful execution of this JCL, COBOL.FILE2 will be identical to COBOL.FILE1.

12.6.2 Loading Data Sets

As stated previously, loading is the term given to restoration of partitioned data sets from tape to direct access devices, such as disk. The COPY command is once again utilized to achieve the desired result. Here's the JCL:

```
//IEBCOPY2    JOB   A123,'J. FOSTER'
//STEP1       EXEC  PGM=IEBCOPY
//SYSPRINT    DD    SYSOUT=A
//SYSUT1      DD    DSN=COBOL.FILE1,
//                  DISP=OLD,
//                  UNIT=TAPE1,
//                  VOL=SER=8888
//SYSUT2      DD    DSN=COBOL.FILE1,
//                  DISP=(NEW,CATLG),
//                  UNIT=DISK1,
//                  SPACE=(TRK,(40,10))
//SYSIN       DD    *
             COPY INDD=SYSUT1,
                  OUTDD=SYSUT2
/*
//
```

In this example, the characteristics of the first file are defined in SYSUT1. The name of this file is COBOL.FILE1; it is an old file, and exists on the device designated as TAPE1, on the volume whose serial number is 8888.

The characteristics of the second file are defined in SYSUT2. The name of this file is also COBOL.FILE1. Since this is a new file, it will reside on the device designated as DISK1. 40 tracks of primary space are allocated to this file.

Next, the SYSIN statement defines the COPY command that identifies the nature of the transaction. The file specified in SYSUT1 will be copied to the file defined in SYSUT2.

12.6.3 Compressing Data Sets

Data sets can be compressed together in order to more efficiently utilize the device space that they are stored on. The JCL that does this is similar to the two examples just presented:

```
//IEBCOPY3    JOB   A123,'J. FOSTER'
//STEP1       EXEC  PGM=IEBCOPY
//SYSPRINT    DD    SYSOUT=A
//SYSUT1      DD    DSN=COBOL.SOURCE,
//SYSIN       DD    *
```

```
              COPY  INDD=SYSUT1,
                    OUTDD=SYSUT1
/*
//
```

If you take another look at this JCL, you will realize that both the INDD and OUTDD statements reference the same data set, i.e., the one defined in the SYSUT1 statement. Executing this job will result in all members of the partitioned data set called COBOL.SOURCE being compressed together, resulting in the release of wasted space between records and data set members.

12.6.4 Including Members of PDS in COPY Command

Specific members of a partitioned data set can be included for the COPY command by coding the SELECT statement immediately after the COPY statement, like this:

```
//IEBCOPY4   JOB    A123,'J. FOSTER'
//STEP1      EXEC   PGM=IEBCOPY
//SYSPRINT   DD     SYSOUT=A
//SYSUT1     DD     DSN=COBOL.SOURCE,
//                  DISP=SHR
//SYSUT2     DD     DSN=COBOL.SOURCE,
//                  DISP=(NEW,KEEP),
//                  UNIT=TAPE1,
//                  VOL=SER=9999
//SYSIN      DD     *
            COPY   INDD=SYSUT1,
                   OUTDD=SYSUT2
            SELECT MEMBER=(FILE1,FILE2,FILE3)
/*
//
```

In this example, the partitioned data set named COBOL.SOURCE is copied to TAPE1. However, instead of all members of the partitioned data set being copied, only FILE1, FILE2, and FILE3 are copied.

12.6.5 Excluding Members of PDS in COPY Command

Specific members can be excluded for the COPY command by coding the EXCLUDE statement immediately after the COPY statement, like this:

```
//IEBCOPY5   JOB    A123,'J. FOSTER'
//STEP1      EXEC   PGM=IEBCOPY
//SYSPRINT   DD     SYSOUT=A
```

```
//SYSUT1    DD    DSN=COBOL.SOURCE,
//                DISP=SHR
//SYSUT2    DD    DSN=COBOL.SOURCE,
//                DISP=(NEW,KEEP),
//                UNIT=TAPE1,
//                VOL=SER=9999
//SYSIN     DD    *
           COPY   INDD=SYSUT1,
                  OUTDD=SYSUT2
           EXCLUDE MEMBER=(FILE1,FILE2,FILE3)
/*
//
```

In this example, the partitioned data set named COBOL.SOURCE is copied to TAPE1. However, this time, FILE1, FILE2, and FILE3 are excluded from the copy.

12.7 IEHPROGM

IEHPROGM provides the following functions:

■ Catalog data sets.

To catalog a data set, the system is told to record its name and other characteristics in the system catalogs.

■ Uncatalog data sets.

Uncataloging a data set results in the system removing an entry from the system catalogs. The data set itself is not purged from the physical location on which it was stored.

■ Rename data sets.

■ Create the index of a Generation Data Group.

In Chapter 11 we created the index for a GDG using the IDCAMS utility. The IEHPROGM utility is another method for achieving the same end.

■ Delete the index of an existing Generation Data Group.

The JCL required to execute the IEHPROGM utility for the cases just listed follows.

12.7.1 Rules for Coding

■ One DD statement is necessary when specifying the characteristics of a permanently mounted direct access volume. The IEHPROGM utility must know this information in order to execute properly.

■ Another DD statement indicating characteristics of the data set that is to be processed, (if this data set is being cataloged), must exist.

12.7.2 Cataloging Data Sets

A data set can be cataloged via the CATLG statement coded for this utility. The syntax of the CATLG statement looks like this:

```
CATLG DSNAME=data-set-name,
      VOL=device-name=volume-number
```

where *data-set-name* is the name of the data set that is to be cataloged, *device-name* is the name of the device on which this data set resides, and *volume-number* is the identifier ID assigned to this volume.

Here's the JCL that catalogs a data set:

```
//IEHPRGM1   JOB     A123,'S. CONNOR'
//STEP1      EXEC    PGM=IEHPROGM
//SYSPRINT   DD      SYSOUT=A
//SYSUT1     DD      UNIT=3390,
//                   VOL=SER=SYS12
//SYSUT2     DD      UNIT=UNIT1,
//                   VOL=SER=9999
//SYSIN      DD      *
           CATLG   DSNAME=FILE1,
                   VOL=UNIT1=9999
/*
//
```

In this example, the IEHPROGM utility is executed.

In SYSUT1, the permanently mounted unit, a 3390 disk, is identified. This is the volume called SYS12.

In SYSUT2, the location of the data set that is to be cataloged is identified. The data set resides on volume 9999 of the device called UNIT1.

Next, the CATLG statement identifies the name of the file (FILE1), and the device and serial number that it currently resides on.

12.7.3 UnCataloging Data Sets

A data set can be uncataloged via the UNCATLG statement coded for this utility. The syntax of the UNCATLG statement looks like this:

UNCATLG DSNAME=data-set-name

where *data-set-name* is the name of the data set that is to be uncataloged.

Here's the JCL that uncatalogs a data set:

```
//IEHPRGM2    JOB      A123,'S. CONNOR'
//STEP1       EXEC     PGM=IEHPROGM
//SYSPRINT    DD       SYSOUT=A
//SYSUT1      DD       UNIT=3390,
//                     VOL=SER=SYS12
//SYSIN       DD       *
             UNCATLG  DSNAME=FILE1,
/*
//
```

In this example, the IEHPROGM utility is executed.

Like the prior example, SYSUT1 identifies the permanently-mounted unit direct access volume. This is the volume called SYS12 on a 3390 disk.

Next, the UNCATLG statement identifies the name of the file (FILE1) that is to be dropped from the system catalogs. There is no need to specify the location of the data set (as we did in the prior example), because the information was recorded by the system at the time that it was cataloged.

12.7.4 Renaming Data Sets

A data set can be renamed via the RENAME statement coded for this utility. The syntax of the RENAME statement looks like this:

RENAME DSNAME=data-set-name,
       VOL=device-name=volume-number,
       NEWNAME=new-member-name

where data-set-name is the name of the data set that is to be renamed, device-name is the name of the device on which it resides, volume-number is the volume identifier, and new-member-name is its new name.

Here's the JCL that renames a data set:

```
//IEHPRGM3  JOB      A123,'S. CONNOR'
//STEP1     EXEC     PGM=IEHPROGM
//SYSPRINT  DD       SYSOUT=A
//SYSUT1    DD       UNIT=3390,
//                   VOL=SER=SYS12
//SYSUT2    DD       UNIT=UNIT1,
//                   VOL=SER=9999,
//                   DISP=OLD
//SYSIN     DD       *
           RENAME    DSNAME=FILE1,
                     VOL=UNIT1=9999,
                     NEWNAME=FILE2
/*
//
```

In this example, IEHPROGM is executed to rename an existing data set.

SYSUT1 identifies the permanently-mounted direct access volume.

SYSUT2 identifies the location of the data set that will be renamed. This is on volume number 9999 on UNIT1.

Next, the RENAME command is used to rename the data set FILE1, on volume number 9999 of UNIT1, to FILE2.

12.7.5 An All-Encompassing Example

Here's the JCL that will rename an existing data set, uncatalog its original name, and catalog the new one.

```
//IEHPRGM4  JOB      A123,'S. CONNOR'
//STEP1     EXEC     PGM=IEHPROGM
//SYSPRINT  DD       SYSOUT=A
//SYSUT1    DD       UNIT=3390,
//                   VOL=SER=SYS12
//SYSUT2    DD       UNIT=UNIT1,
//                   VOL=SER=9999,
//                   DISP=OLD
//SYSIN     DD       *
           RENAME    DSNAME=FILE1,
                     VOL=UNIT1=9999,
                     NEWNAME=FILE2
           UNCATLG   DSNAME=FILE4
           CATLG     DSNAME=FILE2,
                     VOL=UNIT1=9999
/*
//
```

By now you should be able to understand this example without any problems, so we will not explore it any further.

12.7.6 Creating an Index for GDG

Recall that in order to create a Generation Data Group, first its index must be created; then a model prototype for all data sets that will belong to that GDG must also be created. The BLDG INDEX command may be coded on the IEHPROGM utility to create the index. Here's the syntax:

```
    BLDG INDEX=gdg-name,
        ENTRIES=n
or
    BLDG INDEX=gdg-name,
        ENTRIES=n,
        EMPTY
or
    BLDG INDEX=gdg-name,
        ENTRIES=n,
        EMPTY,
        DELETE
```

gdg-name is the name of the GDG. *n* is the maximum number of generations that can exist for that GDG. *EMPTY* is an optional keyword that specifies that all entries are to be removed from the index, if the limit of the number of generations is reached. The *DELETE* keyword is also optional, and is used to specify that the generation data sets are to be physically removed from the volume that they exist on, if their entries are deleted from the index.

Here's the JCL that creates an index:

```
//IEHPRGM4   JOB      A123,'S. CONNOR'
//STEP1      EXEC     PGM=IEHPROGM
//SYSPRINT   DD       SYSOUT=A
//SYSUT1     DD       UNIT=3390,
//                    VOL=SER=SYS12
//SYSIN      DD       *
  BLDG INDEX=FINANCES.MONTHLY,
       ENTRIES=5,
       DELETE
/*
//
```

In this example, SYSUT1 specifies the permanently-mounted direct access volume.

In the SYSIN statement, the BLDG command is used to build the index for a generation data group called FINANCES.MONTHLY. A maximum of five generations will be maintained in this GDG. If this limit is reached, then the earliest generation data set should be physically deleted when the sixth one is created.

12.7.7 Deleting an Index for GDG

The DLTX INDEX command is coded on the IEHPROGM utility to delete the index. Here's the syntax:

    DLTX INDEX=index-name

Here's the JCL that deletes a GDG index:

```
//IEHPRGM5   JOB      A123,'S. CONNOR'
//STEP1      EXEC     PGM=IEHPROGM
//SYSPRINT   DD       SYSOUT=A
//SYSUT1     DD       UNIT=3390,
//                    VOL=SER=SYS12
//SYSIN      DD       *
   DLTX      INDEX=FINANCES.MONTHLY
/*
//
```

The DLTX INDEX command is used to delete the GDG index called FINANCES.MONTHLY. All data sets that may exist for the GDG will also be deleted.

12.8 IEBCOMPR

The IEBCOMPR utility is used to:

- Compare two sequential data sets.

- Compare two partitioned data sets.

If the two data sets are identical, then a condition code of 0 will be returned upon successful execution of the job.

If the two data sets are not identical, then a condition code of 8 will be returned.

12.8.1 Rule for Coding

- The data sets being compared must have the same record length and format. (However, blocksize need not be the same)

12.8.2 Comparing Two Sequential Data Sets

Two sequential data sets can be compared by coding the COMPARE statement for this utility. Here's the syntax:

COMPARE TYPORG=data-set-type

where *data-set-type* specifies the type of data set that is being compared. It is set to *PS* for *Physical Sequential* when comparing sequential data sets.

Here's the JCL that executes a comparison of this type:

```
//IEBCMPR1   JOB       A123,'J. CURTIS'
//STEP1      EXEC      PGM=IEBCOMPR
//SYSPRINT   DD        SYSOUT=A
//SYSUT1     DD        DSN=FILE1,
//                     DISP=SHR
//SYSUT2     DD        DSN=FILE2,
//                     DISP=SHR
//SYSIN      DD        *
           COMPARE   TYPORG=PS
/*
//
```

In this example, the first file to be compared is FILE1; its disposition is specified as shared. The second file to be compared is FILE2; its disposition is also shared.

The SYSIN statement uses the COMPARE command to specify that the two data sets that are to be compared are of type PS, i.e. Physical Sequential.

If these data sets are identical to each other, then a condition code of 0 will be returned. Otherwise, a condition code of 8 will be returned.

12.8.3 Comparing Two Partitioned Data Sets

Two partitioned data sets can be compared by coding the COMPARE statement for this utility, but this time TYPORG is set to PO for *Partitioned Organization*. Here's the syntax:

    COMPARE TYPORG=data-set-type

where *data-set-type* specifies the type of data set that is being compared. TYPORG is set to PO for this type of comparison.

Here's the JCL that executes this type of comparison:

```
//IEBCMPR2   JOB        A123,'J. CURTIS'
//STEP1      EXEC       PGM=IEBCOMPR
//SYSPRINT   DD         SYSOUT=A
//SYSUT1     DD         DSN=COBOL1.SOURCE,
//                      DISP=SHR
//SYSUT2     DD         DSN=COBOL2.SOURCE,
//                      DISP=SHR
//SYSIN      DD         *
           COMPARE     TYPORG=PO
/*
//
```

In this example, the first PDS is called COBOL1.SOURCE. The second PDS is called COBOL2.SOURCE. All members of the same name within these two partitioned data sets will be compared with each other, one by one. If unique member names without a matching pair are encountered in either PDS, the job will terminate unsuccessfully.

If all members with like names are identical to each other, a condition code of 0 will be returned. If they are not identical, then a condition code of 8 will be returned.

12.9 IEFBR14

The IEFBR14 program is nothing more than a *null* program,- its name is derived from an assembler language instruction that is used to exit a procedure or program, and this is exactly what it does. It executes a single statement which specifies the end of the program.

This program is used to code functions that are commonly available on the DD statement, such as the creation, deletion, and updating of data sets, without having to execute any explicit program. The IEFBR14 program is not considered by IBM to be a utility program. However, it is used like a utility in that it does not do anything by itself.

Since IEFBR14 is a do-nothing program, it can also be used to check the syntax of your JCL without affecting any data sets.

You can execute various functions on these data sets without having to execute any specific program via the IEFBR14 utility. To follow are a few examples.

12.9.1 Some Examples

Example 1

```
//UNCATLOG  JOB  A123,'L. HUTTON'
//STEP1     EXEC PGM=IEFBR14
//DD1       DD   DSN=COBOL.FILE1,
//               DISP=(OLD,UNCATLG)
```

In this example, the IEFBR14 program is used to uncatalog the data set called COBOL.FILE1.

Example 2

```
//DELETE1   JOB  A123,'L. HUTTON'
//STEP1     EXEC PGM=IEFBR14
//DD1       DD   DSN=COBOL.FILE2,
//               DISP=(OLD,DELETE)
```

In this example, the data set called COBOL.FILE2 is deleted.

Example 3

```
//CATALOG JOB  A123,'L. HUTTON'
//STEP1   EXEC PGM=IEFBR14
//DD1     DD   DSN=COBOL.FILE3,
//             DISP=(NEW,CATLG)
```

In this example, COBOL.FILE3 is cataloged.

Example 4

```
//CREATE   JOB  A123,'L. HUTTON'
//STEP3    EXEC PGM=IEFBR14
//DD1      DD   DSN=COBOL.FILE4,
//              DISP=(NEW,KEEP),
//              UNIT=UNIT1,
//              SPACE=(TRK,(4,2)),
//              DCB=(LRECL=80,
//                   RECFM=FB,BLKSIZE=800)
//
```

In this example, a dummy data set called COBOL.FILE4 is created. This is a new data set and is to be kept after termination of the job. It is to reside on UNIT1, and will be allocated four tracks of primary space and two tracks of secondary space. It will have a logical record length of 80 bytes, a fixed block format, and a block size of 800 bytes.

12.10 THINGS THAT CAN GO WRONG

We present a general correspondence between some common errors that can occur while coding this utility, and the error codes and messages that are generated from them. Either refer to the JCL error code, or scan through *Probable Cause of Error* to identify the cause of the error in your JCL.

Table 12.2 Some Common Errors on IEBCOPY Utility

JCL Error Code	Description	Probable Cause of Error
IEF212I	Data set not found	Executing IEBCOPY to copy a non-existent data set
IEB1591	No members copied from input data set referenced in xx xx is ddname	Coding SELECT command for a non-existent member A similar message will be displayed if the EXCLUDE command is coded for a non-existent member

12.11 REVIEW

This chapter discussed some of the more commonly used utilities available in an MVS environment. Table 12.3 summarizes the syntax and meanings of the commands described.

Table 12.3 Parameters Coded on Some Common Utilities

Utility	Description and/or Parameters coded on it
IEBGENER	Used to copy one sequential file to another No control statements are required. Therefore, DUMMY is coded on the SYSIN statement Source and destination data sets must be specified on the DD statement
IEBCOPY	Used to copy and compress partitioned data sets COPY command is coded on the SYSIN statement. Input and output files are defined on the DD statements within the same job step Data sets are compressed by coding the same DDname as the input and output files in the SYSIN statement Can include or exclude members in the copy via the SELECT or EXCLUDE statements coded on the SYSIN command

IEHPROGM	Used to catalog, uncatalog, and rename data sets. Also used to create the index of a GDG CATLG DSNAME is coded on the SYSIN statement to catalog a data set VOL command must also be coded UNCATLG DSNAME is coded to uncatalog a data set RENAME DSNAME is coded to rename data sets BLDG INDEX is coded to create a GDG index DLTX INDEX is coded to delete the index
IEBCOMPR	Used to compare sequential or partitioned data sets Data sets being compared must have same record length and format COMPARE TYPORG is coded on the SYSIN statement to compare two data sets
IEFBR14	This is a do-nothing program It is used to code various functions on the DD statement without having to execute a specific program

13

Sort/Merge
Utilities

13.1 INTRODUCTION

In a data processing environment, records are added, updated, or deleted from a data set, as required. Usually, these records have one key identifying field. Each time a record has to be accessed, this key identifying field is referenced.

As records continue to be added and/or deleted as necessary, the end result often is that the contents become disordered. Then, when it comes time to update this data set, finding the record in question takes longer than if the contents had been ordered. Hence, the need to periodically sort files.

IBM provides an excellent sort/merge utility program called DFSORT. SORT is a program that is embedded in DFSORT. This chapter is devoted to describing the *SORT* program.

The SORT program can also be used to merge existing sorted files and combine them into one sequential file. Since the SORT program also provides the functionality for merging data sets, it is called the SORT/MERGE utility.

13.2 HOW THE SORT/MERGE UTILITY WORKS

The sort function in the SORT utility takes records from an input file, sorts the records, and places them in an output file.

The merge function of the SORT utility takes its input from the sorted records of multiple files and combines them into one sequential file.

Records can be arranged in ascending or descending order. Alphanumeric fields are sorted from left to right, based on the collating sequence of the character set of the data set. The collating sequence of the EBCDIC and ASCII character sets is different. You may wish to reference appropriate manuals in order to understand the collating sequence of each set.

Character fields are sorted based on the alphabet, and numeric fields are sorted in order of their algebraic value. The sign is also taken into consideration when sorting numeric fields. Positive values are greater than negative values.

13.3 ISSUES RELATED TO SORTS

In order to sort a file, the following must be addressed:

- The name of the file that is to be sorted.

- The name of the file in which the sorted file is to be stored.

- The location of the record from which to start sorting.

- The location of the record at which to stop sorting, or the length from the starting point, for which the sort is to be implemented.

- Whether the records are to be sorted in ascending or descending order.

- The type of data stored in the data set that is being sorted. For example, it can be character, packed, etc.

13.4 PARAMETERS ON SORT COMMAND

The information listed in the prior section is coded in various statements on the SORT utility. The SORT command is used to specify features specific to the sort itself. Here's the syntax of this command:

SORT FIELDS=(start-location,length,sort-sequence,format)

start-location is the position from which length number of bytes will be used as the sort criteria. *sort-sequence* specifies whether the file is to be sorted in ascending or descending order. *format* specifies the type of data that will be sorted.

The following are the statements and parameters coded in the SORT utility that convey the information listed in the prior section.

Table 13.1 Parameters on the SORT Command

Function	Corresponding Parameter on SORT Command
Name of input file	Coded on the DD statement
Name of output file	Coded on the DD statement
Starting sort location	Coded on the SORT command, first subparameter
Length of field to be sorted	Coded on the SORT command, second subparameter
Type of sort to be implemented	Coded on the SORT command, third subparameter Can be A for Ascending D for Descending
Type of data stored in data set being sorted	Coded on the SORT comamnd, fourth subparameter Can be CH for EBCDIC Character AC for ASCII character PD for Packed Decimal ZD for Zoned Decimal BI for Binary FI for Fixed Point FL for Floating Point

13.5 EXECUTING THE SORT PROGRAM

The SORT program can be executed in two ways:

- Through JCL statements

■ Through the SORT statement coded inside a COBOL, Assembler or PL/1 program

First, we present the method of executing the SORT through a JCL job. Then we will present a complete COBOL program that will execute the SORT.

13.5.1 Executing SORT Through JCL

Here's the JCL that executes the SORT:

```
//SORT1      JOB   (A123),'A. HOPKINS'
//STEP1      EXEC  PGM=SORT
//SYSOUT     DD    SYSOUT=A
//SYSPRINT   DD    SYSOUT=A
//SORTIN     DD    DSN=ADDRESS.BOOK1,
//                 DISP=SHR
//SORTOUT    DD    DSN=ADDRESS.BOOK2,
//                 DISP=(NEW,CATLG,DELETE),
//                 UNIT=UNIT1,
//                 SPACE=(CYL,(2,1),RLSE),
//                 DCB=(RECFM=FB,
//                      LRECL=80,BLKSIZE=800)
//SORTWK01   DD    UNIT=SYSDA,
//                 SPACE=(CYL,(20,10),RLSE)
//SORTWK02   DD    UNIT=SYSDA,
//                 SPACE=(CYL,(20,10),RLSE)
//SYSIN      DD    *
  SORT FIELDS=(2,5,A,CH)
/*
//
```

In this example, the SORT program is executed in the second statement.

The SYSOUT statement specifies the standard print device for messages that are generated by the SORT utility.

The SYSPRINT statement specifies that output is to be directed to the line printer.

The SORTIN statement identifies the name of the file that is to be sorted. This is ADDRESS.BOOK1. This is an old file with a shareable disposition.

The SORTOUT statement identifies the name of the output file, i.e., where the sorted output of ADDRESS.BOOK1 will be stored. The name of this file is ADDRESS.BOOK2. This file will reside on UNIT1, where it will occupy two cylinders of primary space, and one cylinder of secondary space. Any unused space is to be released.

Next, come the definitions of the workfiles that will be used by the SORT utility. These are nothing more than temporary files which are deleted upon completion of the job, and are utilized by the utility in ways that are transparent to the user. How much work area you request depends on many factors, such as the record length of the file being sorted, the number of records contained in the data set, the type of hardware that the data set resides on upon which the work files are being created, and so on. The amount of work area required also depends on the version of the SORT/MERGE program that you are running. Your best bet is to check with the administrators at your installation as to the size that will result in the most efficient sort for your application.

The SYSIN statement defines the kind of sort that you are requesting:

```
//SYSIN     DD    *
   SORT FIELDS=(2,5,A,CH)
/*
```

The SORT utility is instructed to sort ADDRESS.BOOK1 starting at byte 2 of each record. Only five bytes are to be sorted, starting at byte 2. (i.e., the sort is being implemented on bytes 2 through 6 only). The file is to be sorted in ascending order, and the type of data stored in this file is EBCDIC Character.

Assume that there are three records in the input file, and this is what they look like:

```
089134 Ms. Patti Smith, Nevada
012345 Mr. John Henley, California
042345 Mr. Abraham Schneider, New York
```

The file will be sorted starting at the second character, and ending at the sixth. After successful completion of the job,the output file will look like this:

```
012345 Mr. John Henley, California
042345 Mr. Abraham Schneider, New York
089134 Ms. Patti Smith, Nevada
```

13.5.2 Executing SORT Specified in COBOL Program

Here's the JCL that executes a COBOL program that executes a sort:

```
//SORT2      JOB  (A123),'A. HOPKINS'
//JOBLIB     DD   DSN=COBOL.LOAD,
//                DISP=SHR
//STEP1      EXEC PGM=PROGRAM1
//SYSOUT     DD   SYSOUT=A
```

```
//SYSPRINT   DD     SYSOUT=A
//SORTIN     DD     DSN=ADDRESS.BOOK1,
//                  DISP=SHR
//SORTOUT    DD     DSN=ADDRESS.BOOK2,
//                  DISP=(NEW,CATLG,DELETE),
//                  UNIT=UNIT1,
//                  SPACE=(CYL,(2,1),RLSE),
//                DCB=(RECFM=FB,LRECL=80,BLKSIZE=800)
//SORTWK01   DD     UNIT=SYSDA,
//                  SPACE=(CYL,(20,10),RLSE)
//SORTWK02   DD     UNIT=SYSDA,
//                  SPACE=(CYL,(20,10),RLSE)
//
```

The job called SORT2 is executed by A. Hopkins.

The next statement is the JOBLIB DD statement. This is used to specify the location of the program that is executed. In our example, the system is notified that PROGRAM1 is located in the library called COBOL.LOAD.

The EXEC statement follows the JOBLIB statement, and PROGRAM1 is executed.

Next, the SYSPRINT statement is used to specify that all output generated from the run is to be directed to the line printer.

Next, come the SORTIN and SORTOUT statements. These statements are identical to the prior example. They specify the characteristics of the input and output files.

Next come the definitions of the two work files. You could have specified more work files if necessary.

And that's it! There is no SYSIN statement specifying the nature of the SORT that is to be implemented. This is because these details are taken care of by the COBOL program that is being executed.

13.5.3 COBOL Program that Sorts a File

The SORT statement coded inside a COBOL, Assembler, or PL/1 program can also be used to execute the SORT program. We will now present a complete COBOL program that executes the SORT.

```
IDENTIFICATION DIVISION.
PROGRAM-ID.       SORTPGM.
DATE-WRITTEN.     OCT 04, 1993.
DATE-COMPILED.    OCT 6, 1993.
AUTHOR.           ANTHONY H.
*
*
```

```
 ENVIRONMENT DIVISION.
 CONFIGURATION SECTION.
 SOURCE-COMPUTER. IBM-370.
 OBJECT-COMPUTER. IBM-370.
*
 INPUT-OUTPUT SECTION.
 FILE-CONTROL.
    SELECT IN-FILE      ASSIGN TO INPUT1.
    SELECT PRINT-FILE   ASSIGN TO REPORT1.
    SELECT SORT-FILE    ASSIGN TO SORTWK01.
*
*
 DATA DIVISION.
 FILE-SECTION.
 FD  IN-FILE
     BLOCK CONTAINS 0 RECORDS
     LABEL RECORDS ARE STANDARD.
 01 IN-REC             PIC X(40).
 FD PRINT-FILE
    BLOCK CONTAINS 0 RECORDS
    LABEL RECORDS ARE STANDARD.
 01 PRINT-REC          PIC X(133).
*
 SD SORT-FILE
    DATA RECORD IS SORT-REC.
 01 SORT-REC.
    05   SORT-ACCT     PIC X(5).
    05   FILLER        PIC X(5).
    05   SORT-NAME     PIC X(30).
*
 WORKING-STORAGE SECTION.
*
*
 PROCEDURE DIVISION.
 A000-MAIN.
    PERFORM A000-OPEN-FILES.
    SORT SORT-FILE
       ON ASCENDING KEY SORT-ACCT
          INPUT PROCEDURE IS A100-INPUT-PROCEDURE
          OUTPUT PROCEDURE IS B100-OUTPUT-PROCEDURE.
    PERFORM C000-CLOSE-FILES.
    STOP RUN.
*
 A000-OPEN-FILES.
    OPEN INPUT IN-FILE.
    OPEN OUTPUT PRINT-FILE.
*
 A100-INPUT-PROCEDURE SECTION.
 A100-INPUT.
    READ IN-FILE
        AT END
        GO TO A100-EXIT.
    MOVE IN-REC TO SORT-REC.
    RELEASE SORT-REC.
```

```
        GO TO A100-INPUT.
*
  A100-EXIT.
     EXIT.
*
  B100-OUTPUT-PROCEDURE SECTION.
  B100-OUTPUT.
     RETURN SORT-FILE
         AT END
         GO TO B100-EXIT.
     MOVE SORT-REC TO PRINT-REC.
     WRITE PRINT-REC.
     GO TO B100-OUTPUT.
*
  B100-EXIT.
     EXIT.
*
  C000-CLOSE-FILES SECTION.
     CLOSE PRINT-FILE.
     CLOSE IN-FILE.
```

The IDENTIFICATION DIVISION identifies the title and author of the program, and the date it was written and compiled.

The ENVIRONMENT DIVISION identifies the source and object computer that the program will execute on. Take another look at the FILE SECTION:

```
FILE-CONTROL.
     SELECT IN-FILE      ASSIGN TO INPUT1.
     SELECT PRINT-FILE   ASSIGN TO REPORT1.
     SELECT SORT-FILE    ASSIGN TO SORTWK01.
```

The input and output files are defined, in addition to a SORT-FILE. The definition of the sort file in the FILE-CONTROL section is required. It is traditional to name the sort file as follows:

```
SORTWKnn
```

where *nn* is a number.

The DATA DIVISION defines characteristics of each file. Take another look at the definition of the SORT-FILE:

```
SD SORT-FILE
     DATA RECORD IS SORT-REC.
```

Notice that SD is used, instead of FD. This is the required keyword for a sort file.

The PROCEDURE DIVISION opens the input and output files. Take another look at the following statements in the PROCEDURE DIVISION.

```
SORT SORT-FILE
   ON ASCENDING KEY SORT-ACCT
      INPUT PROCEDURE IS A100-INPUT-PROCEDURE
      OUTPUT PROCEDURE IS B100-OUTPUT-PROCEDURE.
```

The SORT keyword is used with the name of the sort file. The next statement specifies that the file is to be sorted in ascending order. INPUT PROCEDURE IS and OUTPUT PROCEDURE IS are sort statements that are required to implement the sort. We now direct your attention to the following statements in these procedures:

```
MOVE IN-REC TO SORT-REC.
RELEASE SORT-REC.
```

The input record is moved to the sort file record. The reserved word RELEASE transfers the contents of the record and places them in the sort file. These contents are now available for processing for the initial phase of the sort operation. Now take a look at this statement:

```
RETURN SORT-FILE
```

RETURN is a reserved word, that is followed by the sort file name. It must be coded, otherwise the program will not execute successfully. It transfers records after the final phase of the sort operation from the sort file to the output file.

After the file is sorted, the input and output files are closed, and the file is produced.

13.6 THE MERGE FUNCTION

The MERGE function combines one or more sorted input files into a single, ordered, sequential file. Merging is faster and more efficient, since the input files are already in sorted order before they are merged together.

The syntax of the MERGE command coded in the SORT utility is identical to the SORT command:

MERGE FIELDS=(start-location,length,merge-sequence,format)

start-location is the starting location in the record from where the merge is initiated. *length* is the number of bytes, from this start location, that are to be used as the merge criteria. *merge-sequence* specifies whether the file is to be merged in ascending or descending order. *format* specifies the format of the data that is being merged.

13.6.1 Rules for Coding

■ The record format of all input files that are being merged must be the same.

■ If the input files are composed of fixed length records, then the logical record length of these files must also be the same.

■ If the input files contain block sizes of different lengths, then those with larger block sizes should be placed before those with smaller block sizes.

■ The ddnames of the input files that are to be merged must begin with the letters SORTIN, followed by digit numbers. The digit number for all files that are to be merged must be in ascending order.

13.7 JCL TO IMPLEMENT MERGE UTILITY

We will present two examples of the MERGE utility. In the first example, three presorted files will be merged together into one. In the second example, the contents of each file would have to be interwoven, in order to produce the final sorted product.

Example 1

Assume that the following three files will be used as input files:

```
FILE1
111 C. KAPOOR
112 S. ZAMIR
113 J. KAPOOR

FILE2
114 R. ENGIRA
115 S. ENGIRA

FILE3
116 A. MAZOREK
117 S. CHAN
```

Here's the JCL that will merge these files together:

```
//JOB1      JOB  (A123),'J. CASH'
//STEP1     EXEC PGM=SORT
//SYSOUT    DD   SYSOUT=A
```

```
//SYSPRINT   DD      SYSOUT=A
//SORTIN01   DD      DSN=FILE1,DISP=SHR
//SORTIN02   DD      DSN=FILE2,DISP=SHR
//SORTIN03   DD      DSN=FILE3,DISP=SHR
//OUTFILE    DD      DSN=ADDRESS.BOOK,
//                   DISP=(NEW,CATLG,DELETE),
//                   UNIT=UNIT1,
//                   SPACE=(CYL,(2,1),RLSE),
//                   DCB=(RECFM=FB,
//                        LRECL=80,BLKSIZE=800)
//SYSIN       DD      *
  MERGE    FIELDS=(1,3,A,CH)
/*
//
```

In this example, the SORT program is executed. The SYSPRINT statement is used to specify that all output is to be directed to the line printer.

Next, the three data sets that will be part of the merge transaction are identified. These are FILE1, FILE2, and FILE3. All three files are shareable.

Next, the name of the output data file is specified. This file will be called ADDRESS.BOOK. It is a new file, and should be cataloged and saved after the successful execution of the job. The file will be created on UNIT1. Two cylinders of primary space will be allocated to it, plus secondary space. Any unused space should be released. The output file will contain fixed length records. The logical record length is specified as 80 blocks, and one block will contain 800 bytes.

The SYSIN statement specifies the nature of the merge to be implemented:

```
//SYSIN       DD      *
  MERGE    FIELDS=(1,3,A,CH)
/*
```

The files to be merged must be sorted starting at the first character, and end at the third. The files are to be merged in ascending order, and each file involved in the merge transaction contains EBCDIC character data.

The contents of ADDRESS.BOOK will look like this, after the successful execution of this job:

```
111  C.  KAPOOR
112  S.  ZAMIR
113  J.  KAPOOR
114  R.  ENGIRA
115  S.  ENGIRA
116  A.  MAZUREK
117  S.  CHAN
```

Example 2

Here's the three input files again.

File 1
```
111  C.  RANADE
116  A.  MAJUREK
118  S.  CHAN
```

File 2
```
113  JEEWAN KAPOOR
115  VINOD  KAPOOR
119  SABA  ZAMIR
```

File 3
```
112  NANCY  ROCKER
114  ANN  DOMINICI
117  HUBERT  DANIELY
```

The same JCL seen in example 1 is submitted. Here's the result:

```
111  C.  RANADE
112  NANCY  ROCKER
113  JEEWAN KAPOOR
114  ANN  DOMINICI
115  VINOD  KAPOOR
116  A.  MAJUREK
117  HUBERT  DANIELY
118  S.  CHAN
119  SABA  ZAMIR
```

13.8 ADDITIONAL CONTROL STATEMENTS ON THE SORT PROGRAM

Table 13.2 lists some additional control statements can be coded on the SYSIN statement when the SORT program is executed.

Table 13.2 Additional Statements on the SORT Program

Control Statement	Function
DEBUG	Used to debug the execution of the SORT program
END	Must be coded on the SYSIN statement, if input is to be discontinued before the actual end of a file
INCLUDE	Used to specify the inclusion of specific records only

ALTSEQ	Used to alter the collating sequence of EBCDIC characters, thereby altering the way the records will actually be sorted
INREC	Used to reformat records before they are processed by the SORT program
OUTREC	Used to specify the format of records before they are written
OPTION	Used to override installation-defined sorting defaults
SUM	Used to sum up equal control fields to produce a single output record, after sorting
OMIT	Used to exclude records from the sort

In this chapter we will be describing some of the more commonly used statements only. These are the INCLUDE and OMIT control statements.

13.9 THE INCLUDE STATEMENT

The INCLUDE statement is coded in the SORT program to select only specific records which meet specified criteria in the sort. Here's the syntax:

INCLUDE COND=(expression)

expression defines a logical relationship between fields in the input records. The general format of an expression looks like this:

fields,comparison,fields or constant

The format for *fields* looks like this:

(start_location,length,format)

As for the SORT command (see Section 13.4), *start_location* is the position from which *length* number of bytes will be used as the sort criteria. *format* specifies the type of data that will be sorted.

comparison can be one of the following:

EQ	Equal
NE	Not equal
GT	Greater than
GE	Greater than or equal to
LT	Less than
LE	Less than or equal to

The comparison can be used against another field, or it can be used against a constant. This can be a character, hexadecimal, or character constant. If a character constant is used, then it must be enclosd in single quotes, and preceded by the letter 'C'. If a hexadecimal constant is used, then it must also be enclosed in single quotes, and preceded by the letter 'X'. A decimal constant can be preceded by a negative sign.

13.9.1 An Example

```
//INCLUDE1   JOB    A123,'R ALPHONSO'
//STEP1      STEP   PGM=SORT
//SYSOUT     DD     SYSOUT=A
//SYSPRINT   DD     SYSOUT=A
//SORTIN     DD     DSN=ADDRESS.BOOK1,
//                  DISP=SHR
//SORTOUT    DD     DSN=ADDRESS.BOOK2,
//                  DISP=(NEW,CATLG,DELETE),
//                  UNIT=SYSDA,
//                  SPACE=(CYL,(2,1),RLSE),
//                  DCB=RECFM=FB,
//                      LRECL=80,BLKSIZE=800)
//SORTWK01   DD     UNIT=SYSDA,
//                  SPACE=(CYL,(20,10),RLSE)
//SORTWK02   DD     UNIT=SYSDA,
//                  SPACE=(CYL,(20,10),RLSE)
//SYSIN      DD     *
   INCLUDE COND=(2,5,CH,EQ,C'BATCH')
/*
//
```

In this example, the INCLUDE statement is used to specify that only those records which meet the specified criteria are to be included in the sort. The specified criteria are the following: Starting at byte number 2, pick up the next five bytes, and compare them to the character constant "BATCH." If there is a match between the fields selected, then include this record in the sort. If there is no match, do not include this record in the sort. The file to be sorted will contain EBCDIC character data (fourth subparameter, CH).

13.10 The OMIT Statement

The OMIT statement does the opposite of INCLUDE. If records meet the criterion specified, then they are omitted from the sort. The syntax of the OMIT is identical to that of the INCLUDE:

OMIT COND=(expression)

Please refer to the prior section for the syntax and meaning of *expression*.

13.10.1 An Example

```
//OMIT1      JOB    A123,'R ALPHONSO'
//STEP1      STEP   PGM=SORT
//SYSOUT     DD     SYSOUT=A
//SYSPRINT   DD     SYSOUT=A
//SORTIN     DD     DSN=ADDRESS.BOOK1,
//                  DISP=SHR
//SORTOUT    DD     DSN=ADDRESS.BOOK2,
//                  DISP=(NEW,CATLG,DELETE),
//                  UNIT=SYSDA,
//                  SPACE=(CYL,(2,1),RLSE),
//                  DCB=(RECFM=FB,
//                       LRECL=80,BLKSIZE=800)
//SORTWK01   DD     UNIT=SYSDA,
//                  SPACE=(CYL,(20,10),RLSE)
//SORTWK02   DD     UNIT=SYSDA,
//                  SPACE=(CYL,(20,10),RLSE)
//SYSIN      DD     *
   OMIT COND=(2,5,CH,EQ,C'BATCH')
/*
//
```

In this example, any records that contain the character constant "BATCH" in bytes 2 through 6 are omitted from the sort.

13.11 Things That Can Go Wrong

A general correspondence between some common errors and the error codes and messages that are generated from them are presented in Table 13.3. Either refer to the JCL error code, or scan through *Probable Cause of Error* to identify the cause of error in your JCL.

Table 13.3 Some Common Errors on SORT/MERGE Utility

JCL Error Code	Description	Probable Cause of Error
ICE027A	Field exceeds maximum record length	Specifying a sort length greater than the record length upon which the sort will be implemented

13.12 REVIEW

In this chapter we discussed the SORT/MERGE utility program called SORT. Input records are taken from an input file, rearranged, and placed in an output file. A sort can be executed from JCL as well as from a COBOL program. Table 13.4 summarizes some of the major features presented.

Table 13.4 The SORT/MERGE Utility

Parameter Coded on the SORT Utility	Description
SORT FIELDS= (start-location, length, sort-sequence, format)	SORT FIELDS are coded on the SYSIN statement of the SORT utility Input and output data set names must be coded on the DD statements Work files are also coded, in order to increase the efficiency of the sort
MERGE FIELDS= (start-location, length, sort-sequence, format)	MERGE FIELDS are coded on the SYSIN statement of the SORT utility Input files should be pre-sorted before they are merged together

INCLUDE COND=expression expression is coded as (fields,comparison,fields/constant) fields is coded as (start-location, length, format) comparison can be EQ, NE, GT, GE, LT, LE constant can be a character, hexadecimal or decimal constant	Used to specify records which are to be included in the sort If the expression evaluates to TRUE, the record is included in the sort If the expression evaluates to FALSE, the record is excluded in the sort
OMIT COND=expression expression is coded as (fields,comparison,fields/constant) fields is coded as (start-location, length, format) comparison can be EQ, NE, GT, GE, LT, LE constant can be a character, hexadecimal or decimal constant	Used to specify records which are to be excluded in the sort If the expression evaluates to TRUE, the record is excluded in the sort If the expression evaluates to FALSE, the record is included in the sort

14

Compile, Link Edit
and Run

14.1 INTRODUCTION

Before a program can be executed, it has to be compiled and linked.
Compilation of a program results in the creation of assembly language
code, which is further converted into machine language code. Machine
language is not the kind of language that you or I can readily understand!
However, this is the only language that a computer knows how to
execute, resulting in its being able to implement the complex tasks that
we assign to it.

This chapter will describe the utilities used to compile and link a
program. Once the program has been compiled and linked (in IBM
terms, link-edited), then the JCL required to execute a program may be
submitted.

14.2 THE LIFE CYCLE OF A PROGRAM

Before we get into the JCL that compiles and link-edits a program, it is
important that you understand the different stages that a program
(whether it be written in COBOL or some other language) goes through
before it becomes an executable module. The various stages are:

- Creation of source code

    In an IBM mainframe environment, a COBOL program is typed at the
terminal using the ISPF editor, and is usually stored as a member of a
partitioned data set. This is called source code.

Once the program has been saved, the next step is its compilation. This is done through a compiler.

- Compilation of source code to create object code

A compiler is a language translator. Many programming languages have their own compiler, and usually several versions exist. The compiler takes the source code program and translates it into relocatable object code. It also supplies the instructions necessary to debug a program, if the program is compiled with the debug option. Relocatable object code also contains machine language instructions which the linker understands. Processing is now transferred to the linkage-editor.

- Link-edit object code to create executable code

The linkage-editor combines the relocatable object code of the source file with the relocatable object code of any pre-compiled subroutines or external procedures that the program may reference. The linkage editor produces the final version of the program that is now in a format that is comprehensible to the computer; this is called executable code.

14.3 CREATION OF SOURCE CODE

In an IBM mainframe environment, the ISPF editor is used to create a data set and store it as a member of a partitioned data set. At most installations, COBOL programs are stored in a library of their own. How to access the ISPF editor was described in Chapter 2. Please refer to this chapter again if you need to refresh your memory about the ISPF editor.

14.4 THE IKFCBL00 COMPILER PROGRAM

The compiler program called IKFCBL00 is executed to compile the COBOL source code. Several options can be specified to this program via the PARM parameter.

14.4.1 Rules for Coding

- A DD statement called SYSLIN must always be coded. The SYSLIN statement is used to indicate the name of the temporary data set that is created by the compiler before it is passed on to the link-edit program.

- A DD statement called SYSLIB must also be coded if precompiled subroutines are referenced by the program that is being compiled. The SYSLIB statement specifies the name of the library containing the object code of the called subroutines. The name of this library is often installation defined.

14.4.2 Some Common Compiler Specifications

Some common specifications that can be coded are:

- Ensure that all lines in the COBOL source code file are numbered in sequence.

- Load subroutines called by the program at the time that the program is executed, instead of when it is compiled.

- Automatically open the data sets and libraries that are referenced in the //SYSLIB statement.

- Produce a sorted cross-reference listing of all data items in the program.

- Produce a condensed listing of the machine language generated upon successful execution of the compilation. This condensed listing will help identify the location of machine language instructions.

14.4.3 Subparameters Coded on the PARM Parameter

Table 14.1 lists the PARM subparameter that conveys the information listed in the prior section.

Table 14.1 Compiler Options for IKFCBL00 Program

Function	Corresponding JCL subparameter
Check line sequence in COBOL source code	SEQ checks line sequence NOSEQ ignores sequence checking

Load submodules dynamically	DYN loads called submodules dynamically This results in a smaller load module file NODYN loads submodules at compile time This is the default
Automatically open data sets referenced in //SYSLIB statement	LIB specifies that all data sets referenced in //SYSLIB should be opened automatically NOLIB specifies the opposite. All data sets must be opened via the JCL submitted NOLIB is the default
Produce sorted cross-reference	XREF produces a sorted cross-reference No cross-reference is the default
Produce condensed listing of machine language object code	CLI produces this listing No listing is produced, if CLI is not coded

14.4.4 JCL that Compiles a Program

The following is the JCL that compiles a COBOL program:

```
//COMPILE1    JOB    (A123),'D. RITCHIE'
//STEP1       EXEC   PGM=IKFCBLOO,
//                   PARM=('NOSEQ,DYN,LIB,XREF,CLI')
//SYSPRINT    DD     SYSOUT=A
//SYSLIB      DD     DSN=COMMON.LIBRARY,
//                   DISP=SHR
//SYSLIN      DD     DSN=&&LOADFILE,
//                   DISP=(NEW,PASS,DELETE),
```

```
//                      UNIT=UNIT1,
//                      SPACE=(CYL,(1,1))
//SYSIN        DD       DSN=PRIVATE.LIBRARY(PROGRAM1),
//                      DISP=SHR
//SYSUT1       DD       SPACE=(CYL(1,1)),UNIT=SYSDA
//SYSUT2       DD       SPACE=(CYL(1,1)),UNIT=SYSDA
//SYSUT3       DD       SPACE=(CYL(1,1)),UNIT=SYSDA
//SYSUT4       DD       SPACE=(CYL(1,1)),UNIT=SYSDA
//
```

D. Ritchie submits a job called COMPILE1. The compiler program IKFCBL00 is executed. The PARM parameter is used to specify that the compiler should *NO*t check the line *SEQ*uence in the source code file, it should *DYN*amically load all subroutines called by the program at execution time, and it should automatically open all *LIB*raries referenced in the SYSLIB statement; it should also produce a sorted cross reference (*XREF*) listing of all data items in the program, and produce a *C*ondensed *LI*sting of the machine language generated for the program.

Next, the SYSPRINT statement specifies that all output generated by the run is to be directed to the line printer.

Next, we see the SYSLIB and SYSLIN statements.

```
//SYSLIB       DD       DSN=COMMON.LIBRARY,
//                      DISP=SHR
//SYSLIN       DD       DSN=&&LOADFILE,
//                      DISP=(NEW,PASS,DELETE),
//                      UNIT=UNIT1,
//                      SPACE=(CYL,(1,1))
```

The SYSLIB statement identifies the name of the library or libraries that contain the object code for the subroutines that are called by the program. This library is called COMMON.LIBRARY.

The SYSLIN statement identifies the name of the temporary file that is created after the successful compilation of the program; it is then passed on to the link-edit program for further processing. The name of this file is LOADFILE. Notice the two ampersands that precede its name, indicating that this is a temporary file.

The characteristics of this file are also specified within the same statement. This will be a new file, that will be passed on to the next step, and it is to be deleted upon unsuccessful execution of the job. The file will reside on UNIT1, and it is assigned a primary space of one cylinder, and a secondary space of the same size.

To follow is the name of the program to be compiled:

```
//SYSIN        DD       DSN=PRIVATE.LIBRARY(PROGRAM1),
//                      DISP=SHR
```

This program is called PROGRAM1 and it exists as a member of the partitioned data set called PRIVATE.LIBRARY.

The next four statements specify the space allocation for the work files that will be used by the compiler as it executes, and the unit on which they will be created:

```
//SYSUT1     DD     SPACE=(CYL(1,1)),UNIT=UNIT1
//SYSUT2     DD     SPACE=(CYL(1,1)),UNIT=UNIT1
//SYSUT3     DD     SPACE=(CYL(1,1)),UNIT=UNIT1
//SYSUT4     DD     SPACE=(CYL(1,1)),UNIT=UNIT1
```

We now present a discussion on the steps required to link-edit a compiled program.

14.5 THE LINKAGE EDITOR PROGRAM

The linkage editor program takes the object code passed to it from the compiler, includes the object code of any subroutines or subprograms called by the program, and creates a load module. The load module is what is called executable code. The IEWL program is executed to implement these functions.

14.5.1 Rules for Coding

- A DD statement called SYSLIN must always be coded. The SYSLIN statement is used to indicate the name of the temporary data set which contains the object module created by the compiler.

- A DD statement called SYSLIB must also be coded if precompiled subroutines are referenced by the program that is being compiled. The SYSLIB statement specifies the name of the library containing the object code of the called subroutines. The name of this library is often installation defined.

- A DD statement called SYSLMOD must be coded. This statement will define the name of the data set that will contain the load module produces by the link-edit program.

- A DD statement (traditionally called SYSUT1), which defines the characteristics of the work file (or scratch data set, as it is commonly called) that will be used by the link-edit program as it executes, must be coded.

14.5.2 Some Common Linkage Editor Specifications

Some common specifications for the linkage editor are:

■ Produce a cross-reference listing of the load module.

■ Produce a listing of the control statements produced by the linkage editor.

■ Produce an executable file, even if minor errors are encountered in the link-edit process.

■ Use 24 or 31 bit addressing.

At this level, it is not necessary for you to understand the differences between these two types of specifications. Check with your installation as to which standard you should use.

■ Print all messages that are directed to the output device.

14.5.3 Subparameters Coded on the PARM Parameter

Table 14.2 lists the options that can be coded on the PARM parameter to convey the information listed in the prior section.

Table 14.2 Options for IEWL Program

Function	Corresponding JCL subparameter
Produce cross reference of load module	XREF
Produce listing of control statements used by linkage editor	LIST produces this listing The default is NOLIST
Create executable code despite minor errors	LET The default is NOLET

Specify type of addressing	AMODE=nn where nn is the number specifying the type of addressing (24 or 31 bit) AMODE=ANY specifies both 24 and 31 bit addressing
Print output messages to specified device	PRINT specifies that all messages be printed to output device NOPRINT is the default
Produce condensed listing of machine language object code	CLI produces this listing No listing is produced, if CLI is not coded

14.6 JCL THAT LINK-EDITS OBJECT CODE

The following is the JCL that link-edits the object code produced by the compiler. Please keep in mind that the statements below are a continuation of the job submitted to the compiler program. And just so that you can see the relationships between the two, (without having to flip through a lot of pages), we re-display the compile portion of the JCL:

```
//COMPILE1   JOB    (A123),'D. RITCHIE'
//STEP1      EXEC   PGM=IKFCBLOO,
//                  PARM=('NOSEQ,DYN,LIB,SRX,CLI')
//SYSPRINT   DD     SYSOUT=A
//SYSLIB     DD     DSN=COMMON.LIBRARY,
//                  DISP=SHR
//SYSLIN     DD     DSN=&&LOADFILE,
//                  DISP=(NEW,PASS,DELETE),
//                  UNIT=UNIT1,
//                  SPACE=(CYL,(1,1))
//SYSIN      DD     DSN=PRIVATE.LIBRARY(PROGRAM1),
//                  DISP=SHR
//SYSUT1     DD     SPACE=(CYL(1,1)),UNIT=SYSDA
//SYSUT2     DD     SPACE=(CYL(1,1)),UNIT=SYSDA
//SYSUT3     DD     SPACE=(CYL(1,1)),UNIT=SYSDA
//SYSUT4     DD     SPACE=(CYL(1,1)),UNIT=SYSDA
```

and here's the link-edit portion:

```
//LINK1   EXEC PGM=IEWL,
//             PARM=
//             ('XREF,LIST,LET,AMODE=ANY,PRINT'),
//             COND=(5,LT,10B)
//SYSLIB DD   DSN=COMMON.LIBRARY,
//             DISP=SHR
//SYSLIN DD   DSN=&&LOADFILE,
//             DISP=(OLD,DELETE)
//SYSLMOD DD  DSN=COMMON.LOADLIB(PROGRAM1),
//             DISP=SHR
//SYSUT1  DD   SPACE=(CYL,(1,1)),UNIT=SYSDA
//
```

LINK1 executes the linkage editor program IEWL.

Next, we see the SYSLIB and SYSLIN statements.

The SYSLIB statement identifies the name of the library or libraries that contain the object code for the subroutines that are called by the program. This library is called COMMON.LIBRARY.

The SYSLIN statement identifies the name of the temporary file that is being passed to it by the compiler. The name of this file is LOADFILE. This time the disposition of LOADFILE is specified as old, and it is to be deleted upon successful execution of the job.

The SYSLMOD statement is next. This DD statement identifies the location where the load module will be kept. In our example this is COMMON.LOADLIB.

Finally, the SYSUT1 statement specifies characteristics of the scratch data set.

14.7 Executing the Program

And now, the JCL that will execute the program, after it has been compiled and link-edited.

Let's assume that this program is using one input file and producing one output file. The following JCL segment can be used to execute the program:

```
//EXEC1     JOB  (A123),'D. RITCHIE',
//               CLASS=0,MSGCLASS=L
//STEP1     EXEC PGM=PROGRAM1
//STEPLIB   DD   DSN=COMMON.LOADLIB,
//               DISP=SHR
//SYSPRINT  DD   SYSOUT=A
//INFILE1   DD   DSN=FILE1.IN,
//               DISP=SHR
//OUTFILE1  DD   DSN=FILE1.OUT,
```

```
//                    DISP=(NEW,CATLG,DELETE),
//                    UNIT=UNIT1,
//                    SPACE=(CYL,(1,1),RLSE),
//                    DCB=(RECFM=FB,
//                        BLKSIZE=800,LRECL=80)
//
```

In this example, EXEC1 is submitted. The JCL should be self-explanatory by now. Please note the STEPLIB statement. Recall that the STEPLIB statement provides an alternative to JOBLIB, and is used to specify the library in which the program being executed resides. In our example, the program resides in COMMON.LOADLIB.

14.8 THINGS THAT CAN GO WRONG

Once again, we present a general correspondence between some common errors and the error codes and messages that are generated from it. Either refer to the JCL error code, or scan through *Probable Cause of Error*, to identify the cause of the error in your JCL.

Table 14.3 Some Common Errors on IKFCBL00 and IEWL

JCL Error Code	Description	Probable Cause of Error
IEC130I	SYSLMOD DD statement missing	SYSLMOD DD statement is not specified
IEC130I	SYSUT2 DD statement missing	Executing IKFCBL00 without specifying work files Similar messages will be output for SYSUT3, SYSUT4, and so on

14.9 REVIEW

In this chapter we described the utilities used to compile, link and execute a program. Specifically, the IKFCBL00 and IEWL programs were discussed. Then, the JCL required to execute the final executable code derived from these two utilities was presented. Table 14.3 summarizes the major features of each of these utilities.

Table 14.4 Compile and Link-Edit Utilities

Utility/Parameter Name	Description
IEKCBL00 program	This utility compiles the COBOL source code SYSLIN is required. It is used to specify the name of the interim (temporary) file created by the compiler, before it is passed on to the loader
PARM	Coded on the EXEC statement for this program Used to specify compiler specific options
IEWL program	This utility loads the object code produced by the compiler SYSLIN is required. This contains the name of the data set sent to it from the compiler
PARM	Coded on the EXEC statement for this program Used to specify linkage-editor specific options

VSAM, JES2 and JES3, and SMS

15

VSAM
Basics

15.1 INTRODUCTION

VSAM stands for *Virtual Storage Access Method*. As the name implies, it is a method by which different types of data sets can be accessed quickly and efficiently. It is used in OS/VS and DOS/VS operating systems.

Chapter 15 is the first of four chapters that are devoted to an explanation of VSAM. In this chapter we will explain some basic concepts related to VSAM. In Chapter 16 you will learn how to define VSAM data sets, and load and print records from them. Chapter 17 will describe the concept of the alternate index. Chapter 18 will define some additional commands in VSAM which are helpful in processing data. You should have a fairly good understanding of VSAM by the time you conclude Part III of this book.

15.2 VSAM, AN OVERVIEW

VSAM is a high performance access method used in OS/VS and DOS/VS operating systems. It is used to organize, store, catalog, retrieve and delete data sets. It is superior to other access methods. This will become apparent in our section titled Advantages of VSAM.

In order for an access method to work, the following must exist:

- Data
  In an IBM mainframe environment, this is called a data set.

■ A method for getting to the data

VSAM provides a superior mode of access to its data sets by virtue of the way it organizes its data, and by supplying a program called AMS (*Access Method Services*), which provides utilities that can efficiently manipulate this data. Therefore, in order to understand VSAM, first, you need to see how data is organized in VSAM data sets; second, you need to understand how to use the utility (specifically the IDCAMS utility) that are available in AMS; and third, you need to know how to use this power to your advantage through a language like COBOL.   In this chapter we give a brief overview of the first two items.   But first, take a look at the advantages that VSAM provides over other access methods.

15.3 ADVANTAGES OF VSAM

VSAM provides superior access to data, when compared to other access methods, in the following ways:

■ Data can be accessed faster, because of the way VSAM data sets are organized.

■ Records can be inserted in a more efficient manner; there is less reorganization of data required after each insertion.

■ Deletion of records results in them being physically removed from the disk (instead of being logically removed).   Thus, free space is more easily available.

■ Records can be accessed sequentially or randomly.

■ VSAM data sets are device independent; thus, VSAM data sets and catalogs can be easily transported between operating systems.

■ The JCL required to access VSAM data sets is much simpler than the JCL for other file structures.

15.4 DISADVANTAGES OF VSAM

■ VSAM data sets require more storage space than other types of data sets; this is because VSAM data sets carry control information in them, in addition to the actual data that they are comprised of.

- VSAM data sets require additional storage due to the free space that must be embedded in them. This free space results in more efficient management of the data contained in them, when records are added, deleted, or changed.

We continue our discussion on the organization of data in VSAM data sets.

15.5 DATA ORGANIZATION OF VSAM DATA SETS

In Parts 1 and 2 of this book, you were exposed to the JCL required to manipulate data sets. For instance, you learned, among other things, how to create, catalog, access, delete, and uncatalog datasets. The organization of the data within the data sets was not stressed since it was not applicable. As we shift our emphasis to VSAM, the organization of data within these files becomes significant. In fact, it is this very feature of the data sets (appropriately called VSAM data sets, or *clusters*), that results in VSAM being the powerful access tool that it is.

VSAM supports four types of file organizations:

- *Key Sequenced Data Sets* (KSDS)

- *Entry Sequenced Data Sets* (ESDS)

- *Relative Record Data Sets* (RRDS)

- *Linear Data Sets* (LDS)

The efficiency with which data is accessed from these four different types of data sets is directly related to the way they are organized.

15.6 KEY SEQUENCED DATA SETS (KSDS)

KSDS data records are organized by a unique key field. KSDS records can be accessed randomly, given that you know the value of its key field. Accessing a KSDS record via the key field is analogous to searching for a topic in a book with the help of an index; the topic is the record, and the entry in the index is the key field. KSDS records can also be retrieved sequentially, and by relative byte address. The concept of a relative byte address will be explained later on in this chapter.

15.6.1 Organization of Data

KSDS data sets consist of two parts. The first part contains information relating to the index component. The index component contains an entry with the key field and a pointer to the location of its corresponding record. The second part contains the data component. The data component contains the individual records belonging to that data set, in addition to the key field. The key field must be unique. KSDS data sets can include an alternate index in addition to the primary index just described. The alternate index need not be unique. KSDS records contain embedded free space and can be of a fixed or variable length.

15.6.2 Other Features

KSDS records are inserted in ascending order of the prime key field. When they are deleted, they are physically removed from the device, resulting in space being freed up for other insertions.

15.7 ENTRY SEQUENCED DATA SETS (ESDS)

ESDS data sets are sequenced in the order in which they are inserted. They can be thought of as sequential files. They can be accessed randomly or sequentially.

15.7.1 Organization of Data

ESDS records contain a data component only, and do not have a prime key index component. They can have an alternate index component. They do not have embedded free space. Records can be of a fixed or variable length.

15.7.2 Other Features

ESDS records are always added at the end of the data set. On a deletion, they continue to reside on the disk that they were originally stored, and are not physically removed. This is why multiple deletes of records in an ESDS can result in wasted space.

15.8 Relative Record Data Sets (RRDS)

An RRDS data set consists of fixed length slots. Records are accessed by their position in the file relative to the first slot. The relative position of each slot is called the *Relative Record Number* (*RRN*). RRDS records can be retrieved randomly by RRN, or sequentially. They are always of a fixed length.

15.8.1 Organization of Data

RRDS data sets contain a data component only. There is no index component. This may very well be due to the fact that there is no need to reorganize them, since the relative location of records contained therein never changes. There are no alternate indexes either.

15.8.2 Other Features

RRDS records may be retrieved, inserted, updated, and deleted randomly or sequentially. On a deletion, the record is removed from its slot, but the slot continues to exist, for subsequent insertions. RRDS records are device-independent.

15.8.3 Linear Data Sets

An LDS data set is similar to ESDS in terms of organization. It is used by DB2, which is IBM's primary relational database management system. LDS data sets contain a data component only.

15.9 Internal Organization of VSAM Data Sets

In this section we explain the internal organization of data inside VSAM data sets. The terminology used for referencing the internal organization of KSDS, ESDS, RRDS, or LDS files is a little different from that of regular data sets. The following terms will be described next.

- *Control Interval* (*CI*)

- *Control Area* (*CA*)

- Free space, as it exists in CIs and CAs.

15.9.1 Control Interval (CI)

The data sets that we have discussed in the prior chapters of this book contains records which are stored in blocks. VSAM data sets are not stored in blocks, in the traditional sense. Instead, they are stored in Control Intervals. A control interval has four components:

- Data

   This contains of the actual data that is processed by a program.

- *Control Interval Description Field (CIDF)*

   This contains information about the free space within the CI. Free space is explained after RDF.

- *Record Description Field (RDF)*

   This contains information about the records within the data space, i.e., whether they are of a fixed length, a variable length, or spanned. This field is three bytes long. A CI can contain one or more RDF's, this depends on whether the records are of a fixed length, a variable length, or spanned. (The concept of spanned records will be explained shortly).

- Free space

   Free space is exactly what its name implies, space that is available to be used as necessary. This free space is used for the internal re-organization of KSDS data records, when records are added, deleted, or updated within CI's.

   Figure 15.1 illustrates the components of a Control Interval.

Data (can consist of multiple records)	Free Space	RDF (can be one or more)	CIDF (four bytes long)

Figure 15.1 Components of a CI

15.9.2 Control Area

A *Control Area* (CA) is a collection of control intervals. One CA must contain at least two CIs. A CA must be at least one track long. The maximum size that it can occupy is one cylinder.

15.9.3 Free Space, as it relates to CIs and CAs

Free space can exist in VSAM data records in three places:

- Free space can exist between CIs. This free space is used when new records are added to the data set, given that the record can fit in that space.

- Free space can exist within a CA. This space is used when new records added to the data set cannot fit between the CIs that exist on it.

- An entire CA can consist of free space. This is the space that is available for insertion of new records when all of the CIs in a particular CA have been used up, and new records cannot be accommodated in them.

15.9.4 Free Space in VSAM Data Sets

KSDS files can have embedded free space in the three areas listed in Section 15.9.3. ESDS files can have free space only at the end of the data set. RRDS files have no free space, since the entire file consists of fixed length slots. The slots can be empty, if records have been deleted from them, but this is not the same thing as free space. LDS files can have free space at the end of the data set; in this respect they are similar to ESDS files.

15.10 How VSAM Fits into this Schema

Now that you have a very basic understanding of the internal organization of VSAM data sets, you should be able to understand why access of these data sets is quicker and more efficient than other types.

When a VSAM data set is updated, it is automatically reorganized, utilizing the free space just described. If a record is added, it is inserted in the appropriate location in the Control Interval. All records subsequent to it are moved down, thereby reducing the amount of available free space at the end of it. If a record is deleted, all records subsequent to it are moved up, thereby increasing the total amount of free space available within it. All pointers referencing the updated data set are also updated at the same time. Management of free space is handled by the VSAM software, and is transparent to the application program.

Figure 15.2 illustrates the internal organization of VSAM data sets.

Control Area1	Record 1	Record 2	Free Space in CI	RDF (3 bytes)	CIDF (4 bytes)
	Record 3		Free Space in CI	RDF	CIDF
Control Area2	Control Interval			RDF	CIDF
Control Area3	Control Interval			RDF	CIDF

Figure 15.2 Sample Organization of Data in a VSAM Data Set

As you take another look at Figure 15.2, notice that in our sample file there are three Control Areas (Control Area1, Control Area2, and Control Area3). Control Area1 contains three records. Records 1 and 2 are stored in the first CI. The RDF and CIDF (*Record Description Field* and *Control Description Field*) follow the CI. Record 3 is located in the second CI, in Control Area1. This record is larger than records 1 and 2, perhaps too large to be stored in the free space in the first CI. Hence, it is stored in the next one.

Control Areas 2 and 3 contain CIs with no records in them, and are available for insertion of new records.

15.11 ACCESSING VSAM DATA SETS

VSAM data sets can be accessed in any of the following ways:

■ Through the index or key of the data set, if one exists

This is the most popular mode of access and involves searching for a record based on its key field. The index component of a data set is searched for a match, and then its corresponding Control Area. KSDS records can be searched by the prime or alternate key. ESDS records can be searched by their alternate key.

■ Through the *Relative Record Number* (RRN)

RRDS records only can be accessed by a relative record number. KSDS and ESDS records do not have a relative record number. This kind of access is very fast, since the RRN is fixed for each slot.

- Through *Relative Byte Address* (RBA)

All VSAM data set organizations are device-independent, therefore they can be easily transferred from one device to another. All addresses are counted relative to the first record in the data set (which is byte 0, not byte 1). Hence, it is a relatively simple matter to access VSAM data sets via the relative byte address. KSDS and ESDS records can be accessed through an RBA.

Relative byte address access is faster than access through an index field. At the same time, it can be dangerous, since the RBA could have been altered through a Control Interval/Control Area split, and therefore should be avoided. Control Interval and Control Area splits are discussed next.

15.12 CONTROL INTERVAL AND CONTROL AREA SPLITS

CI and CA splits occur in KSDS files only. These splits occur as a result of record insertions, and are a result of the structure of these files. A CI split occurs under the following circumstances.

Assume that a new record has to be added to a KSDS file. The system first locates where the record is to be inserted in the file, and then tries to find enough free space in the appropriate CI for that record. If the new record requires more space than is available in the free space area, then the system tries to locate a free CI within the same CA, to store that record. If one is found, then approximately half of the records from the current CI are moved to the available CI. This is called a Control Interval Split. The new record is then placed in the space now made available.

A Control Area split occurs if no free CIs are found within that CA. When this happens, the system attempts to find a free CA. Once space is found, it moves approximately half the records from the existing CA to the new one, and then stores the new record in its appropriate place. This action results in increased space for the original CA, in addition to the space that will be available in the new CA. This kind of reorganization of VSAM data sets is automatically implemented by the system, and is transparent to the users.

15.13 OTHER FEATURES OF VSAM DATA SETS

- VSAM data sets can contain *spanned records*.

A spanned record is created when its size is larger than the available CI size (minus seven bytes, which is utilized by the system). Since it is larger, it needs to be stored in more than one CI; therefore, it *spans* two or more CIs.

- VSAM data sets must be *cataloged*.

VSAM data sets can be cataloged either in the VSAM catalog, or in the ICF (*Integrated Catalog Facility*) catalog.

In an MVS operating system, there is always one master catalog. VSAM, non-VSAM, and user catalogs are created within the master catalog. Usually, there are multiple user catalogs in a master catalog.

User defined data sets can be cataloged either in the VSAM master catalog (not a good practice, not recommended, and rarely used for cataloging data sets), or in user catalogs. Most user-defined data sets are cataloged in user catalogs.

ICF catalogs are an enhancement of the VSAM catalog structure. ICF catalogs offer improved cataloging and recover facilties for data sets, as well as for the catalogs themselves. ICF user catalogs can reside in an ICF master catalog.

- VSAM data sets must reside in space specifically allocated for VSAM data sets.

Often, one or more volumes are allocated to VSAM data sets. This space is called VSAM data space.

- VSAM data sets must reside on direct access volumes.

15.14 ACCESS METHOD SERVICES (AMS)

The AMS program is briefly overviewed in this section. It is described in greater detail in Chapter 16.

Access Method Services is a powerful service program. It is used to perform various functions on VSAM and non-VSAM data sets. AMS utilizes the IDCAMS utility to implement these functions. You have encountered the IDCAMS utility previously in this book. As you will recall, this utility is executed in a JCL job, just like any other IBM-supplied program.

IDCAMS executes various functional commands which are coded on the SYSIN DD statement, or through an input stream. Functional commands can be continued on to the next line via the hyphen (you have encountered the use of the hyphen in previous chapters in this book). The hyphen should be omitted on the last line of a functional command. Multiple functional commands can be executed in the same AMS job step. Multiple AMS job steps can exist within a job.

15.15 SOME COMMON ERRORS

In this section we will give a brief overview of some of the common mistakes that can be made in coding AMS commands. Most of the error messages generated will be prefixed by "IDC;" this indicates that they are AMS or VSAM messages.

Generally speaking, most errors are generated either due to syntax mistakes, or incorrect specifications on parameters. Some of the more common errors are listed below.

- A command or keyword is misspelled

- A positional parameter is not coded in its correct position

- A keyword parameter is coded before a positional parameter

- A command is continued on the next line, without coding a hyphen as the last character

- A hyphen is inserted at the end of a line, even though it is the last line of a command

- Omitting or mismatching parentheses

- Not coding all of the required parameters for a command

- Coding one or more mutually exclusive parameters within the same command

- Specifying the incorrect location of data sets accessed in the job

- Allocating data sets on disks or devices not owned by the user

- Not allocating enough space for a data set

- Defining alternate indexes on non-existent base clusters

15.16 REVIEW

In this chapter we introduced you to VSAM. VSAM supports four types of files:

- Key Sequenced Data Sets (KSDS)

- Entry Sequenced Data Sets (ESDS)

- Relative Record Data Sets (RRDS)

- Linear Data Sets (LDS)

These data sets differ from each other in the way they store data. KSDS records are oganized by a unique key field, and contain a data and index component. ESDS records are sequential and contain a data component only. RRDS records consist of fixed length slots. Each record is relative to the next. LDS is similar to ESDS in terms of organization.

We also discussed the internal organization of VSAM data sets, and learned about terms such as CIs, CAs, free space, and CI splits and CA splits. Finally, we gave a brief overview of the AMS program, and deferred a more detailed description of AMS for the next chapter.

Access Method
Services

16.1 INTRODUCTION

You were briefly introduced to the program called Access Method
Services in Chapter 15. In this chapter we will describe how this
program is used to allocate, process, and print different types of data sets.

16.2 THE IDCAMS UTILITY

The IDCAMS utility is the primary vehicle used by the AMS program to
process VSAM and non-VSAM data sets. You have encountered the use
of this utility several times previously in this book. It is executed just
like any other IBM utility, and the EXEC statement is used to execute
IDCAMS in a job step.

    The commands coded in this utility, regardless of the specific function
that is being implemented, follow the same general pattern. The pseudo-
code required to execute this utility is presented.

```
//jobname    JOB  (accounting-information),
//                'programmer-name'
//stepname   EXEC PGM=IDCAMS
//SYSPRINT   DD   SYSOUT=A
//SYSIN      DD   *
            functional-commands
/*
//
```

As always, the JOB statement is the first statement. Next comes the EXEC statement, which executes the IDCAMS utility. Following this is the SYSPRINT statement, which specifies the output device. Traditionally, SYSOUT=A identifies the line printer. Next, the SYSIN statement is used to input the commands that are to be implemented by the IDCAMS utility.

The following rules apply to coding functional commands for the IDCAMS utility:

- Positional parameters must precede keyword parameters.

- Commands may be continued to the next line (if they don't fit on one line), by coding a hyphen as the last character in the line.

- Comments can be included by coding them between a /* and */. The /* can be coded in any column after column 1.

- Multiple commands can be coded within one job step. However, each command must begin on a new line.

16.3 FUNCTIONS CODED ON IDCAMS UTILITY

The IDCAMS utility can be executed for the following functions on VSAM data sets:

- Define them.

- Load records into them.

- Print them.

The remainder of this chapter describes each one of these functions for the different types of VSAM datasets.

16.4 DEFINING VSAM DATA SETS, AN OVERVIEW

The following items must be addressed when a data set is to be defined:

- The name of the data set

- The name of the volume on which it will be allocated

- The amount of space that is to be allocated to it

- The size of the Control Interval for the data component of the file

- The amount of free space within each Control Interval, and the amount of utilization of each Control Interval

- The size of its key, if it has a key. The location of the key field within each record also has to be specified

- The type of data set

- Its record type

- The name of its data component

- The name of its index component, if it has an index

- The size of the control interval of the index component of data sets with an index

- The name of the VSAM or ICF catalog in which it will be recorded

16.5 CORRESPONDING JCL

Table 16.1 lists the AMS commands, parameters and/or subparameters that are coded for the IDCAMS utility to convey this information.

Table 16.1 AMS Parameters Used to Define VSAM Dataset

Function	Corresponding AMS Commands, Parameters and Subparameters
Define data set	DEFINE CLUSTER
Specification of the name and the type of data set	NAME(name.type) name identifies the data set (cluster) and is a positional parameter name.type can be any data set name

Specification of volume for its storage	VOLUMES(volume-no) CYLINDERS(primary,secondary) volume-no is the serial number of the volume on which the data set will be created
Specification of the size of the Control Intervals for the data component of the file	CONTROLINTERVALSIZE (number-of-bytes) coded on the NAME statement for the cluster
Specification of free space between Control Intervals and within Control Areas	FREESPACE (percent1, percent2) percent1 specifies the percentage of space that must be left free within each control interval percent2 specifies the percentage of unused control intervals that will be maintained in a control area
Size of key if it exists for this particular type of data set	KEYS(n1,n2) n1 is length of key in bytes n2 is starting byte position of key in a record
Specification of record type and size Record type can be fixed or variable	RECORDSIZE(n1,n2) n1 specifies the average record length n2 specifies the maximum record length If both average and maximum record lengths are equal, the implication is that it is a fixed length record Otherwise, it is a variable length record
Specification of name for data component of file	DATA(NAME(data-name))
Specification of name for index component of file	INDEX(NAME(index-name))

Specification of size of Control Interval for index component of the file	CONTROLINTERVALSIZE (number-of-bytes) coded on the NAME statement for the index

16.6 Defining a KSDS Data Set

The following is the JCL that will define a KSDS dataset.

```
//KSDS1       JOB   (A123),'M. ALI'
//STEP1       EXEC  PGM=IDCAMS
//SYSPRINT    DD    SYSOUT=A
//SYSIN       DD    *
    DEFINE CLUSTER                              -
    (                                           -
    NAME(VSAM1.KSDS.CLUSTER)                    -
    VOLUMES(CICT00)                             -
    CYLINDERS(3,1)                              -
    CONTROLINTERVALSIZE(4096)                   -
    FREESPACE(10,20)                            -
    KEYS(5,1)                                   -
    RECORDSIZE(80,80)                           -
    )                                           -
    DATA                                        -
    (                                           -
    NAME(VSAM1.KSDS.DATA)                       -
    )                                           -
    INDEX                                       -
    (                                           -
    NAME(VSAM1.KSDS.INDEX)                      -
    CONTROLINTERVALSIZE(2048)                   -
    )                                           -
    CATALOG(VSAM.USER.PRIVATE)
/*
//
```

In this example, the IDCAMS program is executed in STEP1 and output is directed to the line printer in the SYSPRINT statement.

Next, the SYSIN statement is used to specify input to the IDCAMS utility. The following statements define the cluster (a cluster is a VSAM data set) being created:

```
    DEFINE CLUSTER                              -
    (                                           -
    NAME(VSAM1.KSDS.CLUSTER)                    -
    VOLUMES(CICT00)                             -
    CYLINDERS(3,1)                              -
    CONTROLINTERVALSIZE(4096)                   -
    FREESPACE(10,20)                            -
    KEYS(5,1)                                   -
```

```
RECORDSIZE(80,100)                          -
)                                           -
```

The DEFINE CLUSTER statement is the control statement that allocates the data set. Following the DEFINE CLUSTER statement is an opening parenthesis. All commands between the opening and closing parentheses relate to the cluster being defined.

The name of the VSAM data set is VSAM1.KSDS.CLUSTER. It will be created on the volume identified as CICT00. Three cylinders of primary space and one cylinder of secondary space will be allocated to it. The size of the Control Interval of this cluster will be 4096 bytes. 10% of each CI will be retained as free space. Meanwhile, 20% of all CIs within a Control Area will be left unused. The primary key of this KSDS will be five bytes long, starting at byte location 1 of each record. (Byte counts start at byte 0, hence, this will be the second byte in the record). Finally, the RECORDSIZE parameter specifies that the average length of the record is 80 bytes, while the maximum length of a record that can exist is 100 bytes. Since the two lengths are different, we can assume that this data set will consist of variable length records.

Next come the IDCAMS parameters that define the features of the data component of the cluster:

```
DATA                                        -
(                                           -
NAME(VSAM1.KSDS.DATA)                        -
)                                           -
```

The data component of this file will be called VSAM1.KSDS.DATA.

Next comes the control statements that define the index component of the cluster:

```
INDEX                                       -
(                                           -
NAME(VSAM1.KSDS.INDEX)                       -
CONTROLINTERVALSIZE(2048)                    -
)                                           -
```

The index component of the cluster will be called VSAM1.KSDS.INDEX. The size of its Control Interval is specified as 2048 bytes.

Finally, the name of the catalog in which this data set will be recorded is specified:

```
CATALOG(VSAM.USER.PRIVATE)
```

This data set will be recorded in VSAM.USER.PRIVATE.

Upon successful execution of this job, a condition code of 0 will be returned.

16.7 DEFINING AN ENTRY SEQUENCED DATA SET (ESDS)

Defining an ESDS is similar to defining a KSDS, but with the following differences:

- Parameters related to the key field are not coded when defining an ESDS, since ESDS does not have a key field.

- An ESDS has only the data component, so parameters related to the index component are not coded. The INDEX parameter is replaced by the NONINDEXED parameter.

- The FREESPACE parameter is not coded either, since an ESDS has no embedded free space between records.

The following is the JCL that defines an ESDS:

```
//ESDS1       JOB   (A123),'G.  FOREMAN'
//STEP1       EXEC  PGM=IDCAMS
//SYSPRINT    DD    SYSOUT=A
//SYSIN       DD    *
    DEFINE  CLUSTER                        -
    (                                      -
    NAME(VSAM2.ESDS.CLUSTER)               -
    VOLUMES(CICT00)                        -
    CYLINDERS(3,1)                         -
    CISZ(4096)                             -
    RECORDSIZE(80,100)                     -
    NONINDEXED                             -
    )                                      -
    DATA                                   -
    (                                      -
    NAME(VSAM2.ESDS.DATA)                  -
    )                                      -
    CATALOG(VSAM.USER.PRIVATE)
/*
```

This example is almost identical to the one used to define a KSDS except for the absence of the FREESPACE and INDEX parameters. Also, the CONTROLINTERVALSIZE parameter is abbreviated to CISZ. The NONINDEXED parameter indicates a data component only.

16.8 DEFINING A RELATIVE RECORD DATA SET (RRDS)

Defining an RRDS is similar to defining an ESDS. This is because an RRDS also has a data component only. For this reason, the following applies to defining an RRDS:

- Parameters related to the key field are not coded.

- The FREESPACE parameter is not coded, since an RRDS also has no embedded free space between records.

- The keyword parameter NUMBERED is coded to indicate that this is an RRDS.

- Since an RRDS contains fixed length records only, both values coded in the RECORDSIZE parameter must be identical.

Here's the JCL that defines an RRDS:

```
//RRDS1       JOB  (A123),'L. HOLMES'
//STEP1       EXEC PGM=IDCAMS
//SYSPRINT    DD   SYSOUT=A
//SYSIN       DD   *
    DEFINE CLUSTER                              -
    (                                           -
    NAME(VSAM2.RRDS.CLUSTER)                     -
    VOLUMES(CICT00)                             -
    CYLINDERS(3,1)                              -
    CISZ(4096)                                  -
    RECORDSIZE(80,80)                           -
    NUMBERED                                    -
    )                                           -
    DATA                                        -
    (                                           -
    NAME(VSAM2.RRDS.DATA)                        -
    )                                           -
    CATALOG(VSAM.USER.PRIVATE)
/*
//
```

Notice that the subparameters coded in the RECORDSIZE parameter are both the same, implying fixed length records. Also notice the NUMBERED parameter, which is used to specify that this is an RRDS.

16.9 LOADING VSAM DATA SETS

After a data set has been defined successfully, records can be loaded into it. There are two ways to accomplish this.

■ Code the REPRO command in the SYSIN statement of the IDCAMS utility.

The REPRO command reads records from an input data set and copies them to an output data set. It may be used to load records into VSAM, physical sequential, or member of partitioned data sets.

■ Code a COBOL program to read records from an input data set and write them to an output data set.

We will be describing the use of the REPRO command in this section.

16.10 THE REPRO COMMAND

In order for the REPRO command to work properly, the following must hold true:

■ The input file must be a KSDS, ESDS, RRDS, physical sequential, or member of a partitioned data set.

■ The output file must also be a KSDS, ESDS, RRDS, physical sequential, or member of a partitioned data set.

■ The input file must be sorted on the prime key using the SORT utility.

The following must be specified in the command:

■ The name of the input data set.

■ The name of the output data set.

■ The records that are to be copied from the input data set to the output data set. Please note that entire or partial data sets can be copied. Details follow in subsequent sections in this chapter.

16.10.1 Syntax of REPRO Command

The syntax of the REPRO command is as follows:

```
REPRO INFILE(ddname-of-input-file)
    OUTFILE(ddname-of-output-file)
```

or
```
REPRO INDATASET(input-data-set-name)
     OUTDATASET(output-data-set-name)
```

16.11 LOADING A KSDS

Both forms of the REPRO command are used to illustrate how records can be loaded into a KSDS.

Example 1

```
//KSDLOAD1    JOB   (A123),'J. LOUIS'
//STEP1       EXEC  PGM=IDCAMS
//SYSPRINT    DD    SYSOUT=A
//DDIN        DD    DSN=FILE1.TEST,
//                  DISP=SHR
//DDOUT       DD    DSN=VSAM1.KSDS.CLUSTER,
//                  DISP=OLD
//SYSIN       DD    *
  REPRO                          -
  INFILE(DDIN)                   -
  OUTFILE(DDOUT)
/*
//
```

In this example, the IDCAMS program is executed. The input data set file is FILE1.TEST. The name of the output data set file is VSAM1.KSDS.CLUSTER. Disposition of the output file is specified as OLD and input file SHR.

The REPRO command is executed using the INFILE and OUTFILE statements. The input data set file name is referenced via its *DDname*, which is DDIN, and the output data set file name is also referenced by its *DDname*, which is DDOUT.

Upon successful execution of this job, the data contained in FILE1.TEST will be stored in the Key Sequenced Data Set called VSAM1.KSDS.CLUSTER.

Example 2

```
//KSDLOAD2    JOB   (A123),'J. LOUIS'
//STEP1       EXEC  PGM=IDCAMS
//SYSPRINT    DD    SYSOUT=A
//SYSIN       DD    *
  REPRO                               -
  INDATASET(FILE1.TEST)               -
  OUTDATASET(VSAM1.KSDS.CLUSTER)
/*
//
```

In this example, the data set name is specified in the REPRO command.

16.12 LOADING AN ESDS

The JCL required to load an ESDS follows. It is exactly like the JCL required to load KSDS. The only difference here is that the input file need not be sorted. This is because the ESDS does not have a primary key field.

Here's the JCL required for the job. We use the INDATASET and OUTDATASET statements for the transfer.

```
//ESDSLOAD    JOB  (A123),'J. LOUIS'
//STEP1       EXEC PGM=IDCAMS
//SYSPRINT    DD   SYSOUT=A
//SYSIN       DD   *
  REPRO                            -
  INDATASET(FILE1.TEST)          -
  OUTDATASET(VSAM2.ESDS.CLUSTER)
/*
//
```

16.13 LOADING AN RRDS

The JCL required to load an RRDS is also similar to that used for KSDS or ESDS. Records are loaded starting at Relative Record Number 1.

```
//RRDSLOAD    JOB  (A123),'J. LOUIS'
//STEP1       EXEC PGM=IDCAMS
//SYSPRINT    DD   SYSOUT=A
//SYSIN       DD   *
  REPRO                            -
  INDATASET(FILE1.TEST)          -
  OUTDATASET(VSAM2.RRDS.CLUSTER)
/*
//
```

16.14 OPTIONS AVAILABLE ON THE REPRO COMMAND

Options can be coded on the REPRO command to customize the copy as necessary. Table 16.2 lists the options available, and the parameter that conveys this information. Please note that these parameters relate to partial copies of the data set.

Table 16.2 Options Available on the REPRO Command

Option	Corresponding Parameter and Syntax
Skip selected records from the input file	SKIP(n) n is the number of records from the start of the file which are to be skipped in the copy transaction
Copy select number of records from the input file to the output file	COUNT(n) n is the number of records that are to be copied COUNT starts the copy from the current location. For example, if SKIP is coded before COUNT, the number of records copied will start right after the number of records skipped
Copy records between two keys (KSDS only)	FROMKEY(n1) TOKEY(n2) n1 and n2 specify the two keys
Copy records between two addresses (ESDS only)	FROMADDRESS(n1) TOADDRESS(n2) n1 and n2 specify the two addresses
Copy records between two relative record numbers of RRDS files	FROMNUMBER(n1) TONUMBER(n2) n1 and n2 specify the two relative record numbers

16.15 EXAMPLES OF PARTIAL COPIES

Example 1

```
//KSDSLOAD    JOB   (A123),'J. LOUIS'
//STEP1       EXEC  PGM=IDCAMS
//SYSPRINT    DD    SYSOUT=A
//DDOUT       DD    DSN=FILE1.TEST,
//                  DISP=OLD
//DDIN        DD    DSN=VSAM1.KSDS.CLUSTER,
//                  DISP=OLD
//SYSIN       DD    *
  REPRO                         -
  INFILE(DDIN)                  -
  OUTFILE(DDOUT)                -
  FROMKEY(1111)                 -
  TOKEY(5555)
/*
//
```

In this example, a partial copy is implemented from VSAM1.KSDS.CLUSTER to FILE1.TEST. The copy starts when the key 1111 is encountered and ends on key 5555. The record with the key 5555 will be included in the copy.

Example 2

```
//ESDSLOAD    JOB   (A123),'J. LOUIS'
//STEP1       EXEC  PGM=IDCAMS
//SYSPRINT    DD    SYSOUT=A
//SYSIN       DD    *
  REPRO                              -
  INDATASET(VSAM2.ESDS.CLUSTER)      -
  OUTDATASET(FILE2.TEST)             -
  FROMADDRESS(150)                   -
  TOADDRESS(300)
/*
```

In this example, the input data set is VSAM2.ESDS.CLUSTER, and the output file is FILE2.TEST. Records are copied from address 150 to address 300.

Example 3

```
//RRDSLOAD    JOB   (A123),'J. LOUIS'
//STEP1       EXEC  PGM=IDCAMS
//SYSPRINT    DD    SYSOUT=A
//SYSIN       DD    *
  REPRO                              -
  INDATASET(VSAM2.RRDS.CLUSTER)      -
  OUTDATASET(FILE3.TEST)             -
```

```
    FROMNUMBER(10)
    TONUMBER(20)
/*
//
```

Records are copied from VSAM2.RRDS.CLUSTER from relative record number 10 to relative record number 20.

16.16 PRINTING VSAM DATA SETS

The PRINT command can be coded on the SYSIN statement of the IDCAMS utility to print both VSAM and non-VSAM data sets. Printouts can be obtained in any of the following formats:

■ Hexadecimal

Specifying hexadecimal format results in each character of output being printed as two hexadecimal digits. A maximum of 120 hexadecimal digits can be printed in one print line. If the record length is greater than 120 hexadecimal digits, then the data set is printed in blocks of 120 hexadecimal characters per line.

■ Character

Specification of this type of format results in output being printed as EBCDIC characters. A maximum of 120 characters can be printed per print line. If the record length is more than 120 characters, then the data set is printed in blocks of 120 characters per line.

■ Dump

The dump format results in all characters being printed in hexadecimal as well as character format.

16.16.1 Syntax of PRINT Command

The syntax looks like this:

    PRINT INFILE(ddname-of-dataset)
or
    PRINT INDATASET(data-set-name)

16.16.2 SOME EXAMPLES

Example 1

```
//KSDSPRNT    JOB   (A123),'K. CARSON'
//STEP001     EXEC  PGM=IDCAMS
//SYSPRINT    DD    SYSOUT=A
//SYSIN       DD    *
  PRINT                                  -
  INDATASET(VSAM1.KSDS.CLUSTER)          -
  CHAR
/*
```

This example prints a KSDS in character format. The INDATASET statement names the data set that is to be printed. The contents of the data set are printed in EBCDIC characters. A maximum of 120 characters can be printed on each line. Any combination of bits that do not correspond to a printable character are printed as periods.

Example 2

```
//ESDSPRNT    JOB   (A123),'K. CARSON
//STEP001     EXEC  PGM=IDCAMS
//SYSPRINT    DD    SYSOUT=A
//DD1         DD    DSN=VSAM2.ESDS.CLUSTER,
//                  DISP=SHR
//SYSIN       DD    *
  PRINT                  -
  INFILE(DD1)            -
  CHAR
/*
//
```

In this example, DD1 defines the data set name, which is VSAM2.ESDS.CLUSTER. The PRINT command coded in the SYSIN statement uses the INFILE format to reference the *DDname* that defines the data set that is to be printed. Printout is once again specified in character format.

Example 3

```
//RRDSPRNT    JOB   (A123),'K. CARSON'
//STEP001     EXEC  PGM=IDCAMS
//SYSPRINT    DD    SYSOUT=A
//SYSIN       DD    *
  PRINT                                  -
  INDATASET(VSAM3.RRDS.CLUSTER)          -
  DUMP
/*
//
```

In this example an RRDS file is printed.   Printing will start at Relative Record Number 1.

Example 4

```
//PRINT1      JOB  (A123),'K. CARSON'
//STEP001     EXEC PGM=IDCAMS
//SYSPRINT    DD   SYSOUT=A
//SYSIN       DD   *
  PRINT                               -
  INDATASET(FILE1.REGULAR)            -
  HEX
/*
//
```

This example illustrates how a non-VSAM data set can also be printed via the PRINT command.

16.17 PRINTING SELECT RECORDS

You may code the same key words on the PRINT command as those used in the REPRO command to print selected records from a data set. For example, coding SKIP on the PRINT command will result in the number of records from the start of the data set being skipped before the printing is started.   The syntax of these keywords is the same as that in the REPRO command.

16.18 THINGS THAT CAN GO WRONG

Once again, we present a general correspondence between some common errors and the error codes and messages that are generated from them. Either refer to the JCL error code, or scan through *Probable Cause of Error*, to identify the cause of error in your JCL.

Table 16.3 Some Common Errors

JCL Error Code	Description	Probable Cause of Error
IDC3003I	Data set not found	Executing IDCAMS to process a VSAM data set, and forgetting to code a hyphen as the continuation character on the SYSIN statement Many unrelated error messages will follow, which are generated as a result of the missing hyphen
IDC3013I	Duplicate data set name	Defining a cluster that already exists
IDC3314I	Action error on xxx Record X'xxx' out of sequence xxx is the name of the data set being processed	Using the REPRO command on unsorted data sets

16.19 REVIEW

In this chapter we discussed how to allocate, process, and print VSAM and non-VSAM data sets. The IDCAMS utility is executed to perform these functions. Table 16.4 briefly summarizes the commands discussed.

Table 16.4 IDCAMS, the AMS Utility Program

Parameter Coded on the IDCAMS Utility	Description
DEFINE CLUSTER	Used to define a VSAM data set This is coded on the SYSIN statement of the IDCAMS utility The following parameters should be coded to specify features of the data set: NAME VOLUME CYLINDERS CONTROLINTERVALSIZE FREESPACE KEYS RECORDSIZE
DATA(data-set-name) INDEX(index-name)	Used to define name of data and index components of base cluster
CATALOG(name)	Used to specify name of the catalog in which the data set will be recorded

REPRO INFILE(ddname-input-file)
    OUTFILE(ddname-output-file)
 	
REPRO INDATASET(input-file)
    OUTDATASET(output-file)
	Used to copy one data set into another or load records into a data set
	
	Partial copies can be implemented by coding the following subparameters on the REPRO command:
	SKIP
	COUNT(n)
	FROMKEY(n1) TOKEY(n2)
	FROMADDRESS(n1)
	TOADDRESS(n2)
	FROMNUMBER(n1)
	TONUMBER(n2)

PRINT INFILE(data-set-name) PRINT DATASET(data-set-name)	Used to print VSAM and non-VSAM data sets
	Partial prints can be implemented by coding any of the subparameters listed for the REPRO command

17

Alternate Index

17.1 INTRODUCTION

Suppose you go to a bookstore to buy a book. You search for the book on the bookshelves in the appropriate section, and after a fruitless search, you turn to the salesperson for help. The salesperson asks you if you know the author of the book. You don't. OK, the salesperson says, do you know the title of the book? You happily respond with a "Yes! It's called ...." and the salesperson looks up the book in their inventory file by title.

The simple example that we have just presented illustrates the concept of an alternate index. Suppose a KSDS dataset is created to store inventory information about the books in this store. If this file is indexed by author name, then this would be the primary key. However, there are often occasions when people know the book only by title. Thus, it would be necessary to index the data set by the title, as well as an alternate index.

VSAM gives you the capability of specifying alternate indexes for KSDS and ESDS base clusters. This capability is perhaps one of the most powerful features that VSAM has to offer. Alternate indexes do not exist for RRDS data sets.

Later on in this chapter, we will also describe the concept of a *path*, which is a link between the base cluster and its associated alternate index. But first, let's understand what an alternate index is.

17.2 ALTERNATE INDEX, ILLUSTRATED

We continue with the previous example. Assume that each record of the KSDS data set containing information about the books looks like this:

0 (Byte Number) 35	36 120	121...
Author	Title	Other information

Author name starts at byte 0 and ends at byte 35. Title starts at byte number 36 and ends at byte 120. The remaining fields in the record contain other information.

This record is indexed by author name. Thus, the prime key for this data set would be the author name. (Keep in mind that the prime key of a KSDS must be unique. Author names can be duplicated. In reality, you would probably concatenate some other field with the author name to make it unique. We are bypassing this for now to keep the example simple).

Based on the needs of our customers, it is apparent that we should be able to search the data set by title as well. Figure 17.1 illustrates the structure of the alternate and base cluster index.

Alternate Index

0 4	5 40	41 124
Control Info	Author	Title

Base Cluster

0 35	36 120	121...
Author	Title	Other info

Figure 17.1 Alternate and Base Cluster Index

The alternate index is composed of the primary key of the record, along with the field identified as the secondary key. Bytes 0 through 4 (the first five bytes) contain control information that is used by VSAM for identification purposes.

17.3 RULES FOR CREATING ALTERNATE INDEXES

- An alternate index cannot be created for RRDS or LDS base clusters.

- No more than 253 alternate indexes can be specified for a base cluster.

- Alternate and prime key fields can overlap, but they cannot start at the same location.

A VSAM data set can have only one unique primary index and multiple alternate indexes. Keeping in mind the overhead involved in storing and maintaining alternate indexes, no more than 5 alternate indexes should be specified.

- When an alternate index is defined, it must be cataloged in the same location as its base cluster.

17.4 CREATION OF AN ALTERNATE INDEX

The IDCAMS utility is used to create an alternate index for an existing base cluster. Once the index has been defined, records have to be loaded into it. But before it can be defined, the following items must be specified to the operating system:

- The name of the alternate index

- Name of the base cluster that it relates to

- Key size (length) and starting location in the base cluster record

- The size and type of the individual records that the alternate index will contain

- How much space should be allocated to it

- Whether the alternate index key will contain unique values only or duplicates

- Whether or not the alternate index is to be updated each time its corresponding base cluster is updated

- How much free space should be allocated to its control intervals

Table 17.1 lists the JCL parameters used to convey the information just presented. Explanatory text is added, wherever it would prove useful to achieve a complete understanding of the listed parameter.

17.5 AN EXAMPLE

An example is presented illustrating the JCL parameters listed in Table 17.1.

```
//ALT1      JOB    (A123),'C. CHASE'
//STEP1     EXEC   PGM=IDCAMS
//SYSPRINT DD      SYSOUT=A
//SYSIN     DD     *
  DEFINE AIX                              -
  (NAME(BOOKS.KSDS.AIDX.CLUSTER)         -
  RELATE(BOOKS.KSDS.CLUSTER)             -
  KEYS(84,36)                            -
  CYLINDERS(2,1)                         -
  NONUNIQUEKEY                           -
  UPGRADE                                -
  RECORDSIZE(124,124)                    -
  FREESPACE(20,20)                       -
  DATA                                   -
  (                                      -
  NAME(BOOKS.KSDS.AIDX.DATA)             -
  )                                      -
  INDEX                                  -
  (                                      -
  NAME(BOOKS.KSDS.AIDX.INDEX)            -
  )
/*
//
```

In this example, the program IDCAMS is executed. Output messages are directed to the line printer.

Pay special attention to the SYSIN parameter. This contains the JCL required to define the alternate index.

Table 17.1 Parameters Required for Alternate Index

Function	Corresponding Parameters and Subparameters
Creation or definition of alternate index	DEFINE AIX This command is coded on the SYSIN statement of the IDCAMS utility
Name of index	(NAME(name-of-alternate-index)
Name of corresponding base cluster	RELATE(base-cluster-name)
Size of key and starting point in the base cluster record	KEYS(n1,n2) n1 specifies length of alternate index key in bytes n2 specifies the key's starting location in its corresponding base cluster record
Size and type of records (i.e., fixed or variable)	RECORDSIZE(n1,n2) n1 and n2 are calculated by adding 5 (Control information reserved for VSAM) to length of alternate key plus length of primary key n1 is the average record size, in bytes n2 is the maximum record size, in bytes If n1 is equal to n2, then the index has fixed length records. Otherwise it has variable length records.

Amount of space to be allocated the alternate index	CYLINDERS(n1,n2) n1 is the amount of primary space allocation n2 is the amount of secondary space allocation
Specification of whether it will contain unique or duplicate values	UNIQUEKEY NONUNIQUEKEY UNIQUEKEY specifies that values in the alternate index will be unique for each record NONUNIQUEKEY specifies that the values can be duplicated If the alternate index is NONUNIQUEKEY, multiple rows can be retrieved for that index
Specification of updates to alternate index	UPGRADE VSAM automatically updates the alternate index for all adds, deletes and updates to the base cluster But, you have to specify this parameter at definition time, in order for it to do so
Amount of free space to be allocated to it	FREESPACE This is the amount of available space between each control interval

Subsequent JCL will be explained in small groups. Here's the first group:

```
DEFINE AIX                                  -
(NAME(BOOKS.KSDS.AIDX.CLUSTER)              -
RELATE(BOOKS.KSDS.CLUSTER)                  -
KEYS(84,36)                                 -
```

The DEFINE AIX command specifies that an alternate index is being defined. The name of this index is BOOKS.KSDS.AIDX.CLUSTER. The base cluster that it relates to is BOOKS.KSDS.CLUSTER. The alternate key will be 84 bytes in length, starting at byte 36 of the base cluster record.

```
NONUNIQUEKEY                                 -
UPGRADE                                      -
RECORDSIZE(124,124)                          -
FREESPACE(20,20)                             -
```

Next, the operating system is notified that the alternate index being defined will contain duplicate keys. The system should perform automatic updates of the index each time a record is added, deleted, or updated from the base cluster. This alternate index will contain fixed length records (both values coded for this parameter are identical). Each record will be composed of 124 bytes (5 + length of alternate key (84 bytes) plus length of primary key (35 bytes)). 20 bytes of free space are to be left between each control interval. 20 percent of control intervals are to be left unused.

```
DATA                                         -
(                                            -
NAME(BOOKS.KSDS.AIDX.DATA)                   -
)                                            -
INDEX                                        -
(                                            -
NAME(BOOKS.KSDS.AIDX.INDEX)                  -
)
```

The data component of the alternate index will be called BOOKS.KSDS.AIDX.DATA, and its index component will be called BOOKS.KSDS.AIDX.INDEX.

17.6 BUILDING AN INDEX

Once an alternate index has been defined, records can be loaded into it using the BLDINDEX command on the IDCAMS utility. The following JCL loads records into the index that we just built.

```
//JOB1      JOB    (A123),'C LEHN'
//STEP1     EXEC   PGM=IDCAMS
//SYSPRINT  DD     SYSOUT=A
//BASECLST  DD     DSN=BOOKS.KSDS.CLUSTER,
//                 DISP=SHR
//ALTINDEX  DD     DSN=BOOKS.KSDS.AIDX.CLUSTER,
//                 DISP=OLD
```

```
//IDCUT1    DD    DSN=MI85.WORK.FILE1,
//                AMP='AMORG',
//                VOL=SER=CICTDA,
//                UNIT=PRODDA
//IDCUT2    DD    DSN=MI85.WORK.FILE2,
//                DISP=OLD,
//                AMP='AMORG',
//                VOL=SER=CICTDA,
//                UNIT=PRODDA
//SYSIN     DD    *
  BLDINDEX  INFILE(BASECLST)        -
            OUTFILE(ALTINDEX)
/*
//
```

Let's step through this example. The IDCAMS utility is executed.
Output messages are once again directed to the line printer. BASECLST
identifies the base index, and ALTINDEX identifies the alternate index.
IDCUT1 and IDCUT2 identify the *DDnames* of the two workfiles that
will be used by the BLDINDEX command (it is traditional to use these
DDnames for workfiles). The AMP parameter (*Access Method
Parameter*) is used to allocate I/O buffers for the index and data
components of the file, and is helpful in speeding up performance. We
set the AMP parameter to AMORG (*Access Method Organization*). This
results in the system understanding that a VSAM data set is being
referenced.

Finally, the BLDINDEX command is used to load records from the file
identified in BASECLST to the file identified in ALTINDEX.

17.7 A PATH AND ALTERNATE INDEX

Now that you understand what an alternate index is, let's take a moment
to understand the implications of using an alternate index.

Use of an alternate index is more involved than the use of the primary
index. It requires more coding on the part of the programmer, and it also
requires more activity on the part of the operating system: first, the
alternate index cluster has to be searched for the alternate key; second,
the corresponding prime key or RBA is derived from it; third, the record
in the base cluster is accessed.

There is a way to avoid this extra work, and this is by defining a
PATH between the base cluster and its associated alternate index cluster.
Defining a PATH results in the establishment of a logical link between the
alternate and base index clusters in the VSAM catalog. An actual record
is not created, instead, only a relationship is established.

A PATH is named and created, just like any other data set name.
Then, if a data set is accessed via its path name, both the alternate and

base cluster indexes are opened, and the system *automatically* finds the prime key value, based on the alternate index value, without any extra coding on your part.

17.7.1 Defining a PATH

The DEFINE PATH command is used to define a path. Here's the JCL:

```
//JOB1      JOB    A123,'J FARREL'
//STEP1     EXEC   PGM=IDCAMS
//SYSPRINT DD      SYSOUT=A
//SYSIN     DD     *
  DEFINE PATH                              -
  (NAME(BOOKS.KSDS.PATH1)                  -
  PATHENTRY(BOOKS.KSDS.AIDX.CLUSTER)  -
  UPDATE)
/*
//
```

In this example, the IDCAMS utility is executed. A path called BOOKS.KSDS.PATH1 is defined to establish a bridge between the base cluster and the alternate index. Notice that only the alternate index is named in the PATHENTRY command. PATHENTRY is used to specify the alternate index cluster to which the path will be related to.

When alternate indexes are automatically updated, on addition, deletion or update of a record in the base cluster, they are said to belong to an *upgrade set* of the base cluster. The UPDATE parameter is used to specify that at the time a path is defined, the base cluster and its *upgrade set* should both be opened automatically.

UPDATE is the default. If NOUPDATE had been coded, the base cluster would be opened, but not its upgrade set.

17.8 REVIEW

The alternate index was discussed in this chapter. An alternate index can be created for KSDS and ESDS data sets. It cannot be created for RRDS files. The IDCAMS utility is executed to create this index. An alternate index allows records to be searched by an alternative key, aside from the prime key. A path can be created between the base cluster and its alternate index. Table 17.2 defines some of the subparameters that can be coded on the SYSIN statement of the IDCAMS utility to customize the index as necessary.

Table 17.2 Parameters related to DEFINE AIX Statement

Command	Description
DEFINE AIX	Used to define an alternate index for KSDS and ESDS files The following subparameters can be coded on this command to specify features of the index: RELATE(base-cluster-name) KEYS(n1,n2) RECORDSIZE(n1,n2) CYLINDERS(n1,n2) UNIQUEKEY/NONUNIQUEKEY UPGRADE FREESPACE
BLDINDEX	Used to load records into an AIX after it has been defined

Chapter 18

Additional
VSAM Commands

18.1 INTRODUCTION

This chapter concludes our discussion of VSAM. It describes additional
IDCAMS utility functions that are available through Access Method
Services.

18.2 ADDITIONAL FUNCTIONS OF VSAM DATA SETS

The following functions may be executed on VSAM data sets:

- Modification of attributes of existing VSAM data sets

- Deletion of predefined and existing VSAM data sets

- Creation of backup copies of base clusters and alternate indexes

- Restoration of backup copies of base clusters and alternate indexes

- Control of the execution of Access Method Services Commands

18.3 CORRESPONDING JCL

Table 18.1 lists the commands that are coded on the SYSIN statement of
the IDCAMS utility to implement the functions just listed.

Table 18.1 Additional Parameters on the IDCAMS Utility

Function	Corresponding JCL parameters and Subparameters
Alter data sets	ALTER
Delete data sets	DELETE DELETE can be used to delete both VSAM and non-VSAM data sets
Create backup copies	EXPORT
Restore backup copies	IMPORT
Control execution of statements	MODAL

18.4 THE ALTER COMMAND

The ALTER command of the IDCAMS utility is used to change existing attributes of a VSAM data set. ALTER is a powerful command, and can be used to change many attributes of a data set. In this book, we will discuss:

■ How a partitioned data set name can be updated

■ How a partitioned data set can be write-protected

Although this is a powerful command, it does have some limitations, in that not all attributes of a data set can be modified. The following are some of the limitations of this command. Please refer to your system manual for additional limitations.

■ The keylength and/or offset of a KSDS record cannot be changed, if records have already been loaded into it

■ The average or maximum record size attribute of a data set cannot be changed, it it already contains records

The next two sections describe the JCL requirements for updating and write-protecting a data set.

18.4.1 Altering Name of Partitioned Data Set

The NEWNAME command is used with the ALTER command to alter a partitioned data set name. Here's the JCL:

```
//ALTER1     JOB    A123,'A HELMS'
//STEP1      EXEC   PGM=IDCAMS
//SYSPRINT   DD     SYSOUT=A
//SYSIN      DD     *
  ALTER                                -
  COBOL.LOAD(PROGRAM1)                 -
  NEWNAME(COBOL.LOAD(PROGRAM2))
/*
//
```

In this example, the member name COBOL.LOAD(PROGRAM1) is changed to COBOL.LOAD(PROGRAM2).

18.4.2 Write-Protecting a Data Set

Sometimes it is necessary to write-protect a data set. There can be several reasons for this. For example, suppose a VSAM data set is corrupted, and users need to be prevented from updating it until the problem is fixed. Or perhaps the system is being upgraded, and all updates are to be frozen until the completion of the upgrade. The INHIBIT command is used with the ALTER command to do this. Here's the JCL:

```
//ALTER2     JOB    A123,'A HELMS'
//STEP1      EXEC   PGM=IDCAMS
//SYSPRINT   DD     SYSOUT=A
//SYSIN      DD     *
  ALTER                                -
  BOOKS.KSDS.DATA                      -
  INHIBIT
  ALTER                                -
  BOOKS.KSDS.INDEX                     -
  INHIBIT
/*
//
```

Notice that the ALTER command is used with the data and index components of the KSDS, not with the name of the cluster.

The read-only restriction set by the ALTER command can be removed by coding UNINHIBIT on the ALTER command, like this:

```
//ALTER3     JOB    A123,'A HELMS'
//STEP1      EXEC   PGM=IDCAMS
```

```
//SYSPRINT  DD      SYSOUT=A
//SYSIN     DD   *
  ALTER                                  -
  BOOKS.KSDS.DATA                        -
  UNINHIBIT
  ALTER                                  -
  BOOKS.KSDS.INDEX                       -
  UNINHIBIT
/*
//
```

18.5 THE DELETE COMMAND

The DELETE command of the IDCAMS utility is used to delete different types of data sets.

The following types of data sets can be deleted:

- VSAM data sets (KSDS, ESDS, RRDS, LDS)

- Non-VSAM data sets

- Alternate indexes

- Generation Data Groups

   And here's the syntax of the DELETE command:

   DELETE(name)

or

   DELETE(name) FORCE

where *name* is the data set name assigned to the data set. The *FORCE* parameter is used when a GDG is deleted to physically remove the entry of that GDG. If this parameter is not used, then the entry is not removed from the system catalogs.

18.5.1 Reasons for Deleting

A data set can be deleted for any of the following reasons:

- Multiple splits in the control intervals and control areas of a KSDS

Recall that KSDS data sets have CIs and CAs with embedded free space. The free space area provides space for new data that may be added to the base cluster, and logically needs to be fitted into a particular CI. If the new data being added requires more space than is available in the free space area, then VSAM tries to locate an empty CI within the same CA. Approximately half of the records in the current area are then moved to the new area. The new data is placed in the appropriate CI. This is called a *Control Interval Split*.

Now, assume that VSAM is unable to find enough space within the CA, in which the split is required to take place. In this case, it tries to locate a free CA within the area designated as the primary space. If it is still unsuccessful in its search, then it attempts to find the space within the secondary space. Once space is found, it moves approximately half the records from the existing CA to the new one. This is called a *Control Area Split*.

Multiple CI and CA splits make a KSDS inefficient. In such cases, the KSDS should be reorganized to eliminate the existing splits. The only way to reorganize a KSDS is to back it up, delete it, redefine it, and then restore it from the backup.

A data set may also be eliminated for the following reasons.

- The data set may not be required anymore.

- The data set may have become corrupt due to hardware and/or software errors.

We now present the JCL required to delete the different types of data sets listed. Please note that the command used to delete a data set is the same, regardless of the type of data set.

18.5.2 Deleting a KSDS Data Set

```
//DELETE1  JOB  (A123),'F. ZAMIR'
//STEP1    EXEC PGM=IDCAMS
//SYSPRINT DD   SYSOUT=A
//SYSIN    DD   *
  DELETE BOOKS.KSDS.CLUSTER
/*
//
```

In this example, BOOKS.KSDS.CLUSTER is deleted. Both the data and the index components are deleted. If this data set has any alternate indexes, then they are also deleted.

18.5.3 Deleting a Non-VSAM data set

```
//DELETE2  JOB   (A123),'F. ZAMIR'
//STEP1    EXEC PGM=IDCAMS
//SYSPRINT DD    SYSOUT=A
//SYSIN    DD    *
  DELETE COBOL.SOURCE.FILE1
/*
//
```

In this example, the data set called COBOL.SOURCE.FILE1 is deleted.

18.5.4 Deleting an Alternate Index

```
//DELETE3  JOB   (A123),'F. ZAMIR'
//STEP1    EXEC PGM=IDCAMS
//SYSPRINT DD    SYSOUT=A
//SYSIN    DD    *
  DELETE BOOKS.KSDS.AIDX.CLUSTER
/*
//
```

The alternate index called BOOKS.KSDS.AIDX.CLUSTER is deleted.

18.5.5 Deleting a GDG

```
//DELETE4  JOB   (A123),'F. ZAMIR'
//STEP1    EXEC PGM=IDCAMS
//SYSPRINT DD    SYSOUT=A
//SYSIN    DD    *
  DELETE FINANCES.MONTHLY FORCE
/*
//
```

In this example, the GDG called FINANCES.MONTHLY is deleted. The FORCE parameter physically purges all entries related to the GDG.

18.6 EXPORT AND IMPORT COMMANDS

The EXPORT command makes a backup copy of different types of data sets. The IMPORT command is used to restore the file to the proper device. Backups and restorations can be implemented on the following types of data sets:

- VSAM data sets (KSDS, ESDS, RRDS, LDS)

- Alternate indexes

18.6.1 Features Related to Backing Up and Restoring Data Sets

When a data set is backed up and restored, many factors relating to these transactions have to be specified. Table 18.2 lists these items, and the corresponding parameters used to specify that information:

Table 18.2 Parameters Coded on EXPORT/IMPORT Statement

Function	Corresponding parameters
Make back up of data set	EXPORT name name is the data set name of the VSAM data set
Name of file to which the backup is being sent to	OUTFILE(DDname) DDname is the name assigned to the DD statement which defines the output file If the DCB parameter is defined in this statement, only the BLKSIZE parameter can be coded for it No other data set characteristic can be defined
Indicates whether or not the data set is to be deleted from its original location after it has been backed up	PERMANENT/TEMPORARY PERMANENT specifies it should be deleted This is the default TEMPORARY specifies it should not be deleted

Indicates whether or not the data set can be updated after it has been backed up	NOINHIBITSOURCE/ INHIBITSOURCE NOINHIBITSOURCE specifies that the data set can be updated after backup This is the default INHIBITSOURCE specifies that it cannot
Indicates whether or not the data set can be processed/updated after it is restored via the IMPORT command	NOINHIBITTARGET/ INHIBITTARGET NOINHIBITTARGET specifies that the data set will be available for processing after it is restored. This is the default INHIBITTARGET indicates that it will not be available
Restoring data sets previously backed up	IMPORT
Name of file from which data set will be restored	INFILE(DDname) DDname is the name assigned to the DD statement which defines this file
Name of data set after it has been restored	OUTDATASET(name-of-file)

18.6.2 An Example Using the EXPORT Command

```
//EXPORT1      JOB    (A123),'T. ZAMIR'
//STEP1        EXEC   PGM=IDCAMS
//SYSPRINT     DD     SYSOUT=A
//DD1          DD     DSN=BOOKS.KSDS.BACKUP,
//                    DISP=(NEW,CATLG,KEEP),
//                    UNIT=UNIT1,
//                    DCB=(BLKSIZE=8000)
//SYSIN        DD     *
  EXPORT                          -
  BOOKS.KSDS.CLUSTER              -
  OUTFILE(DD1)                    -
```

```
TEMPORARY                        -
INHIBITSOURCE                    -
INHIBITTARGET
/*
//
```

In this example, the IDCAMS utility is submitted. The output is directed to the line printer. In addition to these preliminaries, DD1 defines a data set called BOOKS.KSDS.BACKUP. Notice that only the BLKSIZE subparameter is coded on the DCB statement. This is required, since this is the DCB definition of the file that the backup will be copied to.

Next, the EXPORT command is coded on the SYSIN statement. The data set which is to be backed up is BOOKS.KSDS.CLUSTER. The DDname of the file to which it will be copied to is specified by the OUTFILE parameter. BOOKS.KSDS.CLUSTER will not be deleted after the backup. After the backup has been made, no updates will be allowed on it. Furthermore, no updates will be allowed on it after it has been restored.

18.6.3 An Example Using the IMPORT Command

```
//IMPORT1       JOB    (A123),'T. ZAMIR'
//STEP1         EXEC   PGM=IDCAMS
//SYSPRINT      DD     SYSOUT=A
//DD1           DD     DSN=BOOKS.KSDS.BACKUP,
//                     DISP=SHR
//SYSIN         DD     *
  IMPORT                -
  INFILE(DD1)           -
  OUTDATASET(BOOKS.KSDS.CLUSTER)
/*
//
```

In this example, the name of the data set to which the backup was copied is defined in DD1. Then, the IMPORT command is used to restore the file defined in DD1. The name of the restored file will be BOOKS.KSDS.CLUSTER.

18.6.4 REPRO Compared to EXPORT command

In Chapter 16 the REPRO command, which also makes a copy of the data set, was discussed. We present a brief comparison of the two commands, so that you may understand exactly which one suits your needs better.

- The REPRO command can be used with VSAM and non-VSAM data sets. The EXPORT and IMPORT commands are used for VSAM data sets only.

- The REPRO command backs up logical records only. If this is a VSAM data set and it has to be restored, this data set has to be redefined and reloaded from the backup copy.

    On the other hand, the EXPORT command backs up not only the logical records, but also its attributes. Then, when the data set is to be restored, the IMPORT command redefines it with these attributes and reloads the data.

18.7 THE MODAL COMMANDS

We conclude this chapter with a discussion of the MODAL commands. These commands are used to control the execution and flow of commands coded for the IDCAMS utility. This feature is useful in those cases where multiple commands are executed, and each command is dependent on the output of the previous one.

18.8 CONDITION CODES GENERATED BY AMS

When an AMS command is executed, a condition code is generated. This condition code indicates the status of the command after execution. Table 18.3 lists the condition codes that can be generated, and what they mean.

18.9 IF-THEN-ELSE AND LASTCC AND MAXCC

The IF-THEN-ELSE modal commands are used to control the execution of JCL statements in AMS. The results are tested via the keywords LASTCC and MAXCC. LASTCC contains the condition code from the most recently executed command. MAXCC contains the highest condition code from any of the previous commands within the same job step. If an immediate exit from the job is required, (this decision would probably be based on the condition code generated by a command), then the SET command can be used to set LASTCC or MAXCC to 16. On doing so, the job will be terminated immediately.

LASTCC and MAXCC can be compared by using the following operators listed in Table 18.4.

Table 18.3 Condition Codes Generated by AMS

Condition Code	Explanation
0	Command executed successfully
4	System encountered a problem in executing the function
8	Requested function was executed, but problems were encountered for the data to be processed For example, if a data set was requested to be deleted, the data set name was not found, duplicate entries were found for it.
12	A logical error was encountered. For example, the JCL being executed had syntax errors, or missing parameters
16	A severe error was encountered When a severe error occurs, execution is immediately terminated

Table 18.4 LASTCC and MAXCC Operators

Operator	Explanation
EQ	Equal to
NE	Not equal to
GT	Greater than
GE	Greater than or equal to
LE	Less than or equal to
LT	Less than

18.9.1 Some Examples

Example 1

```
//MODAL1      JOB   'O. ZAMIR'
//STEP1       EXEC  PGM=IDCAMS
//SYSPRINT    DD    SYSOUT=A
//SYSIN       DD    *
```

```
REPRO                                     -
INDATASET(COBOL.SOURCE.FILE1)   -
OUTDATASET(COBOL.SOURCE.FILE2)
IF LASTCC = 0                             -
    THEN                                  -
    DELETE (COBOL.SOURCE.FILE1)
/*
//
```

In this example, the REPRO command is coded to copy COBOL.SOURCE.FILE1 to COBOL.SOURCE.FILE2. If this command executes successfully, then a condition code of 0 will be generated. The LASTCC command is used to check the condition code generated from this command. If it is, in fact, 0, then COBOL.SOURCE.FILE1 is deleted.

Example 2

```
//MODAL2       JOB    'O. ZAMIR'
//STEP1        EXEC   PGM=IDCAMS
//SYSPRINT     DD     SYSOUT=A
//SYSIN        DD     *
  REPRO                                   -
  INDATASET(COBOL.SOURCE.FILE1)   -
  OUTDATASET(COBOL.SOURCE.FILE2)
  REPRO                                   -
  INDATASET(COBOL.SOURCE.FILE3)   -
  OUTDATASET(COBOL.SOURCE.FILE4)
  IF MAXCC GT 0                           -
    THEN                                  -
    SET MAXCC = 16
  ELSE
    DELETE (COBOL.SOURCE.FILE1)
    DELETE (COBOL.SOURCE.FILE3)
/*
```

In this example, we illustrate the use of the IF-THEN-ELSE loop and the SET command. The IDCAMS utility is executed, and the REPRO command copies COBOL.SOURCE.FILE1 to COBOL.SOURCE.FILE2, and COBOL.SOURCE.FILE3 to COBOL.SOURCE.FILE4. Then, the MAXCC command is used to test the condition codes of all of the prior commands executed within job step STEP1. If the highest condition code generated by any of the prior commands was greater than 0, then MAXCC is set to 16, implying an immediate exit from the job. On the other hand, if the highest condition code was not greater than 0 (implying that all commands generated condition code 0, all commands executed successfully), then the DELETE command is used to delete the two source files.

18.10 Review

Our discussion on VSAM was concluded in this chapter. Table 18.5 summarizes the major features of the commands discussed. The IDCAMS utility is executed to implement these additional functions.

Table 18.5 Additional Commands on the IDCAMS Utility

Command/Parameter Coded on the IDCAMS Utility	Description
DELETE(name)	Used to delete VSAM and non-VSAM data sets. Also used to delete alternate indexes and GDGs
EXPORT name IMPORT name	Used to make a backup copy of a data set and then to restore it Following subparameters can be coded to specify features related to the copy: PERMANENT/TEMPORARY NOINHIBITSOURCE/ INHIBITSOURCE NOINHIBITTARGET/ INHIBITTARGET
MODAL commands	Used to control the execution of JCL statements coded in AMS IF-THEN-ELSE loop construct, along with LASTCC and MAXCC, are used to test the condition codes generated by commands
ALTER name	Used to change attributes of existing data sets

JES2 and JES3
Job Entry Subsystems

19.1 INTRODUCTION

Job Entry Subsystems are additional features of an MVS operating system. The purpose of these subsystems is to manage batch jobs and route output within a group of computers that are a part of the network.

MVS provides two types of Job Entry subsystems: *JES2* and *JES3*. One subsystem does not necessarily provide advantages over the other; whichever one is used is really just a matter of choice. Once the choice has been made, however, it is quite inconvenient to switch from one to another.

In the first half of this chapter the commands available in JES2 will be described. The second part of this chapter will describe the control statements availabe in JES3.

19.2 JES2, AN OVERVIEW

Before getting into the details of JES2, it is important that you understand the difference between a *centralized* and *decentralized* network. In both cases, a group of computers are connected to each other to form a network. Each computer is called a *node*. In a centralized system, a group of computers are assigned the jobs that are to be processed from a job queue through a central computer. In a decentralized system, each computer acts independently in its selection of jobs. JES2 is a decentralized system. JES2 supplies information relating to the execution of jobs within a decentralized network of computers. Table 19.1 lists the corresponding JCL used to supply this information.

Table 19.1 JES2 Control Statements

Function	Corresponding JCL parameters and/or Subparameter
Specify accounting information	NETACCT acct_number acct_number must be the same for all computers in the network
Specify destination node where a job is to execute	ROUTE XEQ node node is the identifier for a computer within the network
Specify destination node where output is to be routed	ROUTE PRINT node node is the identifier for a computer within the network
Specify details of the job	JOBPARM optional-params optional-params are optional parameters that specify additional information about the job
Specify details related to the output of the job	OUTPUT optional-params optional-params are optional parameters that specify information related to the ouput
Specify priority of the job	PRIORITY number number is the priority number assigned to the job
Specify tape volumes that will be used by the job	SETUP vol-number vol-number is the volume serial number of the tapes required for the job
Send messages to the computer operator	MESSAGE text text contains the message

Send messages to specific users within the network	NOTIFY node.userid node is the computer to which the message is to be routed. userid is the identifier assigned to the user to whom the message is to be routed
Start a job at a remote node	SIGNON REMOTEnnn PW1 PW2 SIGNON RMTnnnn SIGNON RMnnnn nnnn is the node number. PW1 and PW2 are the passwords required to sign on to the remote node.
Terminate a job at a remote node	SIGNOFF

19.3 RULES FOR CODING

The following are the rules for coding JES2 control statements:

- All statements must start with a /* in columns 1 and 2, respectively.

- JES2 statements cannot be placed inside cataloged procedures.

   The remainder of this section will illustrate the use of the statements listed in Table 19.1.

19.4 THE NETACCT STATEMENT

The NETACCT statement identifies the account number for the job that is being executed. This account number must be the same for all computers within the network. An example follows.

```
//JOB1      JOB    (A123),'LENNY MANN',CLASS=L
/*NETACCT   777888
```

   NETACCT stands for *NET*work *AC*counT. The NETACCT statement identifies the account number that will be common to all computers in the network.

19.5 THE ROUTE STATEMENT

The ROUTE statement is used to identify the destination of the output of a job. Here's an example:

```
//JOB2       JOB    (A123),'ELY MANSOUR',CLASS=L
/*ROUTE      XEQ    DALLAS
/*ROUTE      PRINT  PRINTER5
```

The first ROUTE statement is used to execute JOB2 at the node identified as DALLAS. The second ROUTE statement is used to route output to PRINTER5.

19.6 THE JOBPARM STATEMENT

The JOBPARM statement specifies additional information for the job. Some of the parameters that can be coded in this statement are:

- LINECT

This is used to specify the number of lines to be printed on each page of output. You can have from 0 to 255 lines on a page.

- NOLOG

This is used to specify that no job log is required for the job that is being executed.

- COPIES=n

This is used to specify the number of copies of output required.

- BYTES=n

This is used to set a limit on the size of the output, in thousands of bytes.

Take a look at this example:

```
//JOB3       JOB    (A123),'DEMI BROWN',CLASS=L
/*JOBPARM    BYTES=20000
```

In this example, the number of bytes of output is limited to 20,000.

■ RESTART=Y or RESTART=N

The RESTART parameter is used to restart a job if it terminates abnormally. Setting RESTART to Y results in the job being restarted from scratch. Setting it to N results in the job being restarted from the step at which it terminated.

■ PAGES=*n*

This is used to set the limit on the number of the pages of output produced by a job. The limit can vary from 1 to 99999.
Take a look at this example:

```
//JOB3        JOB   (A123),'DEMI BROWN',CLASS=L
/*JOBPARM     PAGES=200,LINECT=55,COPIES=5
```

In this example the number of pages of output is limited to 200, each page is to have 55 lines, and 5 copies of output are to be produced.

19.7 THE OUTPUT STATEMENT

The OUTPUT statement is used to route output to specific nodes. Some of the parameters that can be coded on this statement are:

■ LINECT=*n*

This is used to specify the number of lines of output per page of output. This number can range from 0 to 255.

■ FORMS=*forms*

This is used to identify the print forms to which output is to be routed.

■ COPIES=*n*

This is used to specify the number of copies of output. *n* can range from 1 to 255.

■ DEST=*destination*

This is used to specify the destination of the output.

■ UCS=*character-set*

This is used to specify the universal character set of the output.

19.8 THE PRIORITY STATEMENT

The PRIORITY statement is used to specify the priority of the job that is to be executed. It must precede the JOB statement. Priority numbers can range from 0 to 15; note that the higher the number assigned to the job, the higher its priority. Here's an example:

```
/*PRIORITY   4
//JOB1       JOB   (A123),'JACKIE MOE',CLASS=L
```

19.9 THE SETUP STATEMENT

The SETUP statement is used to indicate the tape volumes that will be required in the execution of a job. Here's an example:

```
//JOB1       JOB   (A123),'STACY C',CLASS=L
/*SETUP       00123,00250
```

00123 and 00250 are the volume serial numbers that will be required by JOB1. The volume serial numbers are coded in columns 11 to 71.

19.10 THE MESSAGE STATEMENT

The MESSAGE statement is used to send messages to the computer operator. Here's an example:

```
//JOB2       JOB   (A123),'MARY Z',CLASS=L
/*MESSAGE     PLEASE CALL #2044 AFTER JOB COMPLETION
```

19.11 THE NOTIFY STATEMENT

The NOTIFY statement is used to notify a user of the completion of a job. Here's an example:

```
//JOB3       JOB   (A123),'KATHY S',CLASS=L
/*NOTIFY      NODE1.USER1
```

NODE1 is the node name. USER1 is the ID of the user who will be notified of the termination of JOB3. Both the node name and the user ID can be up to 8 alphanumeric characters each.

19.12 THE SIGNON STATEMENT

The SIGNON statement is used to start a job at a remote location. Here's the syntax:

```
/*SIGNON       REMOTEnnnPW1    ...    PW2
or
/*SIGNON       RMTnnnn
or
/*SIGNON       RMnnn
```

where *nnn* is a number that identifies the remote node. PW1 and PW2 are the passwords associated with the remote node at which the job is to be executed. Passwords are optional. Please note that the keywords REMOTE, RMT or RM must start in column 16 Columns 9 through 15 must be blank. Also, PW1 must start in column 25, and PW2, if it is coded, must begin in column 73. Here's an example:

```
//JOB4       JOB    (A123),'CHARLIE W',CLASS=L
/*SIGNON       REMOTE123ADA
```

19.13 THE SIGNOFF STATEMENT

The SIGNOFF statement is used to terminate a job that has been started at a remote node. Here's an example:

```
//JOB4       JOB    (A123),'CHARLIE W',CLASS=L
/*SIGNOFF
```

19.14 JES3, AN OVERVIEW

Unlike JES2, a JES3 environment is centralized. It has only one computer, called the global processor, which manages and controls the processing of all other computers within the network.   All other computers are called local processors. The global processor schedules the I/O, as well as purge and conversion processes for every job in the system.

In the sections that follow we will describe some common control statements that can be coded in JES3. But first, let us give you some rules about coding.

19.15 RULES FOR CODING

- All JES3 control statements must start with a //* in columns 1, 2 and 3.

- They must follow the JOB statement, unless it is a command statement.

- They cannot be placed inside cataloged procedures.

In addition to this, please note that if any parameters are coded in JES3 control statements, then they will take precedence over any corresponding parameters coded in regular JCL statements.

19.16 SOME JES3 CONTROL STATEMENTS

Table 19.2 lists some of the functions implemented in a JES3 environment and the corresponding control statement. A discussion of each statement follows in subsequent sections.

Table 19.2 JES3 Control Statements

Function	Corresponding Control Statements
Specify processor requirements	MAIN optional-parameters,... Different parameters are used to indicate specific processor requirements for the job
Specify the node within the network at which the job will execute	ROUTE XEQ node node identifies the node at which the job is to execute

Specify accounting information for the node at which the job will execute	NETACCT parameter,... Different parameters can be used to indicate specific accounting information to the system
Supply processing instructions for printed data sets	FORMAT PR parameter,... The parameters will be described in the next section
Specify dependencies between jobs, if any exist, within a network	NET ID=id,parameter,... id is the name of the dependent network
Specify the beginning of an in-stream data set	DATASET DDNAME=name,parameter,.. name is the data set name
Specify the end of an in-stream data set	ENDDATASET
Send messages to the operator	OPERATOR text
Transmit a job or job stream to a JES3 or non-JES3 node	XMIT DEST=destination data destination is the destination node data is passed to the job
Start a job at a remote node	SIGNON parameters
Terminate a job at the remote node	SIGNOFF

19.17 THE MAIN STATEMENT

The MAIN statement is used to identify processor requirements for a job. A description of some of the parameters that can be coded on this statement follows.

- SYSTEM=*option*

This parameter is used to identify the processor to the system. The following options can be coded on the SYSTEM parameter:

Option	Function
ANY	Indicates that any global or local computer can be used as the processor for a job
JGLOBAL	Indicates that the job should use the global processor only
JLOCAL	Indicates that the job is to execute on a local processor
name	Indicates that the job is to execute on the named processor

- USER=*user-id*

This parameter is used to submit the job with a user ID. It may be different from the one who actually submits the job.

- CLASS=*class*

This parameter is used to identify the job class to the remote node. It overrides the CLASS statement on the JOB statement.

- HOLD=*option*

Option can be coded as YES or NO. This parameter is used to hold a job before it finishes executing, or release a job, if it is already being held. This parameter overrides the TYPRUN=HOLD parameter on the JOB statement, if it is coded.

19.17.1 An Example

```
//JOB1       JOB    (A123),'D TUSCAN',CLASS=L
//*MAIN      SYSTEM=JGLOBAL,CLASS=T
```

In this example, the MAIN statement specifies that JOB1 will be processed by the main global processor and CLASS is specified as T.

19.18 THE ROUTE XEQ STATEMENT

This statement is used to identify the remote network node at which a job is to execute.

19.18.1 Rules for Coding

■ This statement should be placed after the JOB statement of the location at which the job is being submitted.

■ It can be coded immediately before the JOB statement of the location at which the job is being executed.

■ It should be placed after the NETACCT statement, if coded.

19.18.2 An Example

```
//JOB1      JOB     (A123),'C SASSOON'
//*ROUTE    XEQ     BOSTON
//JOB2      JOB     (B123),'B SASSOON'
//STEP1     EXEC    PGM=PROGRAM1
```

In this example JOB1 is run locally. However, it is executed at the remote location BOSTON. Notice that the ROUTE statement immediately follows the JOB statement for the current location, and before the JOB statement of the location where it is actually executed.

19.19 THE NETACCT STATEMENT

This statement is used to specify accounting information for a job to a node in the network. A description of the parameters that can be coded on this statement follows.

■ PNAME=*programmer-name*

This parameter is used to specify the programmer name, which can be 1 to 20 characters long.

■ ACCT=*account-number*

The account number can be 1 to 8 characters long.

- DEPT=*name*

name identifies the department number within the network. It can be 1 to 8 characters long.

- BLDG=*building-number*

building-number is used to identify the building number. It can be 1 to 8 characters long.

- USERID=*user-id*

user-id can be 1 to 8 characters long.

19.19.1 An Example

```
//JOB1     JOB     (A123),'A STEVENS',CLASS=L
//*NETACCT PNAME='A STEVENS',DEPT=MIS,BLDG=05
```

The parameters in this example should be self-explanatory.

19.20 THE FORMAT PR STATEMENT

This statement is used to specify processing instructions for print data sets. PR indicates that specifications are for the print data sets only. A description of the parameters that can be coded on this statement follows.

- DDNAME=*name*

name identifies the name of the data set that is to be printed. It may be necessary for you to qualify the data set name by preceding it with the stepname.

In addition to this, DDNAME can be specified as one of the following:

DDNAME	Description
JESJCL	Print JCL statements and associated messages
JESMSG	Print JES3 statements and associated messages
SYSMSG	Print system messages

- DEST=*destination*

This parameter is used to specify the destination of the output data set. If DEST is coded on the DD statement, then it should be the same as that destination. If it is not coded, then output is routed to the default printer.

- PRTY=*priority*

This parameter is used to specify the priority of the print job in the ouptut queue. Priority can be a number between 0 and 255. The higher the number, the higher the priority of the print job.

- COPIES=*n*

This parameter is used to specify the number of copies to be printed for the job.

- CONTROL=*option*

This parameter is used to specify details with reference to the printed output. *option* can be one of the following:

Option	Description
PROGRAM	Used to indicate that each logical record within the print data set begins with a carriage control character
SINGLE	Used to specify forced single spacing of output
DOUBLE	Used to specify forced double spacing of output
TRIPLE	Used to specify forced triple spacing of output

- THRESHLD=*limit*

This parameter is used to specify the maximum size of the output data set in lines. *limit* is a number between 1 to 99999999.

- FORMS=*forms*

This parameter is used to identify the type of form on which the output will be printed. FORMS=STANDARD is the default, implying the size of the installation's standard forms.

19.21 THE NET STATEMENT

The NET statement is used to define dependencies between jobs in a dependent job control network. JES3 organizes the set of dependent jobs in a specific manner, and then executes them.

The syntax looks like this:

//*NET ID=*net-id,parameter,parameter*

where *net-id* is an identifying name for the dependent node. *net-id* can be 1 to 8 characters in length. The first character must be alphabetic.

The following parameters can be coded on the NET statement.

■ ABCMP=*option*

The ABCMP parameter is used to specify the action that should be taken upon abnormal termination of the job. *option* can be one of the following:

Option	Description
KEEP	Used to specify that the job is to be kept until it is resubmitted
NOKP	Used to specify that the job is to be purged, given that it is not resubmitted, within the time frame that other dependent jobs within the node have been executed

■ NHOLD=*n*

This parameter is used to hold a job until the preceding jobs have been completed. *n* is a number specifying the total number of prior jobs that must be completed before the current job can be released for execution. *n* can be a number from 0 to 32767.

If this parameter is skipped, or NHOLD is set to 0, the job is placed on a queue for immediate execution.

■ NORMAL=*option*

This parameter is used to specify the action that should be taken on normal execution of a prior job. *option* can be any of the following:

Option	Description
D	Used to decrease the value stored in NHOLD by 1. The job is scheduled when the count in NHOLD is 0.

F   Used to flush this and subsequent jobs after it. Any output generated from previous jobs will still be printed.

R   Used to retain the job in its current status. The count in NHOLD is not decreased.

- ABNORMAL=*option*

This parameter is used to specify the action that should be taken on abnormal termination of a prior job. option assignments are the same as for the NORMAL parameter.

19.21.1 An Example

```
//JOB5 JOB    (A123),'B LETTERMAN',CLASS=L
//*NET ID=N1234,ABCMP=KEEP,NHOLD=5,ABNORMAL=F
```

In this example, the name of the dependent node for this job is identified as N1234. ABCMP states that the job is to be kept until it is resubmitted, if JOB5 abends abnormally. NHOLD specifies that five jobs (prior to the current job) must be completed before this one is executed. If any prior job executes unsuccessfully, then the entire list of jobs should be flushed from the system.

19.22 THE DATASET STATEMENT

The DATASET statement is used to specify the beginning of an in-stream data set. The in-stream data set can contain JCL and/or data. The following parameters can be coded on this statement.

- DDNAME=*ddname*

This parameter is used to identify the name of the data set. *ddname* must be unique for the job.

- J=YES or J=NO

This parameter is used to identify the kind of statement that will terminate the end of a data set. If NO is coded, it implies that a JOB statement will terminate it. If YES is coded, then a //*ENDDATASET statement is used to imply the same.

- CLASS=MSGCLASS or CLASS=NO or CLASS=*class*

This parameter is used to specify the assignment of class. If MSGCLASS is coded, it implies that CLASS will be assigned the same value as the one assigned to the MSGCLASS parameter. If NO is coded, then the default output class is assigned. You can also code a predefined value for this parameter; this would be the designation for class.

19.22.1 An Example

```
//JOB1       JOB     (A123),'R BECKER'
//STEP1      EXEC    PGM=PROGRAM1
//DD1        DD      DSN=FILE1
//*DATASET   DDNAME=STEP1.PROGRAM1.DD1,J=YES
   THIS IS DATA FOR THE PROGRAM
//*ENDDATASET
```

In this example, PROGRAM1 is executed in STEP1, and a data set called FILE1 is defined in the DD statement called DD1. Next follows the JES3 control statement which defines DATASET. DDNAME refers to STEP1, in which PROGRAM1 is executed, and the data set defined in DD1 is read. Coding a YES for the J parameter indicates that an //*ENDATASET statement will terminate the stream of data.

19.23 THE OPERATOR STATEMENT

This statement is used to send a message to the operator at the time that the JES3 control statements are processed. Here's an example:

```
//JOB1       JOB     (A123),'A BECKER',CLASS=M
//*OPERATOR PLEASE CALL #2044 AFTER BATCH COMPLETES
```

The operator will receive this message at the time that the job will be executed.

19.24 THE XMIT STATEMENT

The XMIT statement is used to transmit a job or job stream to another JES3 or non-JES3 node. The job is transmitted only, not executed. Here's an example:

```
//JOB1        JOB    (A123),'H BECKER',CLASS=M
//*XMIT       DEST=BOSTON
   JOB BEING TRANSMITTED TO BOSTON
/*
```

In this example, the text that follows the XMIT statement, up to the terminating /* is transmitted to the node identified as Boston.

19.25 THE SIGNON STATEMENT

The SIGNON statement is used to start a job at a remote workstation at a remote node. Unlike other JES3 statements, the SIGNON statement contains only a single slash followed by an asterisk. Here's the syntax:

```
/*SIGNON       parameters,...
```

The following parameters can be coded:

■ *work-station-name*

This parameter is used to identify the name of the remote workstation that the job is to be executed at. This name can be 1 to 5 characters long and must begin in column 16.

■ *reader*

This parameter is coded as A, implying an automatic reader for the job. It must be coded in column 22. If an automatic reader is not used, then this parameter should be omitted.

■ *output-spec*

This parameter is coded as R and is used to specify information about the printed output produced by the job. It must be coded in column 23. If it is coded, then it specifies that the printed output of the job is to be suspended, if the device to which the output is to be sent is not ready.

■ *password1*

This parameter is used to identify the password required to execute the remote job. The password can be 1 to 8 characters long and must be coded in column 25.

■ *password2*

This parameter is used to identify the password required to log into the remote workstation. The password can be 1 to 8 characters long and must be coded in column 35.

19.26 THE SIGNOFF STATEMENT

The `SIGNOFF` statement is used to terminate a remote job session. Like the `SIGNON` statement, only one slash precedes the asterisk. The example just presented is continued here.

```
//JOB1      JOB      (A123),'O BECKER'
/*SIGNOFF
```

19.27 REVIEW

In this chapter we described the control statements used in a JES2 and JES3 environment. Job Entry Subsystems control the jobs that execute at remote nodes.

In a JES2 environment, processing is *decentralized* within the network. If your installation requires mostly on-line processing, then a multiple processor complex would be more suitable, hence, the obvious choice would be JES2.

In a JES3 environment, processing is *centralized*. If the processing at your installation is mostly batch oriented, then centralized management of jobs would be required, hence, the obvious choice would be JES3.

Of the two subsystems, JES3 costs more since it requires more central storage. It is also more complex to administer than JES2.

Storage Management
Subsystem (SMS)

20.1 INTRODUCTION

Storage Management Subsystem (SMS) is an optional feature of an MVS operating system, which is activated by your installation. It is a tool that is used to improve the management of available disk space. Developers who code JCL need to specify attributes, such as size and location, about the data sets utilized by their applications to the operating system. Since these specifications are coded by the user, they may not necessarily be the most efficient. SMS allows for better management of disk space by shifting these specifications from the individual application developer, to the data center.

20.2 ADVANTAGES OF SMS

Data sets that are created by SMS are called SMS managed data sets. The following are the advantages associated with an SMS environment.

- The user is relieved of making decisions about resource allocation of data sets, since it is done by SMS.

- SMS provides the capability of concatenating data sets of unlike devices. For example, a tape data set can be concatenated with a disk data set. This capability is not available in a non-SMS environment.

- SMS managed data sets cannot be deleted unless they are first uncataloged. Due to this extra step, erroneous deletion of data sets is minimized.

- Additional features are available in the use of IDCAMS in an SMS environment. For example, the ALTER command can be used to increase the limit of the number of generation data sets in a GDG. This feature is not available in a non-SMS system.

- VSAM data sets created in an SMS environment offer more flexibility than those created through JCL in a non-SMS environment.

20.3 DISADVANTAGES OF SMS

Use of SMS is not devoid of some drawbacks:

- If SMS is used to request space for a data set and there is not enough space left for the secondary allocation, then the job will abend, and this is a serious drawback. For non-SMS managed data sets, subsequent volumes of the device for which the request is issued are searched, and the job does not terminate abnormally.

- In SMS, if a non-existent data set name is created and referenced in the same step, an error is encountered. A data set must exist before the start of a job, if it is referenced in it. For non-SMS managed data sets, a data set can be created and referenced without any errors. This is because the existence of data sets referenced are not verified. The following example will help you understand what has just been said.

```
//JOB1      JOB    (A123),'J MORRISON'
//STEP1     EXEC   PGM=PROGRAM1
//DD1       DD     DSN=TEST.INFILE,
//                 DISP=(NEW,CATLG,DELETE),
//                 UNIT=UNIT1,
//                 SPACE=(CYL,(4,2),RLSE),
//                 DCB=(RECFM=FB,
//                    LRECL=80,BLKSIZE=6160)
//DD2       DD     DSN=TEST.INFILE,
//                 DISP=OLD,
//                 VOL=REF=*.DD1
```

In this example, DD1 defines a data set called TEST.INFILE. The disposition of this file is NEW, indicating that it will be created. Upon successful execution of the job, the data set will be cataloged. Upon unsuccessful execution, it will be deleted. This data set resides on UNIT1. The SPACE and DCB parameters are used to specify other features of the data set.

In the next DD statement, TEST.INFILE is referenced again, and in disposition of this file is specified as OLD.

In a non-SMS environment, this JCL will execute successfully. However, in an SMS environment, the job will abend, since the data set `TEST.INFILE` cannot be created and referenced within the same job.

20.4 DISP DEFAULTS IN AN SMS ENVIRONMENT

Before proceeding with an explanation of SMS parameters, we describe a difference and a similarity in the information conveyed in the `DISP` parameter in an SMS environment, when compared to a non-SMS environment.

- In an SMS-managed environment, the following statement

  `DISP=(NEW,KEEP)`

  defaults to

  `DISP=(NEW,CATLG)`

  In a non-SMS managed environment, the `KEEP` subparameter does not default to `CATLG`. Note that `CATLG` must be explicitly coded if a data set is to be cataloged.

- In an SMS-managed environment, the following statement

  `DISP=(OLD,DELETE)`

  will delete and uncatalog a data set. In a non-SMS managed environment, the same statement will also result in the data set being deleted and uncataloged.

20.5 AN OVERVIEW OF SOME SMS PARAMETERS

Table 20.1 lists some of the functionality that is handled by SMS and the corresponding parameters used to convey that functionality. Explanatory text is added, whenever necessary.

The remainder of this chapter discusses these parameters in detail.

Table 20.1 SMS Parameters

Function	Corresponding Parameters and Subparameter
Specify an SMS managed data set	STORCLAS=class class is the name of a class to which the data set will belong to
Specify parameters coded on the DD statement	DATACLAS=class class is installation defined, and conveys fixed predefined information about the data set
Specify features related to the management of the data set	MGMTCLAS=class class is installation defined and conveys predefined information on: - how unused space in data sets is to be used - how data sets are to be archived - how often the data set is to be backed up
Create VSAM data sets	RECORG=type type is the type of VSAM data set that is to be created
Specify position of key field in VSAM data sets	KEYOFF=key-offset key-offset is the starting position, in bytes, of the key field relative to the beginning of the record
Request space in the number of record units	AVGREC=option option specifies varying methods of figuring out the number of records
Copy attributes of an existing cataloged data set to a new data set	LIKE=model.dataset model.dataset is the name of the cataloged model data set

20.6 THE STORCLAS PARAMETER

STORCLAS is a keyword parameter. It is used to assign a data set to an
SMS defined class. This parameter has significance only if SMS is
active, otherwise it is ignored. Here's the syntax:

STORCLAS=*class*

where *class* is an installation defined name and can be one to eight
characters long.

Use of this parameter results in the data set defined in the DD
statement within that job being SMS-managed. What this means is that
SMS parameters can be used to manipulate this data set.

The VOLUME and UNIT parameters (normally coded at the time that
a data set is created) can be omitted, since these values are now SMS
supplied.

20.6.1 An Example

```
//JOB1       JOB   (A123),'C SIMON'
//STEP1      EXEC  PGM=PROGRAM1
//DD1        DD    DSN=SOURCE.FILE1,
//                 DISP=(NEW,CATLG,DELETE),
//                 SPACE=(CYL,(1,1),RLSE),
//                 LRECL=80,
//                 RECFM=FB,
//                 STORCLAS=SMS1
```

In this example, a new data set called SOURCE.FILE1 is created.
This data set will utilize one cylinder of primary space. The logical
length of its records will be 80 bytes, its records will be of the type *Fixed
Block*. Notice the last parameter, which is STORCLAS. This parameter
is set to SMS1. In this example, SMS1 is an installation defined class, the
use of which indicates that this data set will be SMS managed. Notice
that the VOLUME and UNIT parameters are omitted. These parameters
will be installation defined for the class SMS1.

20.7 THE DATACLAS PARAMETER

DATACLAS is a keyword parameter. It is used to define any or all of the
following parameters for a data set:

LRECL
RECORG

```
RECFM
RETPD or EXPDT
volcount coded on the VOL parameter
SPACE
AVGREC
```

We will now provide an explanation of the *volcount* subparameter only, since most of the other subparameters have already been explained in this book.

volcount is coded on the VOL parameter. It is used to specify the number of tape volumes that can be mounted when a tape data set is being created or expanded.

For SMS managed VSAM data sets, DATACLAS can be used to define the following parameters:

```
CISIZE
IMBED
REPLICATE
SHAREOPTIONS
FREESPACE
```

The data set itself can be any one of the following types:

Physical Sequential (PS)
Partitioned (PO)
VSAM
Direct Access (DA)

Here's the syntax of the DATACLAS parameter:

DATACLAS=*class*

class is installation defined. It can be one to eight characters long. Use of this parameter in a DD statement results in the predefined values for any or all of the above parameters being used for the associated data set. Please note that installation defined values for DATACLAS can be overridden simply by coding the individual parameters within your job.

20.7.1 Some Examples

Example 1

Suppose a class named GENERAL contains the following definitions:

```
SPACE=(CYL,(1,1),RLSE),
DCB=(RECFM=FB,LRECL=80)
```

Now take a look at this JCL:

```
//JOB1       JOB  (A123),'J TAYLOR'
//STEP1      EXEC PGM=PROGRAM1
//DD1        DD   DSN=TEST.DATA1,
//                DISP=(NEW,CATLG,DELETE),
//                UNIT=SYSDA,
//                DATACLAS=GENERAL
```

The space and DCB attributes of the data set TEST.DATA1 will be derived from the predefined installation-defined values for the class called GENERAL.

Example 2

```
//JOB2       JOB  (A123),'RJ MAILER'
//STEP1      EXEC PGM=PROGRAM1
//DD1        DD   DSN=TEST.DATA1,
//                DISP=(NEW,CATLG,DELETE),
//                UNIT=SYSDA,
//                SPACE=(CYL,(5,2),RLSE),
//                DATACLAS=GENERAL
```

This example conveys essentially the same information as Example 1, except that the SPACE parameter of DATACLAS is overridden.

20.8 THE MGMTCLAS PARAMETER

This parameter is used to provide a management class for the associated data set coded in the DD statement. A management class is used to control the migration of data sets, the frequency of back ups, the number of backup versions, and the retention criteria of backup versions. Here's the syntax:

MGMTCLAS=*class*

class is installation defined. It can be one to eight characters long. Parameters defined for this class can not be overridden.

Use of this parameter in a non-SMS managed data sets will result in a JCL error.

20.8.1 An Example

```
//JOB1      JOB    (A123),'R HAVENS'
//STEP1     EXEC   PGM=PROGRAM1
//DD1       DD     DSN=TEST.FILE2,
//                 DISP=(NEW,CATLG,DELETE),
//                 DATACLAS=GENERAL,
//                 MGMTCLAS=ARCHIVE
```

20.9 THE RECORG PARAMETER

This parameter is used to create SMS managed VSAM data sets. It is significant only at the time that a VSAM data set is created. It is ignored if the data set already exists. Here's the syntax:

RECORG=*option*

where *option* can be any of the following:

KS: Key sequenced data set
ES: Entry sequenced data set
RR: Relative record data set
LS: Linear space data set

20.9.1 An Example

```
//JOB1      JOB    (A123),'R CASH'
//STEP1     EXEC   PGM=PROGRAM1
//DD1       DD     DSN=A100.VSAM.DATA1,
//                 DISP=(NEW,CATLG,DELETE),
//                 DATACLAS=GENERAL,
//                 RECORG=ES
```

In this example, an entry-sequenced SMS managed VSAM data set is created.

20.10 THE KEYOFF AND KEYLEN PARAMETERS

The KEYOFF parameter is used in conjunction with the RECORG and KEYLEN parameters. It is required for Key Sequenced data sets. It identifies what is called the key offset, which is the position of the first byte of the key field for that data set, relative to the first byte of the logical record. The first byte of a logical record starts at byte 0.

Here's the syntax:

KEYOFF=*offset*

The KEYLEN parameter is used to define the length of the key. Here's the syntax:

KEYLEN=*n*

where *n* is a number.

20.10.1 An Example

```
//JOB1      JOB    (A123),'R CASH'
//STEP1     EXEC   PGM=PROGRAM1
//DD1       DD     DSN=A100.VSAM.DATA1,
//                 DISP=(NEW,CATLG,DELETE),
//                 RECORG=KS,
//                 KEYOFF=20,
//                 KEYLEN=15
```

In this example, the key offset is specified at byte number 20 (this is the twenty-first byte, since we start counting at byte zero), for the key sequenced data set called A100.VSAM.DATA1. The length of the key is 15 bytes.

20.11 THE AVGREC PARAMETER

The AVGREC parameter is used to request space in units of number of records. Here's the syntax:

AVGREC=U

or

AVGREC=K

or

AVGREC=M

The options coded for AVGREC convey the following information:

- U

This is used to indicate that the primary and secondary allocations of the SPACE parameter will be equal to the number of logical records specified and multiplied by 1.

■ K

This is used to indicate that the primary and secondary allocations of the SPACE parameter will be equal to the number of logical records specified and multiplied by 1024.

■ M

This is used to indicate that the primary and secondary allocations of the SPACE parameter will be equal to the number of logical records which have been multiplied by 1,048,576.

20.11.1 An Example

```
//JOB1      JOB    (A123),'J CARTER'
//STEP1     EXEC   PGM=PROGRAM1
//DD1       DD     DSN=AVG.TEST.FILE,
//                 DISP=(NEW,CATLG,DELETE),
//                 UNIT=SYSDA,
//                 SPACE=(80,(600,200)),
//                 AVGREC=K,
//                 LRECL=80,RECFM=FB
```

In this example, primary space will be calculated as 600 * 1024 bytes of 80 byte records.

The AVGREC parameter should not be coded when requesting space in cylinders (CYL) or tracks (TRK).

20.12 THE LIKE PARAMETER

This parameter is used to copy attributes from an existing cataloged data set to a new data set. The following attributes can be copied over:

    SPACE
    RECFM
    AVGREC
    LRECL

The following attributes can be copied over for VSAM data sets:

    RECORG
    KEYLEN
    KEYOFF

Here's the syntax:

LIKE=*model.dataset*

where *model.dataset* identifies the name of the model data set.

20.12.1 An Example

```
//JOB1      JOB    (A123),'R YANG'
//STEP1     EXEC   PGM=PROGRAM1
//DD1       DD     DSN=TEST.DATA2,
//                 DISP=(NEW,CATLG,DELETE),
//                 LIKE=TEST.MODEL
```

In this example, the attributes of the data set TEST.MODEL is copied to the new data set called TEST.DATA2.

20.13 REVIEW

In this chapter we introduced you to SMS. SMS is an important tool that can significantly reduce the burden placed on JCL programmers as far as coding specifications for data sets is concerned. It can also help increase the efficiency of the system by organizing and storing data in a predetermined manner that is planned by those who are specifically trained to make the correct decisions in this area.

Glossary of Terms

Term	Description
Abend	An abnormal situation that occurs during the execution of a program.
Access Method Services (AMS)	An IBM-developed multifunction service utility program used in the creation and manipulation of VSAM and non-VSAM files.
Allocation	Request for space on a Direct Access Storage Device.
Alphanumeric characters	Alphabetic (letters A to Z) and digit (0 to 9) characters.
Alternate index	A data set that contains alternate keys and one or more pointers to the data set records of a KSDS or an ESDS.
Alternate index cluster	A key sequenced data set cluster containing an index and data component. It keeps key-pointer pair records for a base cluster.
Alternate key	A key, other than the prime key, that provides access to a base cluster

B

Term	Description
Backward reference	Used to copy information from a previous DD statement in a job.
Base cluster	A KSDS, ESDS, LDS or an RRDS.

Backup	A copy of a data set, can be used to reconstruct the data set if necessary.
Block	A physical group of logical records. Each block may contain one or more records. It is the physical unit of transfer between storage and I/O devices.
Byte	The smallest unit of storage in MVS.

C

Cataloged procedure	A group of precoded JCL statements saved in a cataloged partitioned data set.
Condition code	Also known as return code. This is a number between 0 and 4095, which is issued upon successful or unsuccessful execution of a program. A condition code of 0 normally implies the successful execution of a program
Compress	An operation which is used to eiliminate any unusable disk space within a partitioned data set by deleting and replacing applicable members
Control Area (CA)	A group of control intervals used for distributing free space and reorganization of a KSDS
Central Processing Unit (CPU)	Part of a Processor Complex which executes machine instructions
Concatenation	A method by which several identical types of data sets are treated as one data set
Control Interval (CI)	A unit of data that is transferred between auxiliary and virtual storage. It contains records, free space, and control information
Cylinder	An area of data storage on a disk device. It consists of multiple concentric tracks. Data can be accessed in one seek.

D

Data Definition (DD)	JCL statement used to specify the location and attributes of an existing data set, or the attributes and location for a new data set.
Direct Access Storage Device (DASD)	A magnetic data storage device from which data can be accessed directly, there is no need for a sequential search

Disk	A device that contains read-write heads, platters, electronics, and other components
Data component	The component of the cluster or alternate index that contains the data.
Data set	Unit of storage of information that can be read from, or written to, or both.
Define command	An Access Method Services functional command used to allocate VSAM objects
Delete command	An Access Method Services functional command used to delete VSAM objects

E

Entry Sequenced Data Set (ESDS)	A non-indexed VSAM data set, in which records are stored and accessed in physical sequence
Extent	A contiguous area on a DASD allocated to a data set or VSAM space

G

Generation Data Group (GDG)	Group of chronologically related data sets
Generation data set	A data set that is a member of a generation data group

I

Interactive System Productivity Facility (ISPF)	A TSO subsystem which provides full-screen, menu-driven edit and dialog services
Index component	An independent constituent of a KSDS or alternate index that helps in the establishment of the sequence of records in the data component

J

Job Control Language (JCL)	A structured language used by MVS to execute a unit of work
Job Entry Subsystem 2 (JES2)	An MVS subsystem whose installation is mandatory (unless JES3 is used) in order to implement I/O spooling and printing
Job Entry Subsystem 3 (JES3)	An MVS subsystem whose installation is mandatory (unless JES2 is used) in order to implement I/O spooling and printing

JOBLIB	DDname coded on the DD statement. Specifies the library that contains the executable modules used in the job
Jobname	The name field coded on the JOB statement, the job is identified by this name

K

Key Sequenced Data Set (KSDS)	An indexed VSAM data set whose records can be accessed in key sequence
Keyword parameters	Parameters that can be coded in any order, and identified by an equal sign

L

Linear Data Set (LDS)	A sequential VSAM data set having one logical record per control interval

M

Master catalog	Points to other user catalogs that contains pointers to data sets on a DASD. There is always one master catalog for an MVS system, and it is established at initial program load time
MVS/XA	Stands for MVS/Extended Architecture. It is an IBM operating system that supports two gigabytes of address space. It is an extension of MVS/SP
MVS/ESA	Stands for MVS/Enterprise System. It is an IBM operating system that supports additional address space for data. It is an extension of MVS/XA

R

Read/Write heads	Transfers data from the Processor Complex control unit to the surface of the DASD platter and vice versa
Relative Record Data Set (RRDS)	A data set whose records are loaded into fixed-length slots and accessed through the use of a relative record number
Relative Record Number (RRN)	An integer number that specifies the relative position of a slot from the beginning of an RRDS

S

Storage Management Subsystem (SMS)	An IBM product which is available only with MVS/ESA. Its main objective is to simplify the use of JCL by managing disk volumes and data sets defined on them
Secondary space allocation	Space defined on a DASD that is allocated when primary space allocation is used up

T

Temporary data set	A data set whose existence on the Direct Access Storage device is limited for the duration of the job
Track	A predefined path on a Direct Access Storage device
Time Sharing Option (TSO)	An optional feature of MVS that provides time-sharing capabilities

U

Unit affinity	Indicates that two files use the same physical device
User catalog	A catalog that contains information about VSAM and non-VSAM data sets
Utility programs	Used to perform commonly required functions

V

Virtual Storage Access Method (VSAM)	An MVS access method used for Direct Access Storage Device. Resides in virtual storage along with the program that requires its services for manipulation of data
Volume Table Of Contents (VTOC)	Group of records that contain the data set names and attributes of each data set on the Direct Access Storage Device (DASD)
Volume	An electro-magnetic medium. Data can be written to or read from it

Common Abend Codes

Code	Explanation
S0C4	Caused by subscript being out of range
S0C5	Caused by invalid address specification, i.e. the address points to an instruction, control word, or data outside the available real storage
S0C7	Caused by bad data, which the program was unable to detect. The result is an ABEND failure
S222	Caused by job being cancelled by the operator, due to a request by the program for an unavailable resource
S237	Caused by end of volume being encountered
S322	Caused when CPU time assigned to the job, job step, or procedure has been exceeded
S413	This abend occurs if the DD statement referenced by UNIT=AFF statement is not closed before the DD statement that comes before it
S522	Caused when a wait state exceeds an installation defined time limit
SB37	Caused by lack of sufficient secondary space
SD37	Caused by lack of sufficient primary space
SE37	Caused by lack of space for PDS (Partitioned)

Control
Statements

Appendix C shows the format of the MVS JCL control statements listed below. This appendix should prove to be a useful quick-reference.

- The JOB statement

- The EXEC statement

- The DD statement

- JES2 control statements
  - NETACCT
  - ROUTE
  - JOBPARM
  - OUTPUT
  - PRIORITY
  - SETUP
  - MESSAGE
  - NOTIFY
  - SIGNON/SIGNOFF

- JES3 control statements
  - MAIN
  - NETACCT
  - ROUTE XEQ
  - FORMAT PR
  - NET
  - DATASET
  - OPERATOR
  - SIGNON/SIGNOFF
  - XMIT

THE JOB STATEMENT

```
//jobname    JOB    {accounting-information, }

                    {programmer-name, }

                    {CLASS=jobclass, }

                    {COND=number,operator, }

                    {MSGCLASS=output-class-name, }

                    {MSGLEVEL=statements,message, }

                    { (TYPRUN=HOLD)   }
                    { (       SCAN), }

                    {TIME=minutes,seconds, }

                    { (REGION=valueK)  }
                    { (       =valueM) }
```

THE EXEC STATEMENT

```
//stepname    EXEC  { (PGM=program-name  ) }
              { (PROC=procedure-name  ,) }

              { ACCT=account-information,  }

              { (ADDRSPC=VIRT  ) }
              { (       =REAL ), }

              { DPRTY=value1,value2,  }

              { PERFORM=n,  }

              { (REGION=valueK)   }
              { (       =valueM), }

              { (COND=number,operator  ) }
              { (    =number,operator,stepname  ) }
              { (    =EVEN                 ) }
              { (    =ONLY                 ), }

              { TIME=minutes,seconds,  }

              { (RD=R   ) }
              { (  =RNC ) }
              { (  =NR  ) }
              { (  =NC  ), }
```

THE DD STATEMENT

```
//ddname   DD   { (DUMMY ) }
                { (DSN=data-set-name ) }
                { (  =NULLFILE ), }

                { DISP=(status,normal-disp,abnormal-disp),   }

                { (UNIT=device-address ) }
                { (  =device-type ) }
                { (  =device-group-name ) }
                { (  =AFF ) }
                { (  =DEFER ), }

                { (VOL=SER ) }
                { (  =REF ) }
                { (  =PRIVATE ) }
                { (  =RETAIN ) }
                { (  =SEQ ), }

                { SPACE=(unit,(primary,secondary,directory),
                        RLSE,
                        { ( CONTIG) },
                        { ( MXIG ) },
                        { ( ROUND ) }

                { DCB=(LRECL=logical-record-length,
                        RECFM=record-format,
                        BLKSIZE=block-size,
                        BUFNO=number) }
```

The DD statement for in-stream data is:

```
//ddname   DD   { (* ) }
                { (DATA), }

                { DLM=xx }
```

The DD statement for printed output files is:

```
//ddname   DD   { SYSOUT=sysout-class }

                { DEST=destination }

                { HOLD=(YES) }
                {    =(NO), }

                ( OUTLIM=number }
```

JES2 CONTROL STATEMENTS

- **The NETACCT statement**

/*NETACCT account-number

- **The ROUTE statement**

/*ROUTE (XEQ)
    (PRINT)

- **The JOBPARM statement**

/*JOBPARM { BYTES=value }

       { LINES=value }

       { COPIES=copies }

       { RESTART=Y }
       {   =N }

       { PAGES=value }

- **The OUTPUT statement**

/*OUTPUT { LINECT=n }

       { FORMS=forms }

       { COPIES=copies }

       { DEST=destination }

       { UCS=character-set }

- **The PRIORITY statement**

/*PRIORITY priority

- **The SETUP statement**

/*SETUP volume,volume,...,volume

- **The MESSAGE statement**

/*MESSAGE message

- **The NOTIFY statement**

/*NOTIFY   user-id

- **The SIGNON statement**

/*SIGNON   REMOTEnnnPW1   pw2
or
/*SIGNON   RMTnnnn PW1   pw2
or
/*SIGNON   RMnnn   PW1   pw2

- **The SIGNOFF statement**

/*SIGNOFF

JES3 CONTROL STATEMENTS

- ## The MAIN statement

```
//*MAIN    { SYSTEM=main-name }

          { USER=user-id }

          { CLASS=jobclass }

          { HOLD=YES }
          {     =NO }
```

- ## The NETACCT statement

```
//*NETACCT    option,option,...,option
```

- ## The ROUTE XEQ statement

```
//*ROUTE XEQ node-id
```

- ## The FORMAT PR statement

```
//*FORMAT PR,DDNAME={ name-specification }
            { COPIES=n }

              { CONTROL=(PROGRAM ) }
              {         (SINGLE ) }
              {         (DOUBLE ) }
              {         (TRIPLE ) }

              { FORMS=forms }

              { THRESHOLD=limit }

              { PRTY=priority }
```

- ## The NET statement

```
//*NET net-id,{ABCMP=KEEP }
          {     =NOKEEP }

          {NHOLD=number }

          {NORMAL=D }
          {      =F }

          {ABNORMAL=D }
          {        =F }
```

- The DATASET statement

```
//*DATASET DDNAME={ddname,
               CLASS=no,
               MSGCLASS=class }

               {J=NO }
               { =YES }
```

- **The OPERATOR statement**

```
//*OPERATOR message
```

- **The SIGNON statement**

```
//*SIGNON parameters
```

- **The SIGNOFF statement**

```
//SIGNOFF
```

- **The XMIT statement**

```
//*XMIT DEST=node-name
```

Index

About the Authors

SABA ZAMIR is coauthor of the *C++Primer for C Programmers* and *J. Ranade UNIX Primer*, both from McGraw-Hill. She worked as a project manager of a telecommunications system at Teleport Communications Group in Staten Island, New York, and at present is working as a software engineer at Moody's Investor Services, New York. She holds an M.B.A. from Rutgers Graduate School of Management, and a B.S. from St. John's University.

CHANDER RANADE, a VSAM expert, has nearly ten years of experience in the mainframe environment. She is a senior programmer/analyst for the Metro North Commuter Railroad, New York. She holds an M.A. in English Literature and is currently working toward an M.S. in Computer Science at Brooklyn Polytechnic Institute, New York.